Rise to the challenges of scenes from—

and more

Also Edited by
Lorraine Cohen
from Avon Books

MONOLOGUES FOR YOUNG ACTORS
SCENES FOR YOUNG ACTORS

SCENES
FOR
MATURE
ACTORS

**LORRAINE COHEN and
DR. RICHARD A. IMUNDO**

AVON BOOKS  NEW YORK

Permissions, constituting a continuation of the copyright page, are listed on pages v through xvi.

AVON BOOKS, INC.
1350 Avenue of the Americas
New York, New York 10019

Permissions

To any actor who has nervously waited
in the wings for an entrance cue

Acknowledgments

We would like to thank Julie and David and the knowledgeable staff at the Drama Book Shop in New York City for their help and also the many mature actors who have read these scenes so enthusiastically and were really the reason for this collection.

Contents

Scenes for a Man and a Woman

Scenes for Groups of Three or More

How This Book Came to Be

Both of us have spent much of our professional lives associated with the world of theatre. Lorraine, an actor, teaches and lectures on acting. In addition, she has edited *Scenes for Young Actors* and *Monologues for Young Actors*, both of which grew out of the need for material she encountered when working with this age group. Richard is the founder and artistic director of the New Dimension Theatre Studio and its acting school in New York. He has also worked as a director, teacher, and lecturer.

Together we have devoted a considerable amount of time to lecturing mature adults on various aspects of theatre. We realized that many members of our audiences were stimulated by the immediacy of performance and liked the idea of becoming actively involved in theatre. They wanted to move beyond seeing plays or hearing lectures and were eager to discover the rewards of bringing life to the printed word. We, too, were finding the jump from lecturing to scene work much more satisfying.

At the same time, when Richard asked actors in his professional advanced scene study classes to bring in a rehearsed, finished scene of their choice, he was surprised at how often the mature actors in the classes had difficulty finding material, and at how limited they felt their choices were.

Realizing there was no resource on the market to help them, and recalling Lorraine's previous editing experience, Richard suggested she edit a third book: a scene book designed for mature actors, both professionals and amateurs. She saw the merit in such a venture, and persuaded him to join her as a collaborator.

We have tried very hard to balance scenes of different styles and themes in this collection. We have organized the scenes by the number and gender of the characters in order to help actors find appropriate scenes. If the scenes are not familiar to the actors, the brief introductions should be beneficial.

We believe that this is the first book to meet a real need in the mature theatre comunity, from both the professional and amateur sides. We have designed it to be a useful source of audition material with short scenes for new or seasoned professionals, and have tried to make it workshop-friendly as well with longer scenes that could be staged and performed.

Here's to all of you mature professionals, neophytes, and theatre lovers. Good luck, or, if you will, "Break a leg!"

Scenes for
Two Men

Becket or the Honor of God

Jean Anouilh
Translated by Lucienne Hill

This historical play set in twelfth-century England revolves around the complicated relationship between King Henry II and his lifelong friend, Thomas Becket. Because of the king's trust in Becket and their mutual love for each other, the king has appointed Becket to the role of Archbishop of Canterbury. Much to the surprise of Becket himself, and to the surprise and dismay of the king, Becket has undergone a sincere conversion to the life of a devout clergyman, rupturing the extremely close friendship they had enjoyed. Becket's conversion has also brought to the fore the age-old conflict between church and state, a clash Henry had tried to avoid. The following scene clearly reveals the desire of both men to reestablish their relationship in spite of Becket's deep need to be true to his beliefs. The scene occurs upon Becket's return to England after having had an audience with the pope. At Henry's request, they are alone on a bleak winter day, riding on a deserted plain.

KING, BECKET

King.
   You look older, Thomas.

Becket.

You too, Highness. Are you sure you aren't too cold?

King.

I'm frozen stiff. You love it of course! You're in your element, aren't you? And you're barefooted as well!

Becket.

(Smiling.) That's my latest affectation.

King.

Even with these fur boots on, my chilbains are killing me. Aren't yours, or don't you have any?

Becket.

(Gently.) Of course.

King.

(Cackling.) You're offering them up to God, I hope, holy monk.

Becket.

(Gravely.) I have better things to offer Him.

King.

(With a sudden cry.) If we start straightaway, we're sure to quarrel! Let's talk about trivial things. You know my son is fourteen? He's come of age.

Becket.

Has he improved at all?

King.

He's a little idiot and sly like his mother. Becket, don't you ever marry!

Becket.

(Smiling.) The matter has been taken out of my hands. By you, Highness! It was you who had me ordained!

King.

(With a cry.) Let's not start yet, I tell you! Talk about something else!

Becket.

(Lightly.) Has your Highness done much hunting lately?

King.

(Snarling.) Yes, every day! And it doesn't amuse me any more.

Becket.

Have you any new hawks?

King.

(Furiously.) The most expensive on the market! But they don't fly straight.

Becket.

And your horses?

King.

The Sultan sent me four superb stallions for the tenth anniversary of my reign. But they throw every-one! Nobody has managed to mount one of them, yet!

Becket.

(Smiling.) I must see what I can do about that some day.

King.

They'll throw you too! And we'll see your buttocks under your robe! At least, I hope so, or everything would be too dismal.

Becket.

(After a pause.) Do you know what I miss most, Sire? The horses.

King.

And the women?

Becket.

(Simply.) I've forgotten.

King.

You hypocrite. You turned into a hypocrite when you became a priest. (Abruptly.) Did you love Gwendolen?

Becket.

I've forgotten her too.

King.

You did love her! That's the only way I can account for it.

Becket.

(Gravely.) No, my prince, in my soul and conscience, I did not love her.

King.

Then you never loved anything, that's worse! (Churlishly.) Why are you calling me your prince, like in the old days?

Becket.

(Gently.) Because you have remained my prince.

King.

(Crying out.) Then why are you doing me harm?

Becket.

Let's talk about something else.

King.

Well, what? I'm cold.

Becket.

I always told you, my prince, that one must fight the cold with the cold's own weapons. Strip naked and splash yourself with cold water every morning.

King.

I used to when you were there to force me into it. I never wash now. I stink. I grew a beard at one time. Did you know?

Becket.

(Smiling.) Yes, I had a hearty laugh over it.

King.

I cut it off because it itched. (He cries out suddenly, like a lost child.) Becket, I'm bored!

Becket.

(Gravely.) My prince. I do so wish I could help you.

King.

Then what are you waiting for? You can see I'm dying for it!

Becket.

(Quietly.) I'm waiting for the honor of God and the honor of the King to become one.

King.

You'll wait a long time then!

Becket.

Yes. I'm afraid I will. (A pause. Only the wind is heard.)

King.

(Suddenly.) If we've nothing more to say to each other, we might as well go and get warm!

Becket.

We have everything to say to each other, my prince. The opportunity may not occur again.

King.

Make haste, then. Or there'll be two frozen statues on this plain making their peace in a frozen eternity! I am your King, Becket! And so long as we are on this earth you owe me the first move! I'm prepared to forget a lot of things but not the fact that I am King. You yourself taught me that.

Becket.

(Gravely.) Never forget it, my prince. Even against God. You have a different task to do. You have to steer the ship.

King.

And you—what do you have to do?

Becket.

Resist you with all my might, when you steer against the wind.

King.

Do you expect the wind to be behind me, Becket? No such luck. That's the fairy-tale navigation! God

on the King's side? That's never happened yet! Yes,
once in a century, at the time of the Crusades, when
all Christendom shouts "It's God's will!" And even
then! You know as well as I do what private greeds
a Crusade covers up, in nine cases out of ten. The
rest of the time, it's a head-on wind. And there must
be somebody to keep the watch!

Becket.
And somebody else to cope with the absurd wind
i—and with God. The tasks have been shared out,
once and for all. The pity of it is that it should have
been between us two, my prince—who were friends.

King.
(Crossly.) The King of France—I still don't know
what he hopes to gain by it o- preached at me for
three whole days for me to make my peace with you
What good would it do you to provoke me beyond
endurance?

Becket.
None.

King.
You know that I am the King, and that I must act
like a King! What do you expect of me? Are you
hoping I'll weaken?

Becket.
No. That would prostrate me.

King.
Do you hope to conquer me by force then?

Becket.
You are the strong one.

King.
To win me round?

Becket.
No. Not that either. It is not for me to win you
round. I have only to say no to you.

King.

But you must be logical, Becket!

Becket.

No. That isn't necessary, my Liege. Must only do—absurdly—what we have been given to do—right to the end.

King.

Yet I know you well enough, God knows. Ten years we spent together, little Saxon! At the hunt, at the whorehouse, at war; carousing all night long the two of us; in the same girl's bed, sometimes . . . and at work in the Council Chamber too. Absurdly. That word isn't like you,

Becket.

Perhaps. I am no longer like myself.

King.

(Derisively.) Have you been touched by grace?

Becket.

(Gravely.) Not by the one you think. I am not worthy of it.

King.

Did you feel the Saxon in you coming out, despite Papa's good collaborator's sentiments?

Becket.

No. Not that either.

King.

What then?

Becket.

I felt for the first time that I was being entrusted with something, that's all- there in that empty cathedral, somewhere in France, that day when you ordered me to take up this burden. I was a man without honor. And suddenly I found it—one I never imagined would ever become mine o- the honor of God. A frail, incomprehensible honor, vulnerable as a boy-King fleeting from danger.

King.

(Roughly.) Suppose we talked a little more precisely, Becket, with words I understand? Otherwise we'll be here all night. I'm cold. And the others are waiting for us on the fringes of this plain.

Becket.

I am being precise.

King.

I'm an idiot then! Talk to me like an idiot! That's an order. Will you lift the excommunication which you pronounced on William of Aynsford and others of my liegement?

Becket.

No, Sire, because that is the only weapon I have to defend this child, who was given, naked, into my care.

King.

Will you agree to the twelve proposals which my Bishops have accepted in your absence at Northampton, and notably to forego the much-abused protection of Saxon clerics who get themselves tonsured to escape land bondage?

Becket.

No, Sire. My role is to defend my sheep. And they are my sheep. (A pause.) Nor will I concede that the Bishops should forego the right to appoint priests in their own dioceses, nor that churchmen should be subject to any but the Church's jurisdiction. These are my duties as a pastor—which it is not for me to relinquish. But I shall agree to the nine other articles in a spirit of peace, and because I know that you must remain King—in all save the honor of God.

(A pause.)

King.

(Coldly.) Very well, I will help you defend your God, since that is your new vocation, in memory of the companion you once were to me—in all save the honor of the Realm. You may come back to England, Thomas.

Becket.

Thank you, my prince. I meant to go back in any case and give myself up to your power, for on this earth, you are my King. And in all that concerns this earth, I owe you obedience. (A pause.)

King.

(Ill at ease.) Well, let's go back now. We've finished. I'm cold.

Becket.

(Dully.) I feel cold too, now. (Another pause. They look at each other. The wind howls.)

King.

(Suddenly.) You never loved me, did you, Becket?

Becket.

In so far as I was capable of love, yes, my prince, I did.

King.

Did you start to love God? (He cries out.) You mule! Can't you ever answer a simple question?

Becket.

(Quietly.) I started to love the honor of God.

King.

(Somberly.) Come back to England. I give you my royal peace. May you find yours. And may you not discover you were wrong about yourself. This is the last time I shall come begging to you. (He cries out.) I should never have seen you again! It hurts too much. (His whole body is suddenly shaken by a sob.)

Becket.

(Goes nearer to him; moved.) My prince—

King.

(Yelling.) No! No pity! It's dirty. Stand away from me! Go back to England! It's too cold out here!

(Becket turns his horse and moves nearer to the King.)

Becket.

(Gravely.) Farewell, my prince. Will you give me the kiss of peace?

King.

No! I can't bear to come near you! I can't bear to look at you! Later! Later! When it doesn't hurt any more!

Becket.

I shall set sail tomorrow. Farewell, my prince. I know I shall never see you again.

King.

(His face twisted with hatred.) How dare you say that to me after I gave you my royal word? Do you take me for a traitor?

(Becket looks at him gravely for a second longer, with a sort of pity in his eyes. Then he slowly turns his horse and rides away. The wind howls.)

King.

Thomas!

(But Becket has not heard. The King does not call a second time. He spurs his horse and gallops off in the other direction. The lights fade. The wind howls.)

I'm Not Rappaport

Herb Gardner

❧

This play was originally presented in Seattle but transferred to New York City in 1985. The opening scene of the play takes place on a battered bench on an isolated path at the edge of Central Park Lake early October, 1982. It is three o'clock in the afternoon. Two elderly men are dealing with the problems that come with being elderly and alone. Midge, black, wears very thick bifocals and an old soft hat and is reading The Sporting News. *Nat, also about eighty years old and white, is seated across the bench from Midge. He wears a beret and has a finely trimmed beard. A cane with an elegant ivory handle is resting next to him.*

NAT, MIDGE

Nat.
O.K. where was I? (No response. He smacks himself on the forehead.) Where the hell was I? What were we talking about? I was just about to make a very important point here. (To Midge.) What were we talking about?

Midge.

(No response. He continues to read his newspaper for a moment.) We wasn't talking. YOU was talking. (Turns page.) I wasn't talking.

Nat.

O.K. so what was I saying?

Midge.

I wasn't listening either. You was doing the whole thing by yourself.

Nat.

Why weren't you listening?

Midge.

Because you're a goddamn liar. I'm not listening to you anymore. Two days now I ain't been listening.

Nat.

Stop pretending to read. You can't see anything.

Midge.

Hey, how 'bout you go sit with them old dudes in fronta the Welfare Hotel, them old butter brains— (Pointing about the lake.) the babies at the Carousel, them kids in the boat—or some o' them junkie-folk yonder, whyn't you go mess with them? 'Cause I'm not talking to you anymore, Mister. Puttin' you on notice of that. You may's well be talking to that tree over there.

Nat.

It's a lamppost.

Midge.

Sittin' here a week now, ain't heard a worda truth outa you. Shuckin' me every which way till the sun go down.

Nat.

(Slapping the bench) I demand an explanation of that statement!

Midge.

O.K. wise-ass; for example, are you or are you not an escaped Cuban terrorist?

Nat.

(Slapping the bench) I am not!

Midge.

O.K. and your name ain't Hernando—

Nat.

Absolutely not!

Midge.

So it's a lie—

Nat.

It's a cover-story! (Pause.) My line of work, they give you a cover-story.

Midge.

Are you sayin'—?

Nat.

All I'm saying, and that's all I'm saying, is that in my particular field you gotta have a cover-story. More than that I can't divulge at the present time.

Midge.

Honey bun, you sayin' you're a spy?

Nat.

I'm saying my name is Hernando and I'm an escaped Cuban terrorist.

Midge.

But what kinda weirdo, bullshit cover-story is—?

Nat.

You don't think I SAID that to them? That's what I said to them. I said to them, an eighty-one-year-old Lithuanian is a Cuban Hernando? That's right, they said, tough luck, sweetheart; yours is not to reason why. That's how they talk. Of COURSE you don't believe it! You think I believe it? Such dopes. But it's a living. I beg you not to inquire further.

Midge.

But why'd they pick an old—

Nat.

Do I know? You tell ME. A year ago I'm standing in line at the Medicaid, a fellah comes up to me— boom, I'm an undercover.

Midge.

(Impressed.) Lord . . .

Nat.

Who knows, maybe they got something. They figure an old man, nobody'll pay attention. Could wander through the world like a ghost, pick up some tidbits.

Midge.

(Nodding thoughtfully) Yeah . . .

Nat.

So maybe they got something, even though, I grant you, they screwed up on the cover-story. All I know is every month a thousand bingos is added to my Social Security check.

Midge.

Bingos?

Nat.

Bingos. Dollars. Cash. It's a word we use in the business. Please don't inquire further. (Silence.) Please, I'm not at liberty. (Longer silence.) O.K.' they also gave me a code name, "Harry."

Midge.

"Harry"?

Nat.

Harry Schwartzman.

Midge.

What's your real name?

Nat.

Sam Schwartzman. (Outraged.) Can you believe it? Can you BELIEVE it? That's some imaginative group they got up there, right? That's some bunch of geniuses! (Then shrugging.) What the hell, a thousand bananas on your Social Security every month you don't ask fancy questions.

Midge.

Best not, best not. (Leaning closer.) So, do ya . . . do ya ever pick up any information for them?

Nat.

Are you kidding? Sitting on a bench all day with a man who can't tell a tree from a lamppost? Not a shred. (Glances about, leans closer.) Fact is, I think they got me in what they call "deep cover." See, they keep you in this "deep cover" for years; like five, maybe ten years they keep you there, till you're just like this regular person in the neighborhood . . . and then, boom, they pick you out for the big one. Considering my age and general health, they're not too bright. (Reaches into briefcase.) O.K. snack time.

Midge.

(Nodding.) Yeah. Deep cover. I hearda that . . .

Nat.

(Taking foil-wrapped sandwich from briefcase) Here. Tuna salad with lettuce and tomato on whole wheat toast. Take half.

Midge.

(Accepting sandwich.) Thank ya, Sam: thank ya.

Nat.

Yeah, comes three o'clock, there's nothing like a nice, fresh tuna salad sandwich.

Midge.

(Chewing.) Uh-huh.

Nat.

(Chewing.) Crisp.

(Silence for several moments as their old jaws work on the sandwiches.)

Midge.

(Suddenly.) Bullshit! (Sits upright.) Bullshit! Lord, you done it to me AGAIN! You done it! (Throws the sandwich fiercely to the ground.) Promised myself I wouldn't let ya, and ya done it again! Deep cover! Harry Schwartzman! Bingos! You done it again!

Nat.

(Smiling to himself as he continues eating.) That was nice . . . a nice long story, lasted a long time . . .

Midge.

(Shouting, poking Nat sharply) That's IT! That's it, no more conversin'! Conversin' is OVER now, Mister! No more, ain't riffin' ME no more!

Nat.

Please control yourself—

Midge.

MOVE it, boy' AWAY with ya! This here's MY spot!

Nat.

Sir, I was merely—

Midge.

Get offa my spot 'fore I lay you out!

Nat.

YOUR spot? Who made it YOUR spot? Show me the plaque. Where does it say that?

Midge.

Says right here . . . (Remains seated, slowly circling his fists in the air like a boxer.) You read them hands? Study them hands, boy. Them hands wore Golden Gloves, summer of Nineteen and Twenty-Four. This here's MY spot, BEEN my spot six months now, my good and peaceful spot till you show up week ago start playin' Three Card Monte with my head. Want you GONE, Sonny! (Continues circling his fists.) Givin' ya three t'make dust;

comin' out on the count o'three. ONE—
(Midge rises, moving to his corner of the 'ring.'')
Nat.
Wait, a brief discussion—
Midge.
Sound of the bell, I'm comin' out. YOU won't hear
it but I WILL. TWO—
Nat.
How you gonna hit me if you can't see me?
Midge.
Dropped Billy D'Amato in the sixth round with both
eyes swole shut. I just keep punchin' till I hear crun-
chin'. THREE—
Nat.
(Rising, with dignity.) Please, sir—this is an em-
barrassing demonstration—
Midge.
(Moving in Nat's general direction, a bit of remem-
bered footwork, jabbin.) O.K., comin' out, comin'
out, comin' at ya, boy, comin' at ya—
Nat.
(Moving behind bench for protection) Sir, you . . .
you have a depressing personality and a terrible at-
titude!
Midge.
PREPARE yourself, Mister, prepare yourself, get
your—
(Midge suddenly lunges, bumping against the
bench, stumbling—he struggles to keep his balance,
grabbing desperately at the air—then falls flat on
his back in the path. He lies there silently for several
moments.)
Midge.
(Quietly, frightened.) Oh, shit . . .
Nat.
(Aware that Midge is in danger, whispering) Mister . . . ? (No response. He leans forward urgently.)

Mister, Mister . . . ? (Silence. He moves towards Midge as quickly as possible.) Don't move, don't move . . .

Midge.

(Trembling.) I know . . .

Nat.

Could be you broke something . . .

Midge.

(Softly.) I know. Oh, shit. Never fall down, NEVER fall down . . .

King Lear

William Shakespeare

❧

The tragic story of King Lear, the powerful monarch of Great Britain, takes place during the Middle Ages. The king has three daughters. Cordelia, the youngest, who loves her father dearly, has not been diplomatic in her responses to him but always has been honest, unlike her two sisters who have deviously said and done what he wanted. Angry at Cordelia for her honesty, Lear disinherits her, to the advantage of the two older sisters who eventually turn him out. The following scene opens with Lear wandering aimlessly in a state of semi-madness and grief. By chance, he comes across his old trusted friend and subject, the Earl of Gloucestor, who has been cruelly blinded because of a court intrigue. Two short exclamations by Edgar, Gloucestor's

*son, who witnesses this scene unseen, are deleted and marked
with asterisks.*

LEAR, GLOUCESTOR

Lear.
No, they cannot touch me for coining. I am the King
himself.

******

Lear.
Nature's above art in that respect. There's your
press money. That fellow handles his bow like a
crow-keeper. Draw me a clothier's yard. Look, look,
a mouse! Peace, peace; this piece of toasted cheese
will do't. There's my gauntlet' I'll prove it on a
giant. Bring up the brown bills. O, well flown, bird!
I' the clout, i' the clout—hewgh! Give the word.

******

Lear.
Pass.

Gloucester.
I know that voice.

Lear.
Ha! Goneril with a white beard? They flattered me
like a dog and told me I had white hairs in my beard
ere the black ones were there. To say ay and no to
everything that I said ay and no to was no good
divinity. When the rain came to wet me once and
the wind to make me chatter, when the thunder
would not peace at my bidding, there I found 'em,
there I smelt 'em out. Go to, they are not men o'
their words. They told me I was everything. 'Tis a
lie' I am not ague-proof.

Gloucester.
The trick of that voice I do well remember.
Is 't not the King?

Lear.

Ay, every inch a king.
When I do stare, see how the subject quakes.
I pardon that man's life. What was thy cause?
Adultery?
Thou shalt not die. Die for adultery? No.
The wren goes to 't, and the small gilded fly
Does lecher in my sight.
Let copulation thrive; for Gloucester's bastard son
Was kinder to his father than my daughters
Got 'tween the lawful sheets.
To 't luxury, pell-mell, for I lack soldiers.
Behold yond simpering dame,
Whose face between her forks presages snow,
That minces virtue and does shake the head
To hear of pleasure's name;
The fitchew nor the soiled horse goes to 't.
With a more riotous appetite.
Down from the waist they are centaurs,
Though women all above.
But to the girdle do the gods inherit;
Beneath is all the fiends'.
There's hell, there's darkness,
there is the sulfurous, pit,
burning, scalding, stench, consumption. Fie, fie, fie!
Pah, pah! Give me an ounce of civet, good apoth-
ecary,
sweeten my imagination. There's money for thee.

Gloucester.

O, let me kiss that hand!

Lear.

Let me wipe it first; it smells of mortality.

Gloucester.

O ruined piece of nature! This great world
Shall so wear out to naught. Dost thou know me?

Lear.

I remember thine eyes well enough. Dost thou squinny at me? No, do thy worst, blind Cupid; I'll not love. Read thou this challenge. Mark but the penning of it.

Gloucester.

Were all thy letters suns, I could not see.

Lear.

Read.

Gloucester.

What, with the case of eyes?

Lear.

Oho, are you there with me? No eyes in your head, nor no money in your purse? Your eyes are in a heavy case, your purse in a light, yet you see how this world goes.

Gloucester.

I see it feelingly.

Lear.

What, art mad? A man may see how this world goes with no eyes. Look with thine ears. See how yond justice rails upon yond simple thief. Hark in thine ear: change places and, handy-dandy, which is the justice, which is the thief? Thou has seen a farmer's dog bark at a beggar?

Gloucester.

Ay, sir.

Lear.

And the creature run from the cur? There thou mightst behold the great image of authority'' a dog's obeyed in office.

Thou rascal beadle, hold thy bloody hand!

Why dost thou lash that whore? Strip thine own back:

Thou hotly lusts to use her in that kind

For which thou whipp'st her.

The usurer hangs the cozener.
Through tattered clothes small vices do appear:
Robes and furred gowns hide all. Plate sin with
    gold,
And the strong lance of justice hurtless breaks;
Arm it in rags, a pygmy's straw does pierce it.
None does offend, none, I say, none. I'll able 'em.
Take that of me, my friend, who have the power
To seal th' accuser's lips. Get thee glass eyes,
And like a scurvy politician seem
To see the things thou dost not. Now, now, now,
    now!
Pull off my boots. Harder, harder! So.

Lear.

If thou wilt weep my fortunes, take my eyes.
I know thee well enough; thy name is Gloucester.
Thou must be patient. We came crying hither.
Thou know'st the first time that we smell the air
We waul and cry. I will preach to thee. Mark.

Gloucester.

Alack, alack the day!

Lear.

When we are born, we cry that we are come
To this great stage of fools.—This' a good block.
It were a delicate stratagem to shoe
A troop of horse with felt. I'll put 't in proof,
And when I have stolen upon these son-in-laws
Then, kill, kill, kill, kill, kill, kill!

London Assurance

Dion Boucicault

This ribald comedy was first performed in 1841 at the Theatre Royal, Covent Garden. It takes place in England in the mid-nineteenth century. In the preceding scene, Sir Harcourt's son has come home very drunk and has been taken off to bed. This scene is set in the anteroom of Sir Harcourt's house in Belgrave Square. Sir Harcourt is an outlandishly conceited and affected gentleman, foppish, rouged, and dressed in an elegant dressing gown. He is entertaining a visitor, Max, an old friend, because he has designs on Max's young niece and is trying to impress him with his youthfulness. Cool, who appears in this scene but does not speak, is Sir Harcourt's valet.

SIR HARCOURT, MAX

Max.
Why, you are looking quite rosy.
Sir Harcourt.
Ah! Ah! Rosy! Am I too florid?
Max.
Not a bit; not a bit.

Sir Harcourt.

I thought so. (Aside.) Cool said I had put too much on.

Max.

How comes it, Courtly, that you manage to retain your youth? See, I'm as grey as an old badger or a wild rabbit, while you are—are as black as a young rook. I say, whose head grew your hair, eh?

Sir Harcourt.

Permit me to remark that all the beauties of my person are of home manufacture. Why should you be surprised at my youth? I have scarcely thrown off the giddiness of a very boy—elasticity of limb, buoyancy of soul. Remark this position. (Throws himself into an attitude.) I held that attitude for ten minutes at Lady Acid's last reunion at the express desire of one of our first sculptors, while he was making a sketch of me for the Apollo.

Max.

(Aside.) Making a butt of thee for their gibes.

Sir Harcourt.

Lady Sarah Sarcasm started up and, pointing to my face, ejaculated: ''Good gracious! Does not Sir Harcourt remind you of the countenance of Ajax in the Pompeian portrait?''

Max.

Ajax? Humbug!

Sir Harcourt.

You are complimentary.

Max.

I'm a plain man and always speak my mind. What's in a face or figure? Does a Grecian nose entail a good temper? Does a waspish waist indicate a good heart? Or do oily, perfumed locks necessarily thatch a well-furnished brain?

Sir Harcourt.

It's an undeniable fact: PLAIN people always praise the beauties of the MIND.

Max.

Excuse the insinuation. I had thought the first Lady Courtly had surfeited you with beauty.

Sir Harcourt.

No; she lived fourteen months with me, and then eloped with an intimate friend. Etiquette compelled me to challenge the seducer, so I received satisfaction—and a bullet in my shoulder at the same time. However, I had the consolation of knowing that he was the handsomest man of the age. She did not insult me by running away with a damned ill-looking scoundrel.

Max.

That certainly was flattering.

Sir Harcourt.

I felt so, as I pocketed the ten thousand pounds' damages.

Max.

That must have been a great balm to your sore honour.

Sir Harcourt.

It was; Max, my honour would have died without it, for on that year the wrong horse won the Derby—by some mistake. It was one of the luckiest chances—a thing that does not happen twice in a man's life: the opportunity of getting rid of his wife and his debts at the same time.

Max.

Tell the truth, Courtly. Did you not feel a little frayed in your delicacy, your honour, now? Eh?

Sir Harcourt.

Not a whit. Why should I? I married MONEY, and I received it—virgin gold. My delicacy and honour had nothing to do with hers. The world pities the bereaved husband, when it should congratulate. No; the affair made a sensation, and I was the object. Besides, it is vulgar to make a parade of one's feelings, however acute they may be; inpenetrability of countenance is the sure sign of your highly-bred man of fashion.

Max.

So a man must therefore lose his wife and his money with a smile—in fact, everything he possesses but his temper.

Sir Harcourt.

Exactly; and greet ruin with "vive la bagatelle!" For example, your modish beauty never discomposes the shape of her features with convulsive laughter. A smile rewards the BON MOT, and also shows the whiteness of her teeth. She never weeps impromptu; tears might destroy the economy of her cheek. Scenes are vulgar, hysterics obsolete. She exhibits a calm, placid, impenetrable lake, whose surface is reflection but of unfathomable depth—a statue whose life is hypothetical and not a PRIMA FACIE fact.

Max.

Well, give me the girl that will fly at your eyes in an argument, and stick to her point like a fox to his own tail.

Sir Harcourt.

But etiquette, Max, remember etiquette!

Max.

Damn etiquette! I have seen a man who thought it sacrilege to eat fish with a knife that would not scruple to rise up and rob his brother of his birthright in a gambling-house. Your thoroughbred, well-blooded heart will seldom kick over the traces of good feeling. That's my opinion, and I don't care who knows it.

Sir Harcourt.

Pardon me; etiquette is the pulse of society, by regulating which the body politic is retained in health. I consider myself one of the faculty in the art.

Max.

Well, well; you are a living libel upon common sense, for you are old enough to know better.

Sir Harcourt.

Old enough! What do you mean? Old! I still retain all my little juvenile indiscretions, which your niece's beauties must teach me to discard. I have not sown my wild oats yet.

Max.

Time you did, at sixty-three.

Sir Harcourt.

Sixty-three! Good God! Forty, 'pon my life! Forty next March.

Max.

Why, you are older than I am.

Sir Harcourt.

Oh! You are old enough to be my father.

Max.

Well, if I am, I am. (Aside.) That's etiquette, I suppose. (Aloud.) Poor Grace! How often I have pitied her fate. That a young and beautiful creature should be driven into wretched splendour or miserable poverty!

Sir Harcourt.

Wretched! Wherefore? Lady Courtly, wretched? Impossible.

Max.

Will she not be compelled to marry you whether she likes you or not—a choice between you and poverty? (Aside.) And hang me if it isn't a tie! (Aloud.) But why do you not introduce your son Charles to me? I have not seen him since he was a

child. You would never permit him to accept any of
my invitations to spend his vacation at Oak Hall. Of
course, we shall have the pleasure of his company
now?

Sir Harcourt.

He is not fit to enter society yet. He is a studious,
sober boy.

Max.

Boy! Why, he's five and twenty.

Sir Harcourt.

Good gracious! Max, you will permit me to know
my own son's age. He is not twenty.

Max.

I'm dumb.

Sir Harcourt.

You will excuse me while I indulge in the process
of dressing. _ Cool! (Enter Cool.) Prepare my toilet.
(Exit Cool.) That is a ceremony which with me su-
persedes all others. I consider it a duty which every
gentleman owes to society—to render himself as
agreeable an object as possible: and the least compliment a mortal can pay to nature, when she hon-
ours him by bestowing extra care in the manufacture
of his person, is to display her taste to the best possible advantage' and so, au revoir. (Exits.)

Max.

That's a good soul. He has his faults, and who has
not? Forty years of age! Oh, monstrous! But he does
look uncommonly young for sixty, in spite of his
foreign locks and complexion.

The Master Builder

Henrik Ibsen

This play was written in 1892 by this most significant play-wright, who, along with Anton Chekhov and August Strindberg, is considered a father of modern theatre. It is set in a middle-sized town in Norway in 1892. Many have believed that Halvard Solness, the master builder, is like Ibsen himself: successful, proud, idealistic, but with very human flaws. The play takes place in a plainly furnished office in Solness's house. The following scene occurs early in the play. Two young workers have left the office, leaving Knut Brovik, described as a "thin old man dressed in a somewhat worn but carefully preserved black tail coat," and Solness, the master builder, a "middle-aged man, strong and vigorous." Solness has just had a mild altercation with Brovik's son, Ragnar, who is one of the workers.

SOLNESS, BROVIK

Brovik.
  May I have a few words with you?
Solness.
  Certainly.

Brovik.

(Lowers his voice.) I don't want the children to know how seriously ill I am.

Solness.

Yes, you look rather poorly these days.

Brovik.

I haven't much longer. My strength gets less every day.

Solness.

Sit down for a moment.

Brovik.

Thank you, may I?

Solness.

(Moves the armchair a little.) Here. Well?

Brovik.

(Sits down with difficulty.) It's this question of Ragnar. That's what weighs most on my mind. What's to become of him?

Solness.

Your son? He'll stay here with me, for as long as he wants to.

Brovik.

But that's just it. He doesn't want to. He doesn't feel he can—now.

Solness.

Well, he's doing quite well for himself, I should have thought. Still, if he wants a little more, I wouldn't be unwilling to—

Brovik.

No, no, that's not it. (Impatiently.) It's time he was given the chance to do something on his own.

Solness.

(Not looking at him.) Do you think he's got the ability?

Brovik.

That's what's so dreadful. I've begun to have doubts about the boy. In all these years you've never uttered so much as a single word of encouragement about him. But it must be there. I can't believe he hasn't got the ability.

Solness.

But he doesn't know anything. Not really. Except how to draw.

Brovik.

(With suppressed hatred.) You didn't know much either, when you were working for me. But you managed to get started all right. (Breathes heavily.) Fought your way up. Put me out of business—and plenty of others.

Solness.

Yes, things worked out for me.

Brovik.

That's right. Everything worked out nicely for you. But surely you won't let me die without seeing what Ragnar can do. And I would like to see them married before I go.

Solness.

(Sharply.) Does she want that?

Brovik.

Not Kaja so much. It's Ragnar—he talks about it every day. (Pleadingly.) You must—you MUST help him to stand on his own feet now! I must see the lad do something on his own. Do you hear?

Solness.

(Angrily.) But, damn it, I can't conjure contracts out of the air for him.

Brovik.

He could get a commission right away. A nice big job.

Solness.

(Startled, uneasy.) Could he?

Brovik.

If you agree.

Solness.

What kind of job would that be?

Brovik.

(A little diffidently.) He could build that villa out at Lovstrand.

Solness.

That! But I'm going to build that myself.

Brovik.

Oh, you don't really want to do that.

Solness.

Don't want to? Who dared to say that?

Brovik.

You said so yourself, just now.

Solness.

Oh, never mind what I SAY. Could Ragnar get that contract?

Brovik.

Yes. He knows the family, you see. And then, he's—just for the fun of it, you know—he's made drawings and estimates and so on—

Solness.

And these drawings—are they satisfied with them? These people who are going to live there?

Brovik.

Yes. If only you'd just look through them and approve them, they—

Solness.

They'd like Ragnar to build their home for them?

Brovik.

They were very taken with his idea. They thought it was so new and original.

Solness.

Oh! New! Not the old-fashioned junk I build?

Brovik.

They thought this was—different.

Solness.

So it was Ragnar they came to see—while I was out.

Brovik.

They came to talk to you. And to ask if you'd be willing to give way—

Solness.

I? Give way for your son!

Brovik.

Rescind the contract, they meant.

Solness.

What's the difference? (Laughs bitterly.) So that's it! Halvard Solness is to retire! Retire to make way for younger men! For apprentices! Make way for the young! Make way! Make way!

Brovik.

Good heavens, there's room in this town for more than one—

Solness.

Oh, there's not so much room round here either. But that's not the point. I shall never give way! I shall never make way for anyone! Not of my own free will. Never, never!

Brovik.

(Gets up with difficulty.) Won't you let me die in peace? Happy—believing in my own son? Won't you let me see him do one thing on his own?

Solness.

(Turns half aside and mutters.) Don't ask me that now.

Brovik.

Yes, answer me! Must I die so poor?

Solness.

(Seems to fight with himself, then says, quietly but firmly.) You must die as best you can.

Brovik.

So be it. (Walks away.)

Solness.

(Follows him, almost desperately.) I can't do otherwise, don't you understand? I am what I am. And I can't create myself anew.

Brovik.

No, no. You can't do that. (Stumbles and stops by the sofa table.) May I have a glass of water

Solness.

Of course. (Pours one out and hands it to him.)

Brovik.

Thank you.

Scenes for
Two Women

The Curious Savage

John Patrick

This light comedy, which opened in New York City in 1955, takes place in the living room of the Cloisters in a town in Massachussetts in 1949. The Cloisters is a sanitarium for people with social and emotional problems who have difficulty adjusting to the world around them. Mrs. Savage, eccentric in style, appearance, and mannerisms, has been committed by her three grown stepchildren. The children have designs on her huge fortune, which Mrs. Savage intends to use for charitable purposes. While the children have taken advantage of her bizarre behavior to have her committed, Mrs. Savage is by no means unstable. She is diminutive and fragile, dressed too youthfully with a capricious feathered hat and carrying a large teddy bear somewhat the worse for wear. In the following scene, she has just been admitted, the children have left, and she is alone with a mature female attendant.

MRS. SAVAGE, MISS WILLIE

(Mrs. Savage continues to stare out window with her back to Miss Willie. For the first time she becomes aware of confinement. She bows her head and presses her handkerchief to her mouth. Miss Willie crosses to her.)

Miss Willie.

We've a lovely garden out there—you'll be able to see it in the morning. (Mrs. Savage does not answer.) When I was a child—we always said—THIRTY needles and thirty pins. You've added twenty more dirty Republi-kins.

Mrs. Savage.

(Looks up—smiles and turns to Miss Willie.) It's a fault of mine—exaggeration. It's stupid of me to try to irritate them like this—I just irritate myself. Well, I suppose it has to be exasperating now to be funny later. (She crosses down to sofa and deposits her bear on a pillow beside her.)

Miss Willie.

(Continues affably.) I notice one of its eyes is gone. It must have dropped out in the office. I'll look as soon as they go.

Mrs. Savage.

Don't bother. It fell out last fall at the opera. I'd have found it but the usher was so nasty about my lighting matches during the Magic Fire music. (She looks from the bear to Miss Willie.) You know what this is, don't you?

Miss Willie.

(Hesitates.) Suppose you tell me.

Mrs. Savage.

It's a teddy bear. Surely you've seen one before?

Miss Willie.

Not that big.

Mrs. Savage.

Do you know what I do with it?

Miss Willie.

I couldn't possibly guess.

Mrs. Savage.
I sleep with it.

Miss Willie.
Do you?

Mrs. Savage.
Yes, I do. Are you going to talk to me as if I were an imbecile, too?

Miss Willie.
Here—here—we mustn't be hostile. (Sits in chair facing Mrs. Savage.)

Mrs. Savage.
Of course not—you haven't harmed me. Would you care to know why I sleep with it?

Miss Willie.
If you'd care to tell me.

Mrs. Savage.
I don't care. And I'll tell you. I get lonely. I'm too old to have a lover and too fastidious to sleep with a cat.

Miss Willie.
Then, by all means, you must take it to bed with you here. Would you care to take off your hat?

Mrs. Savage.
If I'm going to spend the rest of my life here—I might as well. (Takes it off.)

Miss Willie.
It's a mighty saucy hat.

Mrs. Savage.
A ten cent piece of felt and three chicken feathers. Eighty-five dollars. Why economy should be expensive—I don't know.

Miss Willie.
It takes imagination.

Mrs. Savage.
And the blood of pirates. But I wanted it. I wanted a hat like this since I was sixteen. For all the good

it does me now. (Strokes the feathers fondly.)
Well—I won't need a hat here. (She holds the hat
out.) Maybe you can use it for something—I'm not
at all sure what.

Miss Willie.

Oh, you'd better keep it. You might need it.

Mrs. Savage.

(Sees herself in mirror on L. wall.) Dear, dear! My
hair looks like the matted end of a cocoanut.
(Crosses to mirror.)

Miss Willie.

Oh, I don't think so. It's a heavenly color.

Mrs. Savage.

(Brightens.) You should have seen it last year. (She
laughs.) It was bright red. Then just to be different,
I dyed it black with a white streak in the middle. I
looked like nothing so much as a skunk. Finally, I
just gave up and tinted it blue. It goes with everything.

Miss Willie.

It'll certainly go with your room. Wouldn't you like
to go up and get settled?

Mrs. Savage.

Is it time to lock me up?

Miss Willie.

I wouldn't dream of locking you up. Did you bring
a suitcase?

Mrs. Savage.

My daughter did. I wasn't consulted.

Miss Willie.

I'll get it and take you up. There'll be time to ex-
plore your surroundings tomorrow. (Starts for door
and Mrs. Savage follows her.) You can wait here.

Mrs. Savage.

Alone?

Miss Willie.
Of course.
Mrs. Savage.
No handcuffs?
Miss Willie.
We have the honor system.
(A short interlude with others.)
Mrs. Savage.
Do you think I belong here?
Miss Willie.
We're understaffed, Mrs. Savage. I'm kept too busy
to have any opinions.
Mrs. Savage.
I'd like to know what they told you about me.
Miss Willie.
Was there anything to tell?
Mrs. Savage.
Did they mention my Memorial Fund?
Miss Willie.
Not to me.
Mrs. Savage.
Then they probably told you that my husband's
death affected—my reason.
Miss Willie.
That would be understandable.
Mrs. Savage.
But untrue.
Miss Willie.
Why—weren't you happy with your husband?
Mrs. Savage.
I married Jonathan when I was sixteen. I loved him
from the moment I met him until the moment he
died. Do you know what that meant?
Miss Willie.
I think so.

Mrs. Savage.

Well, you don't, my dear. It meant that my only aim in life was to make him happy—to want what he wanted—to anticipate what would please him. And that meant that all the other things I ever wanted had to be forgotten.

Miss Willie.

But surely you had no regrets.

Mrs. Savage.

None. While he lived. But after he was gone—I remembered all the foolish things I'd always wanted to do.

Miss Willie.

What had you always wanted to do?

Mrs. Savage.

Things that would have shocked poor Jonathan.

Miss Willie.

Such as dying your hair blue?

Mrs. Savage.

That. And studying French. And ballet dancing— and people. As a girl, I was sure I could have been a great actress. So, with no responsibilities and time running out—I decided to be one.

Miss Willie.

But don't you think you waited too long, Mrs. Savage?

Mrs. Savage.

I certainly do. Had I been a fool in my youth—no one would have noticed the difference in my old age.

Miss Willie.

Oh—I'd never think of you as old, Mrs. Savage.

Mrs. Savage.

Well, having kicked over the traces myself—and learned once again the importance of unimportant things—I decided I'd help others have the foolish things they'd always wanted.

Miss Willie.

How were you going to do that?

Mrs. Savage.

By establishing the Jonathan Savage Memorial Fund—a foundation for giving money away in memory of my husband. And that insane idea has brought me here.

Miss Willie.

Well, you won't find it too unpleasant here. (Rises.) Shall we go up to your room now? (Picks up Mrs. Savage's grip and starts for door.)

Mrs. Savage.

Well, at least I learned one thing from my French lessons. (Crosses to pick up teddy bear on window seat.)

Miss Willie.

What's that?

Mrs. Savage.

What I am. I'm a "Mort canard." That's a "dead duck"—I think.

Miss Willie.

Now it's not as bad as that.

Mrs. Savage.

Yes, it is. Some day you'll realize that a great injustice was done me. You'll know that I was always quite sane. But here I am—and here they'll try to keep me—with my few foolish years taken from me. (Miss Willie goes to door R. and stands waiting. Mrs. Savage starts toward door, but instead of crossing a direct line, she follows the edge of the carpet until it leads her up to Miss Willie. She looks up brightly.) If people would walk around the edge of the carpet once in a while, it would save wearing it out in the middle. (She goes out.)

The Dark at the
Top of the Stairs

William Inge

This play by the well-known playwright opened on Broadway in 1957 and is set in a small Oklahoma town in the early 1920s. It takes place in the home of Rubin and Cora Flood. Rubin has left the house and not returned after another argument with Cora. Cora has made a major decision and has invited her sister, Lottie, over to ask if she and her teenage children can stay at Lottie's home. As the scene opens, Lottie's husband, Morris, is just leaving for one of his usual walks. The two women are alone.

LOTTIE, CORA

Lottie.
(Following him to the door.) Oh. Well, don't be gone long. We've got to get started back soon.
Cora.
Oh, please don't talk about going.
Lottie.
My God, Cora, we can't stay here all night. (She

peers out the window now, wondering about Morris.) Morris is funny, Cora. Sometimes he just gets up like that and walks away. I never know why. Sometimes he's gone for hours at a time. He says the walk helps his digestion, but I think it's because he just wants to get away from me at times. Did you ever notice how he is with people? Like tonight. He sat there when all the young people were here, and he didn't say hardly a word. His mind was a thousand miles away. Like he was thinking about something. He seems to be always thinking about something.

Cora.

Morris is nice to you. You've got no right to complain.

Lottie.

(Joining Cora at table C.) He's nice to me . . . in SOME ways.

Cora.

Good heavens, Lottie! He gave you those red patent leather slippers, and that fox neckpiece . . . you should be grateful.

Lottie.

I know, but . . . there's SOME things he hasn't given me.

Cora.

Lottie! That's not his fault. You've got no right to hold that against him!

Lottie.

Oh, it's just fine for you to talk. You've got two nice kids to keep you company. What have I got but a house full of cats.

Cora.

Lottie, you always claimed you never wanted children.

Lottie.

Well . . . what else can I say to people?

Cora.

(This is something of a revelation to her.) I just never knew.

Lottie.

(Having suddenly decided to say it.) Cora . . . I can't let you and the kids come over and live with us.

Cora.

(This is a blow to her.) Oh . . . Lottie.

Lottie.

I'm sorry, Cora. I just can't do it.

Cora.

Lottie, I was depending on you . . .

Lottie.

Maybe you've depended on me too much. Ever since you were a baby, you've run to me with your problems, and now I've got problems of my own.

Cora.

What am I going to do, Lottie?

Lottie.

Call up Rubin and ask him to come back. Beg him to come back, if you have to get down on your knees.

Cora.

I mustn't do that, Lottie.

Lottie.

Why not?

Cora.

Because we just can't keep from fighting, Lottie. You know that. I just don't think it's right, our still going on that way.

Lottie.

Do you still love him?

Cora.

Oh . . . don't ask me, Lottie.

Lottie.

Do you?

Cora.

Oh . . . yes.

Lottie.

Cora, I don't think you should listen to the stories those old Werpel sisters tell you.

Cora.

He's as good as admitted it, Lottie.

Lottie.

Well, Cora, I don't think it means he likes you any the less, because he's seen Mavis Pruitt a few times.

Cora.

No . . . I know he loves me.

Lottie.

(Asking very cautiously.) Does he still want to be intimate?

Cora.

That's only animal, Lottie. I couldn't indulge myself that way if I didn't feel he was being honorable.

Lottie.

(Breaks into a sudden raucous laugh.) My God, a big, handsome buck like Rubin! Who cares if he's honorable?

Cora.

(A little shocked.) Lottie!

Lottie.

(We see now a sudden lewdness in Lottie that has not been discernible before.) Cora, did you hear what the Old Maid said to the burglar? You see, the burglar came walking into her bedroom with this big, long billy club and . . .

Cora.

Lottie!

Lottie.

(Laughing so hard she can hardly finish the story.) And the old maid . . . she was so green she didn't know what was happening to her, she said . . .

Cora.

Lottie! That's enough. That's enough.

Lottie.

(Shamed now.) Shucks, Cora. I don't see what's wrong in having a little fun just telling stories.

Cora.

Sometimes you talk shamefully, Lottie, and when I think of the way Mama and Papa brought us up . . .

Lottie.

Oh, Mama and Papa, Mama and Papa! Maybe they didn't know as much as we gave them credit for.

Cora.

You're changed since you were a girl, Lottie.

Lottie.

What if I am!

Cora.

I never heard such talk.

Lottie.

Well, that's all it is. It's only talk. Talk, talk, talk.

Cora.

Lottie, are you sure you can't take us in?

Lottie.

It'd mean the end of my marriage too, Cora. You don't understand Morris. He's always nice and quiet around people, so afraid of hurting people's feelings. But he's the most nervous man around the house you ever saw. He'd try to make the best of it if you and the kids came over, but he'd go to pieces. I know he would.

Cora.

Honest?

Lottie.

I'm not joking, Cora. My God, you're not the only one who has problems Don't think that for a minute.

Cora.

A few moments ago, you said YOU had problems, Lottie . . .

Lottie.

Problems enough.

Cora.

Tell me, Lottie.

Lottie.

Oh, why should I?

Cora.

Doesn't Morris ever make love to you any more?

Lottie.

(It takes her several moments to admit it.) . . . No. It's been over three years since he even touched me . . . that way.

Cora.

(Another revelation.) Lottie!

Lottie.

It's the God's truth, Cora.

Cora.

Lottie! What's wrong?

Lottie.

How do I know what's wrong? How does anyone ever know what's wrong with anyone else?

Cora.

I mean . . . is there another woman?

Lottie.

Not unless she visits him from the spirit world. (This releases her humor again and she is diverted by another story.) Oh, say, Cora, did I tell you about this woman over in Oklahoma City who's been holding seances? Well, Marietta went to her and . . . (But suddenly again, she loses her humor and makes another sad admission.) Oh, no, there isn't another woman. Sometimes I wish there was.

Cora.

Lottie, you don't mean that.

Lottie.

How the hell do YOU know what I mean? He's around the house all day long, now that he's got his dental office in the dining room. Day and night, day and night. Sometimes I get tired of looking at him.

Cora.

Oh, Lottie . . . I'd always felt you and Morris were so devoted to each other. I've always felt you had an almost perfect marriage.

Lottie.

Oh, we're still devoted, still call each other "honey" just like we did on our honeymoon.

Cora.

But what happened? Something must have happened to . . .

Lottie.

Did you notice the way Morris got up out of his chair suddenly and just walked away, with no explanation at all? Well, something inside Morris did the same thing several years ago. Something inside him just got up and went for a walk, and never came back.

Cora.

I . . . just don't understand.

Lottie.

Sometimes I wonder if maybe I've been too bossy. Could be. But then, I always supposed that Morris LIKED me because I was bossy.

Cora.

I always envied you, having a husband you could boss.

Lottie.

Yes, I can boss Morris because he just isn't there any more to fight back. He doesn't care any more if I boss him or not.

Cora.

Just the same, he never hit you.

Lottie.

I wish he would.

Cora.

Lottie!

Lottie.

I do. I wish to God someone LOVED me enough to hit me. You and Rubin fight. Oh, God, I'd like a good fight. Anything'd be better than this NOTH-ING. Morris and I go around always being so sweet to each other, but sometimes I wonder maybe he'd like to kill me.

Cora.

Lottie, you don't mean it.

Lottie.

Do you remember how Mama and Papa used to caution us about men, Cora?

Cora.

Yes, I remember.

Lottie.

My God, they had me so afraid of ever giving in to a man, I was petrified.

Cora.

So was I.

Lottie.

Yes, you were until Rubin came along and practically raped you.

Cora.

Lottie! I don't want Sonny to hear talk like that.

Lottie.

Why not? Let him hear!

Cora.

(Newly aghast at her sister's boldness.) Lottie!

Lottie.

Why do we feel we always have to protect kids?

Cora.

Keep your voice down. Rubin never did anything like that.

Lottie.

Didn't he?

Cora.

Of course not!

Lottie.

My God, Cora, he had you pregnant inside of two weeks after he started seeing you.

Cora.

Sssh.

Lottie.

I never told. I never even told Morris. My God, do you remember how Mama and Papa carried on when they found out?

Cora.

I remember.

Lottie.

And Papa had his stroke just a month after you were married. Oh, I just thought Rubin was the wickedest man alive.

Cora.

I never blamed Rubin for that. I was crazy in love with him. He just swept me off my feet and made all my objections seem kinda silly. He even made Mama and Papa seem silly.

Lottie.

Maybe I shoulda married a man like that. I don't know. Maybe it was as much my fault as Morris's. Maybe I didn't . . . respond right from the very first.

Cora.

What do you mean, Lottie?

Lottie.

Cora, I'll tell you something. Something I've never told another living soul. I never did enjoy it the way some women . . . say they do.

Cora.

Lottie? You?

Lottie.

Why do you say ME like that? Because I talk kinda dirty at times? But that's all it is, is talk. I talk all the time just to convince myself that I'm alive. And I stuff myself with victuals just to feel I've got something inside me. And I'm full of all kinds of crazy curiosity about . . . all the things in life I seem to have missed out on. Now I'm telling you the truth, Cora. Nothing ever really happened to me while it was going on.

Cora.

Oh, Lottie!

Lottie.

That first night Morris and I were together, right after we were married, when we were in bed together for the first time, after it was all over, and he had fallen asleep, I lay there in bed wondering what in the world all the cautioning had been about. Nothing had happened to me at all, and I thought Mama and Papa must been makin' things up.

Cora.

Oh, Lottie!

Lottie.

So, don't come to me for sympathy, Cora. I'm not the person to give it to you.

Lettice and Lovage

Peter Shaffer

❧~❧

This scene from the play, which opened in England in 1987, takes place in the late 1980s. The scene opens in a grand hall of the gloomy sixteenth-century home of a once-renowned British family in Wiltshire, England. It is called Fustian House and at the opening of the play, Miss Lettice Douffet, a middle-aged woman dressed somewhat theatrically, is leading a tour. Just as Lettice is ending her lecture, a somberly dressed middle-aged woman, Lotte Schoen, approaches. A few "good-byes" and "thank yous" spoken in chorus by the tour group are omitted and marked with asterisks.

LETTICE, LOTTE

(Lettice has just about finished her tour. Lotte finally speaks, unable to restrain herself any longer.)

Lotte.

This is intolerable!

Lettice.

I beg your pardon?

Lotte.

I find this absolutely intolerable!

Lettice.

I'm sorry. I don't understand.

Lotte.

Miss Douffet, is it not?

Lettice.

That is my name, yes.

Lotte.

Yes! Well I would like to speak to you at once, please—in private.

Lettice.

On what subject?

Lotte.

I said private, please.

Lettice.

I find this extremely odd . . . I am not used to having my tours interrupted with brusque demands.

Lotte.

(Sharply to the Public.) Would you please excuse us now? It is most urgent that I speak to this lady alone. The tour is at an end at this point anyway, I believe.

Lettice.

It is. But its conclusion is a graceful adieu—not an abrupt dismissal. And it is spoken by me.

Lotte.

I'm sorry but I really have to insist. (To the Public.) Please forgive me, but I do have the most imperative business with this lady. (She looks at them hard, and her look is very intimidating.) Please!

                    (They stir uneasily.)

Lettice.

(To the Public.) Well—it seems I have to let you go—regrettably without ceremony . . . What can be so urgent as to preclude manners I cannot imagine . . . I do hope you have all enjoyed yourselves.

Lettice.

The way out is over there. You will find placed by the exit a Staffordshire soup-bowl into which, if you care to, you may deposit such tokens of appreciation as you feel inclined to give. Thank you and good-bye.

******

(They go out . . .)

Lotte.

You are not permitted to receive tips, I believe.

Lettice.

I do not regard them as that.

Lotte.

What then?

Lettice.

What I called them. Some people are appreciative in this world. They warm to the thrilling and ro-mantic aspects of our great History.

Lotte.

Others however warm to accuracy, Miss Douffet. And others again—a few—are empowered to see that they receive it.

Lettice.

I don't understand you.

Lotte.

Myself, for example. My name is Miss Schoen, and I work for the Preservation Trust. In the Personnel Department.

(A pause.)

Lettice.

Oh.

Lotte.

(Grimly.) Reports have been coming in steadily for some time now of bizarre inaccuracies in your tour here. Gross departures from fact and truth. I have myself heard with my own ears a generous sample of what you have been giving the Public, and every one of those reports falls far short of what you are actually doing. I can hardly think of one statement you made in my presence that is correct.

Lettice.

The gastronomic references for a start. They are all correct. I would like you to know I am an expert in Elizabethan cuisine.

Lotte.

(Crisply.) I am not talking about gastronomic references—which in any case form no part of your Official Recital. Today I listened to a farrago of rubbish unparalleled, I should say, by anything ever delivered by one of our employees. That tale of Arabella Fustian, for example was virtually fabrication from beginning to end. The girl was crippled by a fall, certainly—but it was not known how she fell. Her engagement was broken off, yes, but it is not known why, or who broke it. And so far from staying in her room SINGING thereafter, she lived to become a respected figure in the vicinity, noted for her work among the poor. The composer Henry Purcell was not, to my knowledge, involved in her life in any way.

(A pause.)

Lotte.

WELL? . . . WHAT DO YOU HAVE TO SAY?

(A long pause.)

Lettice.

I'm sorry but I cannot myself get beyond your own behaviour.

Lotte.

Mine?

Lettice.

What you have just done.

Lotte.

I don't understand.

Lettice.

What you have done here, Miss Schoen, today—pretending to join my group as a simple Member of the Public. I find that quite despicable.

Lotte.

I beg your pardon?

Lettice.

It is the behaviour actually of a spy.

Lotte.

Well that is what I am. I came here with that specific intention. To observe unnoticed what you were doing.

Lettice.

To spy.

Lotte.

To do my duty.

Lettice.

Duty?

Lotte.

Precisely. My duty . . . the precise and appropriate word.

Lettice.

To embarrass your employees—that is your duty? . . . To creep about the Kingdom with a look of false interest, guidebook in hand—and then pounce on them before the people in their charge? . . . Is that how you conceive your duty?—to humiliate subordinates?

Lotte.

This is a side track.

Lettice.

It is not. It really is not.

Lotte.

A total sidetrack and you know it! . . . MY behaviour is not the issue here. Yours . . . YOURS is what we are discussing! It is that which needs explaining! . . . You will report tomorrow afternoon at my office in London. I believe you know the address. Fourteen Architrave Place. Three o'clock if you please.

Lettice.

(Alarmed.) Report? . . . For what—report? . . . I don't understand. What do you mean?

(Pause.)

Lotte.

(Coldly.) I suggest you now attend to the next group of tourists awaiting you. And that you confine yourself strictly to the information provided by the Trust. I will see you at three tomorrow. Good-afternoon. (She goes out.)

(Lettice stands, appalled.)

Lettice.

(Calling after her, in rising panic.) I . . . I'm to be tried then? . . . I'm to be judged? . . . Hailed to Judgement?

(A pause. Miss Schoen has gone.)

Lettice.

(In dismay.) Oh dear.

(Grim music. The lights fade.)

Lettice and Lovage

Peter Shaffer

❧

This scene takes place in London at an office of the Preservation Trust. Lettice Douffet, a tour guide, has been chastised for giving inaccurate information during her tours and has been told to report to the office of her superior, Miss Lotte Schoen. For more background, see the introduction to the prior scene from this play on page 56.

LETTICE, LOTTE

Lotte.
Ah, Miss Douffet: good-afternoon. Please sit down.
(Lettice sits in a chair on the other side of the desk.)

Lotte.
I hope you had a pleasant journey up to London.

Lettice.
That is not very likely, is it?—considering one is about to be arraigned.

Lotte.
I'm sorry?

Lettice.

I'm at the Bar of Judgement, am I not?

Lotte.

Your position is to be reviewed, actually. I'm sure you see the inevitability of that . . . I have no choice in the matter.

Lettice.

Like the headsman.

Lotte.

I'm sorry.

Lettice.

The headsman always asked forgiveness of those he was about to decapitate.

Lotte.

I would really appreciate it if we could exclude historical analogies from this conversation.

Lettice.

As you please.

Lotte.

It is after all solely to do with your job, and your fitness to perform it. We both know what we have to talk about. As an official of the Department which employs you I cannot possibly overlook what I witnessed yesterday afternoon. I cannot understand it, and I cannot possibly condone it. Do you have anything to say in extenuation?

(A pause.)

Lettice.

It is not my fault.

Lotte.

I'm sorry?

Lettice.

Except in a most limited sense of that word.

Lotte.

Then whose is it?

Lettice.

I respect accuracy in recounting History when it is

moving and startling. Then I would not dream of
altering a single detail.

Lotte.

That is gracious of you.

Lettice.

In some cases however I do confess I feel the need
to take a hand . . . I discovered this need working at
Fustian House this summer. It is wholly the fault of
the House that I yielded to it.

Lotte.

Of the House?

Lettice.

Yes.

Lotte.

You are actually blaming the House for those gro-
tesque narrations?

Lettice.

I am. Most definitely . . . Fustian House is quite simply the DULLEST HOUSE IN ENGLAND! It is
actually IMPOSSIBLE to make interesting! Not
only is its architecture in the very gloomiest style
of Tudor building—NOTHING WHATEVER
HAPPENED IN IT!—OVER FOUR HUNDRED
YEARS! A queen almost fell downstairs but
DIDN'T. A girl did fall—not even downstairs—and
survived to be honoured by the poor. How am I
expected to make anything out of that?

Lotte.

You are not expected to make things OUT of the
house, Miss Douffet. Merely to show people round
it.

Lettice.

I'm afraid I can't agree. I am there to enlighten
them. That first of all.

Lotte.

Enlighten?

Lettice.

Light them up! "Enlarge!— Enliven!— Enlighten!"— that was my mother's watchword. She called them the three Es. She was a great teacher, my mother.

Lotte.

Really? At what institution?

Lettice.

The oldest and the best. The Theatre.

(Miss Schoen bristles.)

Lettice.

All good actors are instructors, as I'm sure you realize.

Lotte.

(Coldly.) I'm afraid I don't at all.

Lettice.

But certainly! "Their subject is Us—Their sources are Themselves!"—Again, my mother's phrase. She ran a Touring Company of players, all trained by her to speak Shakespeare thrillingly, in the French tongue.

Lotte.

The French?

Lettice.

Yes. She moved to France after the war, unable to find employment in her native England equal to her talent. We lived in an agricultural town in the Dordogne. It was not really very appreciative of Shakespeare.

Lotte.

The French peasantry is hardly noted for that kind of enthusiasm, I understand.

Lettice.

Nor the intellectuals either. Voltaire called Shakespeare "barbare"—did you know that? Barbarian.

Lotte.

I'm not surprised. The Gallic mind imagines it invented civilization.

Lettice.

My mother set out to correct that impression. Her Company was called in pure defiance—''Les Barbares!''

Lotte.

She was evidently not afraid of challenge.

Lettice.

Never! Every girl was trained to phrase faultlessly.

Lotte.

And every man also, one presumes.

Lettice.

There were no men.

Lotte.

You mean it was an All-girl Company?

Lettice.

Indeed. My mother married a Free French soldier in London called Douffet, who abandoned her within three months of the wedding. She took no pleasure thereafter in associating with Frenchmen. ''They are all fickle,'' she used to say. ''Fickle and furtive.''

Lotte.

A fair description of the whole nation, I would say.

Lettice.

She brought me up entirely herself. Mainly on the road. We played all over the Dordogne—in farmhouses and barns—wherever they would have us. I was the Stage Manager, responsible for costumes, props, and fights. Fights, I may say as ferocious as they can only be, enacted by a horde of Gallic girls in armour when their dander is really up! We performed only the History plays of Shakespeare—because History was my mother's passion She herself was famous for her Richard the Third. She used to wear a pillow on her back as a hump. It was brilliantly effective. (Springing up.) No-one who heard it will ever forget the climax of her performance— the cry of total despair wrung from her on the battlefield! (Stooping, as the royal hunchback.) "UN CHEVAL! UN CHEVAL! MON ROYAUME POUR UN CHEVAL!"

    (Lotte stares astounded.)

Lettice.

All the translations were her own.

Lotte.

(Drily.) A remarkable achievement.

Lettice.

Not for her. Language was her other passion. As I grew up I was never permitted to read anything but the grandest prose. "Language alone frees one!" she used to say. "And History gives one place." She was adamant I should not lose my English Heritage—either of words or deeds. Every night she enacted for me a story from our country's past— fleshing it out with her own marvellous virtuosity! . . . King Charles the First marching to his execution on a freezing January morning—putting on two shirts, lest if he trembled with cold his enemies should think it was from fear! Or his son, Charles the Second, hidden in the branches of an oak tree— his enemies hunting furiously for him below! One creak of a bough and the whole future of royalty is finished in the land! . . . (Rapt.) Wonderful! . . . On a child's mind the most tremendous events were engraved as with a diamond on a windowpane . . . And to me, MY TOURISTS—simply random holiday-makers in my care for twenty minutes of their lives—are my children in this respect. It is my duty to enlarge them. Enlarge—enliven—enlighten them.

Lotte.

With fantasies?

Lettice.

Fantasy floods in where fact leaves a vacuum.

Lotte.

Another saying of your mother's?

Lettice.

My own! . . . When I first went to Fustian House I spoke nothing but fact! Exactly what was set down for me by your office—in all its glittering excitement. By the time I'd finished my whole group would have turned grey with indifference . . . Fustian is a haunted house, Miss Schoen. It is haunted by the Spirit of Nullity,—of Nothing Ever Happening! That had to be fought.

Lotte.

With untruth.

Lettice.

With ANYTHING!

Lotte.

(Implacably.) With untruth.

Lettice.

(Grandly.) I am the daughter of Alice Evans Douffet—dedicated to lighting up the world, not dousing it in dust! . . . My tongue simply could not go on speaking that stuff! . . . No doubt it was excessive. I was carried—I can't deny it—further and further from the shore of fact down the slipstream of fiction. But blame the House—not the spirit which defied it!

Lotte.

And this is your defence?

Lettice.

Where people once left it yawning they now leave ADMIRING. I use that word in its strict sense—

meaning a state of Wonder. That is no mean defence.

Lotte.

It is completely irrelevant!

Lettice.

Last month I put a soup bowl by the Rear Exit. Not from greed—though heaven knows I could be forgiven for that, with what you pay me . . . I wanted proof! People express gratitude the same way all over the world: with their money. (Proudly.) . . . MY SOUP BOWL BRIMS! It BRIMS every evening with their coins—as they themselves are brimming! I watch them walking away afterwards to the Car Park—and those are BRIMMING PEOPLE. Every one!

Lotte.

Really? If you were to look through those letters you might discover quite a few who were not actually brimming—except with indignation.

(Lettice approaches the desk and examines a letter.)

Lettice.

Churls are always with us. Curmudgeons are never slow to come forward.

Lotte.

(Furious.) TWENTY-TWO letters! I have twenty-two letters about you, Miss Douffet! None of them exactly written in a state of wonder!

Lettice.

(Loftily.) Twenty-two—what's that? . . . I have fifty! . . . Sixty! . . . Here—look for yourself! . . . Here! Behold! . . . Here! (She grabs her satchel and empties its contents over the desk—a small avalanche of envelopes.) VOX POPULI! The Voice of the People! . . . I wrote my address beside my bowl. This is the result!

Lotte.

(Protesting.) Please, Miss Douffet! . . . This is my desk!

Lettice.

Read them! Read for yourself! There is my defence! The Voice of the People! . . . Read!

Lotte.

(Exploding and standing up.) I WILL NOT! . . . I WILL NOT! . . . This is nonsense all of it! . . . They don't matter! . . . None of this matters!—Your mother—your childhood—your Car Park—I DON'T CARE! (Pause; struggling to control herself.) I am not in the Entertainment Business—and nor are you. That is all. We are guarding a heritage. Not running a theatre. THAT IS ALL! (She glares at Lettice.)

The Oldest Profession

Paula Vogel

❧

This play about five older members of the world's oldest profession is set in New York City in 1980. The author has set up this play with blackouts and in each succeeding scene we are aware that one less of the original group is alive. In this scene Edna and Vera, the two remaining women, are again sitting on a park bench, relaxed and enjoying the sun. The previous

*madam, Ursula, has died and Edna has inherited that position.
Vera is clutching a small white bag of chocolates. Please refer
to the introduction to a previous scene from this play on page
430 for more detailed background.*

EDNA, VERA

Edna.
I thought she'd never die.

Vera.
Edna!

Edna.
Well, it's true. Ursula was mean enough to live to
a hundred.

Vera.
I don't think she was that bad. She was cranky; but
after forty-five years, you kind of get attached even
to that.

Edna.
Maybe you got attached. I didn't.
(Vera opens her small white bag and smiles.)

Vera.
Would you care for some chocolate, Edna?

Edna.
What kind are they?

Vera.
Turtles. I felt like a little treat.

Edna.
Thank you.
(Edna, with great deliberation, chooses one. Vera
looks in the bag, takes one out and puts it in her
mouth. The two women pause a moment, and let
the chocolate melt.)

Edna.
They're very good.

Vera.

(Happy.) Yes. They're sweet. (Looks into her bag.) Still, who would have suspected that she was so batty?

(Edna and Vera laugh.)

Edna.

"You're going to need two strong arms to carry away what's left. . . ." "More solid than gold, more stable than oil . . ."

(Pause.)

Vera.

Edna, what are we going to do with all that sugar?

Edna.

Dump it.

Vera.

All that sugar? How much do you think she has?

Edna.

Well, the back room's piled ceiling to floor with five-pound bags. You can figure there's more than a thousand pounds—no wonder the floor's been sagging.

Vera.

That explains why she insisted on having the large rooms at the back. And why she never invited us to her room.

Edna.

She must have been collecting those sugar bags before 1945 . . . some of those bags are rotting through . . . and the roaches . . . (Shudders.) Mr. Zabar says it's up to us to clear out the room and exterminate. There may be more than roaches back there, too. I'll hire someone to do it first thing next week. I'm not stepping foot in there. As Ursula would say, "You can catch more roaches with sugar . . ."

Vera.

Poor Ursula. . . . Edna

Edna.

Hmmm?

Vera.

What happened to the certificate . . . certificate . . .

Edna.

Of deposit? Well, I got the money out. We had to pay a substantial penalty. So much for money making money.

(Pause.)

Vera.

What are we going to do about the customers?

Edna.

Well, this is how I figure it, Vera. Let's just keep the ones we fancy.

Vera.

Really? You mean it?

Edna.

There's no sense in us working ourselves to death.

Vera.

Well, Edna, now that you're in charge . . . you know, you don't have to do any of the work at all . . . (Bravely.) I could arrange things and keep the books, if you want . . . the others did . . .

Edna.

No—I don't want to do that. . . . I like my work. Besides, Mr. Benjamin would be furious if I left the Life. You know, I think that's what happened to Ursula . . . she quit working when she became Madam, and I think the . . . inactivity killed her. (Pause; then low.) Or maybe it was the strike. I don't feel good about that.

Vera.

Why?

Edna.

I don't know—it just wasn't right. It upset . . . the way things are supposed to be. I feel bad about it.

Vera.

Why, Edna, we meant no harm about it. It was fun. If Ursula had wanted to, she could have joined us— she could have gone on strike too.

Edna.

No, she couldn't—she was Management.

Vera.

Oh. Well, I had a good time on strike. Edna, do you suppose we could go on strike again?

Edna.

You can if you like—I can't. I'm Management now.

Vera.

Oh, yes, of course . . .

Edna.

You know, Vera, I don't much care if I'm in charge or not . . . you could take over the operations if you want . . .

Vera.

Why, goodness, no, Edna, I couldn't take over the business. I have no head at all for numbers and dates . . . You're much better at that sort of thing. Besides, you're older.

Edna.

Yes, I guess you're right. It feels funny to be in charge. It doesn't feel right. I don't know..

Vera.

You're doing a great job. Really. Besides, Mae would want it this way. Keeping to the order of things.

Edna.

Yes.

Vera.

So, who are we going to ditch?

Edna.

First one to go: Mr. Ezra! No wonder he never talks—his breath could kill a horse at ten paces!

Vera.

Mr. Adam?

Edna.

Mr. Warren!

Vera.

Mr. Julius?

Edna.

Let's keep Mr. Sidney and Mr. Brett . . .

Vera.

Oh, yes. Lillian's friends . . . and of course, Mr. David and Mr. Andrew.

Edna.

Mr. Samuel, Mr. Lawrence, Mr. Sheldon, and of course, Mr. Benjamin. And Mr. Francis when he gets out. How is he doing?

Vera.

Oh, he's much better this week. His appetite is back. They might let him come back any day now . . .

Edna.

Vera? Do you think maybe you could visit Mr. Francis tonight instead of this afternoon? Mr. Zabar's charging us for the fumigation; that's going to put us back at least forty dollars . . .

Vera.

Well, I suppose so. I think if I took a cab, I could keep my appointment with Mr. Brett and still get to Roosevelt in time for dinner. I like to be there with Mr. Francis when he eats. It's so awful to eat dinner alone. Mr. Francis acts just like a child if I'm not there.

Edna.

Sometimes Mr. Benjamin acts just like a child when it's time to leave. He holds me around the waist and says he's not going to let me out of his sight. Then I have to slap his face, and say, "Mr. Benjamin, let go this instant. What makes you think any woman would have you?'' And I rub the bristle on his face and say, ''Shave this mug!'' And then he rubs his beard on my face and I scream. And sometimes he says, ''Edna, you've got to marry me! I can't afford to keep this up . . .'' He doesn't really mean it, though. It's just one of our games . . . he's my good-time papa, that's what I call him. I like to sit on his knee and put my hands under his shirt; I like his smell—I know it after all these years. There was a time when he was still working on Wall Street that Mae would schedule me in regular for him at lunch time; I had the key to his apartment. He'd come through the door, three-piece suit and briefcase, and say ''What's for lunch?'' And I'd jump on him and wrap my legs around him . . . He's got a picture of himself in uniform on the night table, twenty-five years old and smiling. Gives me the willies to look at it. I don't like to think of Mr. Benjamin as a young man. It makes me sad. Don't you think young men are awfully sad?

BLACKOUT

Save Me a Place at Forest Lawn

Lorees Yerby

∽✦∾

This one-act play, which opened in 1963, presents a small but perceptive slice of the lives of the two characters, Clara and Gertrude, both octogenarians. They are tired, lonely, and need each other. They reveal their characters as they talk, touching on many subjects with wisdom and humor. The scene is set in a cafeteria where they meet daily, in the early 1960s. The women are having one of their not unusual altercations when the scene opens.

CLARA, GERTRUDE

Clara.
(Staring stiff-necked straight ahead.) Never in my life have I ever made a public exhibition of myself. Never. THAT was going to be my epitaph. It COULD have been a fitting memorial and now I've thrown it all to the wind! Why I had to join YOU in that absurd song . . .

Gertrude.
No, no, Clara, you were wonderful . . .

Clara.

That absurd song drained me of every ounce of dignity. I can feel every single eye in the place staring at us. I am mortified!

Gertrude.

(Looking about guiltily.) They hardly noticed . . .

Clara.

For God's sake, Gertrude, stop looking like a cocker spaniel . . . and maybe it'll pass over. Maybe they'll think they were hearing things. Eat your custard so we can leave . . . we'll never be able to come back HERE again. (She resumes eating her dessert with a haughty, defiant air.)

Gertrude.

(Eating obediently.) I don't really like custard, but Henry loved it so it takes me close to Henry, and so I eat it.

Clara.

Humph!. . . . Probably better for you than Henry was . . .

Gertrude.

Oooooh, I hope his poor soul didn't hear you . . . Do you suppose you'll be seeing your Charlie and me my Henry again . . . I mean if we go to heaven if there is one?

Clara.

. . . Tch . . . tch . . . your life stutters with if. . . . if, if, if. . . . Yes, I suppose we'll be running into them again, but I don't suppose we'll recognize them.

Gertrude.

I wouldn't know MY Henry?

Clara.

Well, I don't know . . . could you recognize YOUR Henry if he weren't a man?

Gertrude.

(Very perplexed.) Oh, my . . . let me see . . . (Concentrating hard.) my Henry not as a man . . . oh, my!

It's very hard to say . . . perhaps his smells . . . yes.
I remember them . . . yes, I'd know Henry ANY-
WHERE.

Clara.
Gertrude, sometimes I really wonder why I spend
so much time with you . . . can't you possibly be . . .
abstract?

Gertrude.
Of course I can. I can be anything you can be, but
I can't talk about it.

Clara.
Well, you know that the Henry you knew is still
here underfoot . . . underground.

Gertrude.
(Smiling wryly.) No, underfoot . . . ha . . . ha

Clara.
It's nothing to laugh about, Gertrude. You have to
think of, what is Henry in heaven?

Gertrude.
If he's not a man, then a woman?

Clara.
OF COURSE HENRY'S NOT A WOMAN IN
HEAVEN! Look, Gertrude, the difference in the
sexes on earth is just . . . emphasized here . . . it really matters very little . . .

Gertrude.
(Wide-eyed.) You mean we've been making a
mountain out of a molehill!

Clara.
Noooo . . . I think it's just another of nature's . . .
mistakes, (Pause.) . . . but a necessary one, you understand, here, anyway. But not there. (She discreetly points a finger on her lap toward heaven.) In
heaven . . . such mistakes are corrected . . .

Gertrude.
Oh, my. I don't think Henry's enjoying himself
much, then; he can't stand being corrected.

Clara.

(Very impatient.) Gertrude, it's impossible even discussing this whole thing with you . . . you can't see
Henry as an abstraction . . .

Gertrude.

(Staring away at the line.) Don't look now, Clara,
but Albert Hoagbarth is in line, and he's looking
this way . . . Don't look!

Clara.

(Hunching her shoulders and turning her head away
from the line.) Oh, bother! I hope he doesn't see
us..we'll never get rid of him if he does. Has he
seen us yet?

Gertrude.

I think he's seen me, but not you yet. He doesn't
give a whit about me. It's you he's after, Clara. . . .

Clara.

Ugh, that's disgusting. You'd think he'd have some
sense at his age . . . he must be ninety.

Gertrude.

Now, Clara, be charitable. He's only lonely . . . he
just likes your company.

Clara.

(Straightening herself.) Humph! No man just likes
your company. . . . I went to see a travelogue with
him once. . . . and we were no sooner flying over the
Andes when he reached right over in my lap and
took my hand in HIS. Oh, the MUSH of it all . . .
Where is he now, Gertrude?

Gertrude.

(Looking around.) He got away from the line!
Oooops, I'm afraid I've lost him. . . . I can't make
out the faces up close . . . Do you have your glasses,
Clara?

Clara.

Of course I don't have my glasses. They're only for
reading, and I don't read in public.

Gertrude.

Well, I can't find him without glasses, Clara. (Searches her purse.) I have my magnifying glass. Shall I use that? I use it for looking at price tags . . .

Clara.

GOOD GAWD! PUT THAT MAGNIFYING GLASS AWAY! You can't look at PEOPLE with a MAGNIFYING GLASS!

Gertrude.

(Grumpily.) If I ever thought I'd still be scolded at my age . . . (Puts away glass.) Oh, where will it all end? (Eating and mumbling.) . . . Treated like a child . . .

Clara.

You act like one . . .

Gertrude.

Oh, if I knew then what I know now. . . . I never would have tried to act otherwise . . . Ah! What dear little friends I had. . . . where are they all now? Ring around the rosey, pocket full of posey. . . . ashes, ashes . . . all fall. . . . (Sadly pausing.) They won't get up again for all the tea in China . . .

Clara.

(Loudly whispering.) . . . Just keep it up! . . . Let yourself wander down memory lane . . . you'll end up in a rest home, that's what! They won't let you manage your own affairs.

Gertrude.

I don't have affairs.

Clara.

And when they ask me if you're incompetent, I'll tell them!

Gertrude.

What'll you tell them?

Clara.

I'll tell them you're not to be trusted!

Gertrude.

Who is?

Clara.

(Exasperated.) Me. You can trust me, Gertrude.

Gertrude.

Oh, yes. I've always trusted old people . . . but I didn't trust you when you were forty, Clara.

Clara.

What a horrible thing to say . . . After all these years of devotion I've given you . . .

Gertrude.

You used to repeat everything I told you in confidence to Henry. I know you did, Clara. Henry said so.

Clara.

Why did you keep telling me things then, Gertrude?

Gertrude.

(Shrugging her shoulders.) Oh, I don't know . . . maybe I just wanted to see how far you and Henry would go. I so wanted him to like you . . .

Clara.

(Astonished.) You mean. . . . you think that . . . Henry DIDN'T like me?! Did HE say that???!!

Gertrude.

Don't get upset, Clara. He said in the beginning that he didn't . . . to throw me off the track. Later he told me he loved you.

Clara.

And you didn't leave him?

Gertrude.

No . . . no. Once I was going to, but I decided against it.

Clara.

But why?

Gertrude.

Well, I figured there was always an end to everything . . . end of happiness . . . end of suffering . . .

end of love . . . and I thought if I could just LAST
long enough, I'd outlive your love . . . and I did!

Clara.

(Very upset) My secret . . . the one secret I was taking to the grave . . . you've stolen! Oh, Gertrude,
how could you . . .

Gertrude.

(Soothingly.) Clara . . . my dear . . . Clara. . . . my
friend! I haven't meant to hurt you. . . . I thought I'd
bring us closer. . . . You've always meant so much
to me, Clara. When I decided against leaving Henry.
. . . oh, I was miserable . . . I was thinking of you. I
knew if I left him, I'd lose you, and at forty you
think twice about losing a friend. So I thought and
thought, and I figured out that YOU'D probably live
MUCH longer than Henry, and while I was sure I
could continue my life without a husband, because
I'd spent a good portion of it without one . . . I really
wasn't sure about continuing my life without a
friend. And it's one of the few decisions I've made
that I still think was right!

Clara.

(Shaking her head woefully.) All these years you've
known . . . you've placed all your faith in a friend
. . . me . . . and I've been so untruthful . . .

Gertrude.

(Brightly.) No, you haven't.

Clara.

Of course I have! Henry and I loved each other . . .
right up to his death . . .

Gertrude.

Yes, and you'll be my friend right up to mine . . .

Clara.

GERTRUDE! HAVE YOU NO PRIDE? Do you realize that Henry, even on his deathbed, repeated his

love for ME! And he asked me to look after you.
... like ... like a favorite pet!!!

Gertrude.

(Unflustered.) Hmmmmmmm. . . . how nice . . .

Clara.

Doesn't it matter to you that your husband and your
dearest friend were. . . . loving behind your back???

Gertrude.

Love is so rare . . . who am I to criticize where it's
found. . . . ? I'm happy to know that Henry discovered it before he died . . . and to think he found it
so close to home . . . Henry never did wander far
from home . . . he loved my meat loaf . . . my muf-
fins . . . my friends . . .

Clara.

Ooooh! To think I thought I knew every hair on
your head. . . . oh my. . . . oh, my . . .

Gertrude.

(Eyes upward.) As you say, it'll all be different in
heaven, Clara . . . can't tell one from another. . . . Or
did you tell Henry you'd meet him there, too?

Clara.

Oh, my. . . . it was so long ago I don't know what I
told him . . .

Gertrude.

No matter . . . no matter, Clara . . . what's done is
. . . Better to know whatever's to know, heh, Clara?
After all there's only so much room behind my
back . . .

Clara.

Gertrude, there's always room for two behind anybody's back . . .

Gertrude.

Not in heaven, my friend. There are no backs in
heaven . . . only wings . . . now there's a place for
you and Henry . . . under my . . .

Clara.

Gertrude! Henry and I . . . I don't want . . . we wouldn't hide . . . any more . . . we wou . . .

Gertrude.

Getting too old to hide, Clara?

Clara.

Now listen here . . . I needn't remind you . . . you know to the day how old I am . . . why, you were practically walking before I saw my first day . . .

Gertrude.

Sixteen months and she's trying to tell me I lost Henry to a younger woman.

Clara.

I'm simply trying to say I'm old enough . . . YOU'RE old enough to know the truth.

Gertrude.

That's what I say. You're old enough to trust me now. I wonder what's happened to Henry?

Clara.

Henry's gone.

Gertrude.

But his love . . . is it with him?

Clara.

I doubt it . . . you can't bury love . . .

Gertrude.

Then maybe it went upstairs . . .

Clara.

I don't know . . . I've never been upstairs.

Gertrude.

But if love isn't in heaven, wherever is it, Clara?

Clara.

(Confidentially.) It's somewhere around. . . . (They both look about and lean closer.)

Gertrude.

Yes?

Clara.

(Beckoning her friend a little closer.) Something different, dear, than we suspected . . .

Gertrude.

Oh, God, I don't care WHAT it is as long as I know it when it happens. . . .

Clara.

Maybe that's the difference, Gertrude . . . we'll know it . . .

Gertrude.

Didn't you and Henry know, Clara?

Clara.

I'm embarrassed to tell. . . .

Gertrude.

Oh, go ahead anyway . . . be embarrassed . . . it's good for your circulation.

Clara.

I don't think Henry and I knew it as much as we DEDUCED it . . . know what I mean?

Gertrude.

No.

Clara.

Henry and I knew we hadn't found it elsewhere, so we got the idea that we had it . . . you know, if you can't find the pea under the other walnut shell, then you deduce it's under yours.

Gertrude.

That's what I wanted to know, Clara. Did Henry look under your walnut shell?

Clara.

No.

Gertrude.

Why?

Clara.

Because we were afraid to.

Gertrude.

Afraid of me?

Clara.

No, afraid the pea wasn't there.

Gertrude.

(Folding her hands with finality.) That's all I wanted to know. It was the one part I wanted to know. I knew you and Henry did a heckuva lot of talking, but I didn't know about the other. . . . (Pause.) Now I'll never mention it again.

Clara.

I don't mind talking about it any more . . . in fact, it'd be a relief.

Gertrude.

Humph! . . . I think I'd be a bloody bore . . .

Clara.

My story of our unfulfilled love BORES you??? Of all the heartless creatures I've ever known . . .

Gertrude.

Sticks and stones may break my bones, but names can never hurt me . . . AND THAT INCLUDES YOURS AND HENRY'S! He . . . ha . . . so there! (Plunking her hat down firmly on her head and pushing all her plates away, she folds her arms.)

Clara.

(Trembling.) I find it very difficult to keep my promise to Henry . . . If he only could've heard you today . . . tch . . . tch . . . it's I who needs the care . . .

Gertrude.

WHY, CLARA! . . . I THOUGHT THE MOMENT WOULD NEVER COME when you'd say THAT to me. After all these years . . . YOU NEED ME!

Clara.

(Petulant.) I didn't specify who . . . I need.

Gertrude.

PICK ME, CLARA ... PICK ME (Looking about the room.) ... who else, but me ... your best friend? ...

Clara.

I need the care of poor Gertrude who can barely maneuver across the street. ... poor Gertrude, my love's wife! Humph, you'll probably push me off some sidewalk when the light is red!

Gertrude.

Clara, you've trusted my ignorance this long ... our last few years won't matter for more ... I know no more than I did, and perhaps a little less ... I'm not angry. I couldn't be. We're on a desert island together, Clara, and I couldn't hate the only other survivor!

The Shadow Box

Michael Cristofer

❦

This play opened in 1977 and is set in 1970 in three separate cottages at a Midwestern hospice where family members may live with the hospice patients. In this scene, Felicity, an elderly patient, is being cared for by her daughter, Agnes, a very plain, middle-aged woman. Because Felicity looks forward to letters from another daughter, Claire, Agnes has made a decision to

not inform her of Claire's death. In so doing, Agnes has had to
fabricate the existence and contents of the letters.

AGNES, FELICITY

Felicity.
   (Calling out in her sleep.) Agnes.
Agnes.
   Mama, if I told you the truth now, would it matter?
Felicity.
   (Waking up.) Agnes!
Agnes.
   Yes, mama?
Felicity.
   . . . sons of bitches . . . Did we get any mail today,
   Agnes?
Agnes.
   (Every word of this lie is now more and more un-
   bearable.) Yes, mama . . . we did . . .
Felicity.
   From Claire?
Agnes.
   Yes, we did. Another letter from Claire. Another
   letter from Claire.
Felicity.
   (As if she never said it before.) I get so lonesome
   for Claire . . .
Agnes.
   (Cutting her off.) I know, mama . . .
Felicity.
   Will you read it to me, Agnes?
Agnes.
   Yes, mama.
Felicity.
   (Like a phonograph, skipping back.) I get so lone-
   some for Claire . . .

Agnes.
(Unable to bear any more.) Mama, please . . .
Felicity.
I get so lonesome for Claire . . .
Agnes.
Please!
Felicity.
I get so lonesome . . .
Agnes.
(A cry.) Mama!! (And then silence.)
Felicity.
Agnes?
Agnes.
Yes.
Felicity.
Could I have some tea?
Agnes.
(Almost in a trance pours the tea and carefully puts the cup in Felicity's hands.) Yes.
Felicity.
(Holding the cup, but not drinking from it yet.) Could you read me the letter, now?
Agnes.
Yes.
Felicity.
The letter from Claire.
Agnes.
Yes. Yes. Yes. (She takes the letter from her pocket—the one she was writing earlier. She opens the envelope and begins reading.) Dear Mama, I am writing today from Mexico. We are finally out of the swamp and onto high dry ground. What a relief after so much rain and dampness . . . Because of some unexplainable mechanical difficulties, we found ourselves stranded today in a beautiful little mountain village called San Miguel . . . It's a lovely

little town clinging for dear life to the side of a great
ghostly mountain in the middle of nowhere . . . a
very curious place to be. Nothing has changed in
hundreds of years and nothing WILL change, I
guess, for hundreds more . . .

Felicity.

(Mumbling.) . . . my bright-eyed . . . girl . . .

Agnes.

. . . There are so many things to see during the day,
but then the nights grow bitter cold . . . (Agnes
watches her, making up the words to the letter.) and
I can hear the wind blowing . . . outside the door,
whistling and . . . and whispering . . . and when I
look out the window, nothing is there . . . nothing
. . . mama I think . . . I think it's because I miss
you . . . because it hurts not being close to you . . .
and . . . and touching you . . . (Agnes breaks down
and can't go any further.)

Felicity.

Agnes?

Agnes.

Yes, mama. Yes.

Felicity.

What time is it now?

Agnes.

Oh, four . . . five . . . I don't know.

Felicity.

(Still holding her cup.) Could I have some tea, Agnes? (Agnes just looks at her.) Could you read me
the letter now?

Agnes.

Mama . . .

Felicity.

Could you read me the letter now?

Agnes.

Mama . . .

Felicity.
    The letter from Claire? (Pause.)
Agnes.
    Yes. Yes. (She starts to read the letter again.) Dear
    mama, I am writing today from Mexico. We are
    finally out of the swamp and onto high dry ground.
    What a relief after so much rain and dampness . . .
    Because of some unexplainable mechanical difficul-
    ties . . .

Waiting in the Wings

Noël Coward

❧

*This scene takes place in the lounge of a comfortable home for
retired, aging actresses. May has been at the home for a few
years; Lotta is a newcomer. The two had a serious conflict with
each other in the past and there was a period of open hostility
some thirty years ago which has never been resolved, resulting
in total estrangement. They are both very attractive and in their
seventies. In this scene, another woman has just left and they
are alone for the first time. For general background, set location,
and circumstances, we suggest you refer to the introduction to
a prior scene from this play on page 500.*

MAY, LOTTA

(There is a long silence. May takes up her workbag, which is by her chair, and takes out her embroidery frame. She shoots Lotta another swift look and, fumbling in her bag again, produces her wool, needle and spectacle case. She gives a little grunt of satisfaction. Lotta sits quietly staring in front of her. The silence continues.)

May.

(At last.) They were here all the time. (Lotta without replying looks at her inquiringly. May meets her eyes and forces a wintry little smile.) My glasses. They were here all the time—in my work bag.

Lotta.

(Gently)   'And frosts were slain and flowers begotten   And in green underwood and cover Blossom by blossom the Spring begins'.

May.

The fire's nearly out.

Lotta.

There's enough heat left, really. It's not very cold.

May.

Were you happy with him?

Lotta.

Yes. I was happy with him until the day he died.

May.

That's something gained at any rate, isn't it?

Lotta.

(Lightly.) He was a monster sometimes, of course. Those black Irish rages.

May.

Yes. I remember them well. (She looks at Lotta curiously and says, without emotion.) Why did you take him from me?

Lotta.

I didn't. He came to me of his own free will. You must have known that. He wasn't the sort of character that anyone could take from anyone else.

May.

(Dispassionately.) You were prettier than I was.

Lotta.

You know perfectly well that that had nothing to do with it. The spark is struck or it isn't. It's seldom the fault of any one person.

May.

Any one person can achieve a lot by determination.

Lotta.

Would you like a scrap of accurate but rather unpleasant information?

May.

What do you mean?

Lotta.

I can tell you now. I couldn't before. You never gave me the chance anyhow.

May.

What are you talking about?

Lotta.

There was somebody else.

May.

Somebody else?

Lotta.

Yes. Between the time he left you and came to me.

May.

I don't believe it.

Lotta.

It's quite true. Her name was Lavinia, Lavinia Parsons.

May.

(Incredulously.) Not that dreadful girl who played Ophelia with poor old Ernest?

Lotta.

That's the one.

May.

Are you telling me this in order to exonerate yourself?

Lotta.

(With a touch of asperity.) No, May. I'm not apologising to you, you know, not asking for your forgiveness. I see no reason to exonerate myself. Charles fell in love with me and I fell in love with him and we were married. I have no regrets.

May.

(Drily.) You are very fortunate. I have, a great many.

Lotta.

Well, don't. It's a waste of time.

May.

What became of your first husband, Webster Whatever-his-name-was?

Lotta.

(Evenly.) His name was Webster Bennet. After our divorce in 1924, he went to Canada and died there a few years later.

May.

You had a son, didn't you?

Lotta.

Yes. I had a son.

May.

Is he alive?

Lotta.

Yes. He went to Canada with his father. He is there still. He has had two wives, the first one apparently was a disaster, the second one seems satisfactory. They have three children.

May.

Does he write to you often?

Lotta.

I haven't heard from him for seventeen years.

May.

(Gruffly.) I'm sorry, Lotta, very sorry.

Lotta.

Thank you, that's kind of you. I was unhappy about it for a long time but I'm not any more. He was always his father's boy more than mine. I don't think he ever cared for me much, except of course when he was little.

May.

Why did you come here? Was it absolutely necessary?

Lotta.

(Looking down.) Yes, absolutely. I have a minute income of two hundred pounds a year and nothing saved; the last two plays I did were failures and—and there was nothing else to be done, also I found I couldn't learn lines any more—that broke my nerve.

May.

That's what really finished me, too. I was always a slow study at the best of times, the strain became intolerable and humiliating, more humiliating even than this.

Lotta.

I refuse to consider this humiliating. I think we've earned this honestly, really I do.

May.

Perhaps we have, Lotta, perhaps we have.

Lotta.

Bonita's left her bottle of whisky. Would you like a sip?

May.

A very small one.

Lotta.

(Going to the table and pouring out two drinks.) All right.

May.

(Ruminatively.) Lavinia Parsons. He must have been mad!

Lotta.

(Handing her her drink.) She was prettier than you and prettier than me and a great deal younger than both of us.

May.

(Thoughtfully.) I must buy a bottle of whisky to-morrow in Maidenhead. What is really the best sort?

Lotta.

Oh, I don't know. There's Haig and Black and White—they're all much of a muchness unless one happens to be a connoisseur, and we're neither of us that.

May.

(Rising and holding up her glass.) Well, Lotta, we meet again.

Lotta.

Yes, May dear, we meet again. (She also holds up her glass.) Happy days!

May.

Happy days!

(They both drink and then stand quite still for a moment looking at each other. In their eyes there is a glint of tears.)

CURTAIN.

The Whales of August

David Berry

❧

This play was first presented as a staged reading in 1980 and opened in Providence, Rhode Island in 1981. The play is set at a summer cottage on an island off the Maine coast. It is an August weekend in 1954. The cottage's two inhabitants are Sarah, seventy-five years old, and her sister Libby, eighty-six years old. In this play the entire cast of five characters are in their seventies or eighties and the play deals with their differing attitudes toward age, dying, and living. In the author's own words, "cliches and carictures of old people must be avoided in playing these roles, just as the play itself avoids them. These minds are not slow; these bodies are not infirm beyond the normal lessening of physical strength in old age. These people are trying to choose HOW TO LIVE, not to die . . . that spirit of life-affirmation." Sarah is described as having a quality of Yankee competence and strength while still maintaining a strong femininity. Libby is described as handsome and possessing an imperious dignity. Both women are casually dressed. The following scene opens the play.

The entire play is very appropriate for a senior citizens group as all five characters are elderly.

SARAH, LIBBY

(Sarah enters onto the porch carrying a wicker laundry basket which she sets on a porch rocker. She withdraws from the basket a red rose and a white rose which she sniffs briefly, then carefully lays the roses back in the basket and removes several dish towels to hang over the porch rail to dry. When she finishes hanging the towels, she straightens, looks at the sea for the first time, and takes a deep breath.)

Sarah.

Not a cloud, not one. (Peering intently forward and down.) Is that a seal? I think it is! (Pause.) No . . . just a log. (Looks seaward again, and follows the flight of a single gull as it cries and flies from right to left.) The herring are running! (Movement on the rocks below catches her eye, withdraws hanky from bosom and waves.) Yoo-hoo! Mr. Maranov! Yoo-hoo! (Final wave, replaces hanky, enters living room with basket.) Libby, it's a beautiful morning. You should take some sun. (Puts basket away in kitchen upstage right, returns to living room with dust cloth.) Where does it all come from? (Starts about the room with a determined brushing of the dust-catchers.) Gracious . . . look at that brass. . . . (Pauses at mantel photograph, dusts it gently and blows a kiss to it.) Forty-two years, Philip. Just think. (Libby's bedroom door opens and she enters.)

Libby.

Is someone here?

Sarah.

No, dear. Just talking to myself.

Libby.

Anybody answer?

Sarah.

Not today.

Libby.

(Making slow and careful way to her platform rocker.) Wouldn't we be surprised if someone did?

Sarah.

We certainly would. (Notices breakfast tray on Libby's side table.) Libby, you didn't eat a speck of your breakfast again.

Libby.

I don't want it.

Sarah.

Your tea must be cold.

Libby.

Yes.

Sarah.

Your cereal, too.

Libby.

Logical.

Sarah.

Libby, you haven't eaten breakfast all week.

Libby.

I don't need it.

Sarah.

It's the most important meal of the day.

Libby.

(Sitting.) I'm not hungry, not hungry at all.

Sarah.

You shouldn't do without breakfast.

Libby.

This is the mauve dress, isn't it?

Sarah.

(Looks, notices the uneven buttoning, goes to Libby to re-button her dress.) You're not wearing your shoes.

Libby.

I couldn't find them.

Sarah.

Perhaps you kicked them under your bed.

Libby.
I don't know.
Sarah.
You really should eat something.
Libby.
Mauve was always a favorite colour of mine.
Sarah.
(Finished re-buttoning, rises.) I'll get your shoes for
you.
Libby.
You didn't answer me.
Sarah.
Answer what, dear?
Libby.
I asked if this were the mauve dress.
Sarah.
Oh. Yes, dear, it is. (Resumes dusting.)
Libby.
I didn't forget that I asked.
Sarah.
No, dear.
Libby.
I don't forget things, y'know.
Sarah.
No, dear.
Libby.
What are you doing?
Sarah.
Dusting.
Libby.
You dusted yesterday.
Sarah.
I did?
Libby.
Yes.
Sarah.
Well . . . I can't keep up with it.

Libby.

Busy, busy, busy . . .

Sarah.

I've simply given up on the brass.

Libby.

I always like it better tarnished.

Sarah.

It's the ocean dampness . . .

Libby.

I'm glad the silver's stored away. You'd be at THAT all the time.

Sarah.

Oh Libby . . .

Libby.

Are your duties finished for the Fair?

Sarah.

I've hardly made a dent in them.

Libby.

You're usually finished in July.

Sarah.

I know, but with one thing and another, I just can't keep up. (Pause.) The summer's going so quickly.

Libby.

I wish we were back home in Philadelphia now.

Sarah.

Libby, it's so hot in Philadelphia now!

Libby.

I like the heat. YOU can't be busy in it.

Sarah.

I've almost finished with the aprons I'm making for the Fancy Goods Table. (Pauses in her dusting.) And I've collected some things for the White Elephant Table . . . and . . . what else . . . ?

Libby.

Potholders? Those knitted things?

Sarah.

Not this year.

Libby.

Argyle socks?

Sarah.

Last year, Libby, I do them only on the odd numbered years.

Libby.

Salt water taffy for the Candy Table?

Sarah.

No . . . (Pause.) I am donating that old stereopticon to the Silent Auction Table. They say they're quite valuable nowadays.

Libby.

We'd be pretty valuable, too, if we were stereopticons.

Sarah.

I should think so. A matched pair.

Libby.

My, my . . . what would the Annual Fair BE without Sarah Webber?

Sarah.

It's a worthy cause, dear. (Resumes dusting.)

Libby.

The world is full of worthy causes.

Sarah.

Yes, indeed.

Libby.

And you're always in line for most of 'em.

Sarah.

I was trained to do for others.

Libby.

Well . . . Mr. Barnum said there was one born every minute.

Sarah.

(Pause.) I did promise to make something else for the Fair . . .

Libby.

Plans.

Sarah.

No. (Pause.) What did you say?

Libby.

I said, "plans." (Brief pause, then quickly.) Remember your plans for the Grand Tour? You never got past Cousin Minnie's house in Belfast, though.

Sarah.

No, I didn't.

Libby.

Barnum's maxim again, Sarah.

Sarah.

Now Libby, Aunt Mary was very ill.

Libby.

Yes. And, besides, "doing for others is a way of doing for one's self." (Sarcastically.)

Sarah.

Libby, I did see quite a bit of Ulster. County Down, County Antrim, the Giant's Causeway. (Pauses in her dusting to turn briefly to Libby.) I even bowled on the green in Bangor—TWICE. (Resumes dusting.)

Libby.

(After a pause.) November is a time for departures, you know.

Sarah.

Hmm?

Libby.

August isn't bad as a choice, but November is more appropriate.

Sarah.

(Exiting to kitchen.) Well, thank goodness it isn't November!

Libby.

Ishmael joined Captain Ahab's crew when it was November in his soul.

Sarah.

(Off.) Who, dear?

Libby.

Ishmael, Sarah! In Mr. Melville's book!

Sarah.

(Off.) Oh . . .

Libby.

MOBY DICK. Didn't you ever read MOBY DICK?!

Sarah.

(Enters carrying a tall white taper for the mantel candlestick.) You were always the reader in the family, dear, but I know the book you mean . . . the one about the white whale. (Places taper in candlestick.)

Libby.

That's the one.

Sarah.

(Brief pause at mantel.) Stuffed animals! THAT'S what I forgot! For the Toy Table. Right after the aprons. (Resumes dusting.)

Libby.

(After a pause.) You sailed for Belfast in November. November, nineteen and ten.

Sarah.

I believe I did.

Libby.

Yes, and you considered returning on the Titanic.

SARAH.

It's a good thing I didn't!

Libby.

Oh, I don't know. If you'd survived, you'd have had a lot to talk about for the rest of your life.

Sarah.

Indeed. But, I came back on the Olympic instead, without incident.

Libby.

Shipwreck would have been so thrilling.

Sarah.

I'm not cut out for that sort of thrill.

Libby.

Is that so?

Sarah.

Yes. (Pauses in her chore.) You know, I believe we'll see the whales this weekend.

Libby.

Now THAT would be a surprise.

Sarah.

It's time for them.

Libby.

They don't come anymore.

Sarah.

They were here last summer.

Libby.

Right out here, in the sound?

Sarah.

Of course.

Libby.

I didn't hear them.

Sarah.

(A slight pause.) Well, they were too far offshore.

Libby.

I see.

Sarah.

Besides, the herring are running. That's a sure sign.

Libby.

Signs fail, y'know.

Sarah.

Libby Strong, I shall see them and you will hear them, right out front, just as we always have! (She exits into kitchen with dust cloth.)

Libby.

(Pause.) When you were a little girl, Sarah, you thought the whales made the seasons change.

Sarah.

(Re-entering and pausing in her cross.) I did?

Libby.

Yes, you told Father that the whales caught the wind with their tails and hauled it down from the Arctic.

Sarah.

I DO remember that.

Libby.

Tisha's coming, isn't she?

Sarah.

Yes, dear.

Libby.

Then I should have my shoes.

Sarah.

Of course, dear. (Crosses to exit into Libby's room.) With all this reminiscing, I forgot.

Libby.

I want to look presentable.

Sarah.

(Off.) What did you do with them?

Libby.

I didn't do anything.

Sarah.

(Off.) Did you look for them?

Libby.

Yes, Sarah!

Sarah.

(Off.) I found them. (Enters with shoes.) You must have kicked them under the bureau. (Gives shoes to Libby.)

Libby.

(Starts putting on shoes, hands slippers to Sarah.) You needn't hover, Sarah.

Sarah.

(Doing just that, she retreats a small distance to observe Libby's efforts.) Of course not, dear.

Libby.

(After her shoes are on.) Will you have time to brush my hair?

Sarah.

I do have some more tidying to do.

Libby.

Oh, if it's SUCH a bother . . .

Sarah.

No, dear, no bother. (Exits to Libby's room with slippers.)

Libby.

Perhaps outside would be nice.

Sarah.

(Off.) Yes, there's no breeze.

Libby.

(Rises, crosses slowly to porch.) Will you bring my brooch, too?

Sarah.

(Off.) Yes, dear. (Libby makes her way outside through the screened door, takes a deep breath once on porch landing, then crosses D. to her porch rocker. Sarah enters from bedroom, follows to porch with brush, comb, hairpins and brooch.)

Libby.

(Sitting in rocker.) Do make me look presentable.

Sarah.

You always look presentable. (Arranges items on side table, and takes her place behind Libby after placing brooch in Libby's hand.)

Libby.

I expect I'm a great bother to you.

Sarah.

Nothing of the sort. (Pause; Sarah begins the brushing.) Mr. Maranov is fishing on our rocks.

Libby.

I hope he doesn't offer his catch to us.

Sarah.

He usually gets a fine bunch of cunners.

Libby.

I will not eat any of those fish!

Sarah.

Oh, for heaven's sake—

Libby.

Sewer fish—that's what they are.

Sarah.

Nonsense. The currents are very strong.

Libby.

I will not eat anything caught off these rocks.

Sarah.

The fish are perfectly delicious.

Libby.

They are disgusting! Our sewage goes right out that ugly pipe.

Sarah.

Do you think that I would eat them if I were worried?

Libby.

You'd do anything to flatter that fraud.

Sarah.

He's NOT a fraud.

Libby.

BARON Maranov, indeed.

Sarah.

Helen Parsons has seen photographs of him and his mother at the Tsar's court.

Libby.

That was so long ago it could be anybody.

Sarah.

According to Helen, the resemblance is unmistakable.

Libby.

I will not eat his fish.

Sarah.

You don't have to!

Libby.

There, you see. I AM a bother.

Sarah.

You're just being silly about those fish.

Libby.

You're not much for complaining, but I can feel it from you.

Sarah.

I remind you, Elizabeth Mae, that I was the one who volunteered to move into your house in Germantown after your operations.

Libby.

You had just lost your Philip.

Sarah.

Yes.

Libby.

Well, I suppose you could change your mind.

Sarah.

Whatever for?

Libby.

I do have my Anna.

Sarah.

Your Anna has never wanted to be involved in our lives.

Libby.

She IS my daughter.

Sarah.

Only at Christmas, it would seem.

Libby.

I know what you're thinking.

Sarah.

Yes, and we've had this very same discussion since the Depression. She's never been very daughterly and you've never been very motherly, and that's THAT. Now, hold still while I get out this snarl.

Libby.

Ouch! (Pause.) Do you remember the swans in the park when we were children?

Sarah.

Yes.

Libby.

Mother had hair like that. I suppose you wouldn't remember.

Sarah.

No.

Libby.

Is my hair as white as the swans?

Sarah.

I expect it is.

Libby.

You're not fibbing?

Sarah.

Why should I?

Libby.

Not yellowing at all?

Sarah.

No, dear.

Libby.

I've always had beautiful hair.

Sarah.

Um-hmn.

Libby.

Matthew thought it was my crowning glory.

Sarah.

Matthew was right.

Libby.

What colour is your hair now?

Sarah.

Grey. The brown's all gone.

Libby.

Nothing's forever.

Sarah.

So you always say.

Libby.

I do?

Sarah.

Several times a week.

Libby.

Some things bear repeating.

Sarah.

I suppose.

Libby.

Many times.

Sarah.

I hear them.

Libby.

I don't think so.

Sarah.

Hold still, dear.

Libby.

(Pause.) Quite white you say?

Sarah.

What?

Libby.

My hair.

Sarah.

Oh, yes . . . quite.

Libby.

(Pause.) Matthew and I used to sit in the park. (Pause.) Parks are for children, and lovers in springtime.

Sarah.

Ah . . . yes . . .

Libby.

I haven't been to a park for a long time.

Sarah.

Being here is like being in a park.

Libby.

No swans, though. (Pause.) Swans mate for life, you know.

Sarah.

Is that a fact?

Libby.

Yes. (Pause.) Did you and Philip think it was for life?

Sarah.

Why . . . yes.

Libby.

Life fooled you.

Sarah.

Yes, it did.

Libby.

Always does.

Sarah.

(Pause.) Tomorrow is Philip's and my forty-second anniversary.

Libby.

Last Valentine's Day, it was sixty-six years for Matthew and me.

Sarah.

Gracious . . .

Libby.

Yes. . . . you were only nine when I married him.

Sarah.

Wasn't I a good flower girl?

Libby.

You stepped on my train. (Pause.) Matthew died in November.

Sarah.

So he did. November, nineteen and . . .

Libby.

Thirty-four.

Sarah.

Has it really been twenty years?

Libby.

Yes. I was sixty-six when he died. (Pause.) When did the four of us take that trip out West?

Sarah.

Right after the War, dear. Not too long after Philip came home from France.

Libby.

Yes . . . you two were always creeping away to be alone.

Sarah.

It WAS our anniversary.

Libby.

It wasn't an important one.

Sarah.

It was to ME.

Libby.

(Slight pause.) Wasn't it nice of Teddy Roosevelt to put those National Parks all over the place?

Sarah.

Very thoughtful of him.

Libby.

Trouble is, they're always in the middle of nowhere. He didn't put any of 'em close to home. (Pause.) It would be lovely to sit in a park for a while. It's such a nice day for November.

Sarah.

(Halts brushing.) Libby. . . .

Libby.

I know what month this is! This August I know.

Sarah.

(Resumes brushing.) Good, dear.

Libby.

I don't forget things.

Sarah.

I think you forgot your breakfast.

Libby.

That was a CHOICE.

Sarah.

All right, dear. (Finishes brushing, starts combing.)

Libby.

I had such trouble taking care of your hair. A little ragamuffin you were.

Sarah.

A bit of a tomboy, I guess.

Libby.

Always creeping about and hiding in trees.

Sarah.

No more trees for me.

Libby.

Why not?

Sarah.

I creak too much around the edges. (Stops combing, begins wrapping Libby's hair in an elegant, simple twist.)

Libby.

Just close your eyes and climb a tree.

Sarah.

Haven't got time. (In silence, places hairpins in Libby's coif.) There, there, there. All done.

Libby.

Do you know why old ladies sit on park benches, Sarah?

Sarah.

Why, dear?

Libby.

To hold them for springtime lovers. Even the benches want to get away in November.

Sarah.

Libby, this is August.

Libby.

Whatever you wish, Sarah. The time doesn't matter.

Sarah.

Of course it does.

Libby.

Only if you wear it like a wet blanket.

Sarah.

(Gathering up hair things.) Are you going to stay outside a while?

Libby.

Yes, Sarah.

Sarah.

All right, dear. (Starts to exit with hair things.)

Libby.

Bring me that hat from Albuquerque.

Sarah.

I'll get it for you, dear. (Enters living room to re-trieve outsized "tourist" sombrero.)

Libby.

(While Sarah is inside.) You think I forget the time, but I don't. All the time is mine. It's what's left to me.

Sarah.

(Enters porch, pauses.) Are you sure you want to stay outside, dear?

Libby.

Yes, go about your chores, Sarah. I'll hold the bench. (Puts on sombrero.)

Sarah.

Your favorite programs are coming on. It's almost time for Arthur Godfrey and Break the Bank.

Libby.

I don't need the radio anymore. (She shivers slightly.)

Sarah.

Are you all right, dear?

Libby.

He's so close, Sarah. My bones are in his November reach.

Sarah.

(Pause.) Whose reach, Libby?

Libby.

The escort. Not so very far away, the door will open and in he'll come, wearing an old bathrobe soiled with the residues of all the times, the stains and streaks and smears ... and tears ... tears from a thousand eyes.

Sarah.

Libby!

Libby.

A time for departure, damp and drizzly—November, you see! Matthew's month will be mine!

Sarah.

Elizabeth Mae, I won't listen to this!

Libby.

Hush, child. You must!

Sarah.

No! We don't have much time left, Libby. I'd like the last of it to be pleasant!

Libby.

Then stop making plans!! (Sarah exits into living room.)

(Moderate fade to black)

Scenes for a Man and a Woman

The Cave Dwellers

William Saroyan

The following introduction is in the author's own description of the play in his foreword. "The Cave Dwellers happens on the stage of an abandoned theatre. . . . Two of the leading characters of the play, called the King and the Queen, are professional actors, old, unemployed, ill and comic, because while all people are inevitably actors of one sort or another, who else but rejected actors would find sanctuary on the stage of an abandoned theatre, with a silent and empty auditorium? Who else would return with regret and hope to a fallen empire except a King and Queen driven long ago from their own realms?" Two very short lines by a Girl are deleted and marked with asterisks. The following scene from Act I, Scene 3 takes place at a table. The King and the Queen are chewing the last of the bread.

KING, QUEEN

King.
 Well, that's the end of the bread.
Queen.
 (Brightly, almost gaily.) Yes, we've eaten it all.

121

King.

Uptown the lights are on. The theatres are ready. The tickets are sold. The players are putting on their makeup and getting into their costumes. In a moment the curtains will go up, and one by one the plays will begin and The Great Good Friend out there—(He gestures toward the auditorium.)—will look and listen. And little by little something will stir in his soul and come to life—a smile, a memory, a reminder of an old forgotten truth, tender regret, kindness. In short, the secret of the theatre.

******

Queen.

Love, of course. Without love, pain and failure are pain and failure, nothing else. But WITH love they are beauty and meaning themselves.

******

Queen.

(Acts.) Entreat me not to leave thee: for whither thou goest, I will go: and where thou lodgest, I will lodge: thy people shall be my people, and where thou diest, will I die.

King.

Bravo, you did that very well.

Queen.

Oh, King, do a clown's bit. A KINGLY clown's bit.

King.

I belong uptown. I STILL do. I was born there, and then I was put out.

Queen.

Are you an actor, or a sad old man like all the other sad old men? I thought it was agreed. We are of the theatre. You are to perform, not to be performed UPON.

King.

(Puts a crumb in his mouth.) I'm still eating. Would you have eating a performance, too?

Queen.

Would you have it something else? Could it possibly BE something else? Do a bit about EATING!

King.

We just did that bit, didn't we? (He puts a crumb between his upper and lower teeth and crushes it with one deliberately large chomp.)

Queen.

This time WITHOUT bread. For its own dear sake.

King.

I AM challenged, Woman. You know I would kill myself for art.

Queen.

Or US—from the wonder of it.

King.

(He gets up quickly.) The great man comes to the famous restaurant, hungry and hushed, and thoughtful, because he remembers when he was nobody and the world was still faraway. Now, he wears the unmistakable SCOWL of superiority, and so the ARROGANT headwaiter's offer to sit—(He indicates the drawing-out of a chair.)—he stands a moment to notice who else has come to the holy joint, and to be noticed by them. (The Queen leans forward, delighted both with his work and her success in having provoked him into it.) But who is he? (Pause, extra clearly, now loud, now soft, inventing wildly.) Is he perhaps the new Secretary of State, before his first flight to—(Searches for an inept destination.) DUBROVNIK? The Spanish pianist from Palma of the Canary Islands? The man who discovered the FLAW in the theory of cycles? He who invented the law of loss, or was it only the lollipop?

Or is he perhaps the man who learned the language of the Arab tribes, brought the warring chiefs together, engineered the business of the oil? (Slight pause.) Let them try to guess, it's good for them. In any case, it's time to sit and eat. He eats, and eats, one rare dish after another. (Comically astonished.) But what's this with the crepe suzettes? A FLY, isn't it? A COMMON FLY? (He stops.)

(The Queen waits expectantly. He does not go on.)

Queen.

(Softly.) Well, why do you stop?

King.

(Earnestly.) It's part of the bit. A man stops, doesn't he? Suddenly? Unaccountably? He remembers, and he thinks, doesn't he? IS it worth it? All the TRYING, and all the eating? (Slowly, very clearly.) Joe's dead. Mary's divorced. Johnny's boy is stealing automobiles. Pat's girl is breaking up the home of a dentist.

Queen.

Bravo!

King.

Thank you for stopping me. I might have gone on forever, from loneliness and despair.

Come Back, Little Sheba

William Inge

❧

The play, produced in l950, is set in a Midwestern city in 1949 and deals with Doc, a middle-aged chiropractor, who, many years before, had had to quit medical school to marry his girl-friend Lola, whom he had impregnated. This and other disappointments, as revealed in this scene, have been factors in his struggle with alcohol. To help make ends meet, Doc and Lola have taken in a boarder, a young, attractive college girl, Marie, whose presence seems to have affected Doc's behavior patterns. Although Marie has been spending time with a college boy, Turk, she is expecting a visit from her fiancé. This has motivated Lola, whose housekeeping leaves much to be desired, to make a real effort toward making the house presentable. This scene opens with Doc washing the dishes and Lola puttering around putting the finishing touches on her housecleaning. The "Little Sheba" of the title refers to a lost puppy.

DOC, LOLA

Lola.

(At stove) There's still some beans left. Do you
want them, Doc?

Doc.

(At sink) I had enough.

Lola.

I hope you got enough to eat tonight, Daddy. I been
so busy cleaning I didn't have time to fix you much.

Doc.

I wasn't very hungry.

Lola.

(To table, cleaning up) You know what? Mrs. Coffman said I could come over and pick all the lilacs
I wanted for my centerpiece tomorrow. Isn't that
nice? I don't think she poisoned Little Sheba, do
you?

Doc.

I never did think so, Baby. Where'd you get the new
curtains?

Lola.

I went out and bought them this afternoon. Aren't
they pretty? Be careful of the woodwork; it's been
varnished.

Doc.

How come, Honey?

Lola.

(Gets broom and dust pan from closet) Bruce is
comin'. I figured I had to do my spring housecleaning sometime.

Doc.

You got all this done in one day? The house hasn't
looked like this in years.

Lola.

I can be a good housekeeper when I want to be,
can't I, Doc?

Doc.

(kneels, holding dustpan for Lola) I never had any complaints. Where's Marie now?

Lola.

I don't know, Doc. I haven't seen her since she left here this morning with Turk.

Doc.

(Rises. A look of disapproval) Marie's too good to be wasting her time with him.

Lola.

Daddy, Marie can take care of herself. Don't worry. (To closet—returns broom.)

Doc.

(Goes into living room) 'Bout time for Fibber McGee and Molly.

Lola.

(Untying apron. To closet and then to back door) Daddy, I'm gonna run over to Mrs. Coffman's and see if she's got any silver polish. I'll be right back. (Doc goes to radio. Lola exits. At the radio Doc starts twisting the dial. He rejects one noisy program after another, then very unexpectedly he comes across a rendition of Shubert's famous "Ave Maria," sung in a high soprano voice. Probably he has encountered the piece before somewhere, but it is now making its first impression on him. Sits davenport. Gradually he is transported into a world of ethereal beauty which he never knew existed. He listens intently. The music has expressed some ideal of beauty he never fully realized and he is even a little mystified. Then Lola comes in the back door, letting it slam, breaking the spell, and announcing in a loud, energetic voice:)

Lola.

(Comes into living room) Isn't that funny?? I'm not a bit tired tonight. You'd think after working so hard all day I'd be pooped.

Doc.

(He cringes) Baby, don't use that word.

Lola.

(Sets silver polish down and joins Doc on davenport) I'm sorry, Doc. I hear Marie and Turk say it all the time, and I thought it was kinda cute.

Doc.

It—it sounds vulgar.

Lola.

(Kisses Doc) I won't say it again, Daddy. Where's Fibber McGee? (Starts record)

Doc.

Not quite time yet.

Lola.

(Sits chair down Right) Let's get some peppy music.

Doc.

(Tuning in a sentimental dance band) That what you want?

Lola.

That's O.K. (Doc takes a pack of cards off radio, returns to davenport and starts shuffling them very deftly.) I love to watch you shuffle cards, Daddy. You use your hands so gracefully. (She watches closely. Rises, crosses to Doc) Do me one of your card tricks.

Doc.

Baby, you've seen them all.

Lola.

But I never get tired of them.

Doc.

O.K. Take a card. (Lola does.) Keep it now. Don't tell me what it is.

Lola.

I won't.

Doc.

(Shuffling cards again) Now put it back in the deck. I won't look. (He closes his eyes.)

Lola.

(With childish delight) All right.

Doc.

Put it back.

Lola.

Uh-huh.

Doc.

O.K. (Shuffles cards again, cutting them, taking top half off, exposing Lola's card, to her astonishment) That your card?

Lola.

(Unbelievingly) Daddy, how did you do it?

Doc.

Baby, I've pulled that trick on you dozens of times.

Lola.

But I never understand how you do it.

Doc.

Very simple.

Lola.

Docky, show me how you do that.

Doc.

(You can forgive him a harmless feeling of superiority) Try it for yourself. (Rises; crosses Right.)

Lola.

Doc, you're clever. I never could do it.

Doc.

Nothing to it.

Lola.

There is too. Show me how you do it, Doc.

Doc.

And give away all my secrets? (Sits down Right) It's a gift, Honey. A magic gift.

Lola.

Can't you give it to me?

Doc.

(Picks up newspaper) A man has to keep some things to himself.

Lola.

It's not a gift at all, it's just some trick you learned.

Doc.

O.K., Baby, any way you want to look at it.

Lola.

Let's have some music. How soon do you have to meet Ed Anderson?

Doc.

(Turns on radio) I still got a little time. (Pleased.)

Lola.

Marie's going to be awfully happy when she sees the house all fixed up. She can entertain Bruce here when he comes, and maybe we could have a little party here and you can do your card tricks.

Doc.

O.K.

Lola.

I think a young girl should be able to bring her friends home.

Doc.

Sure.

Lola.

We never liked to sit around the house 'cause the folks always stayed there with us. (Rises—starts dancing alone) Remember the dances we used to go to, Daddy?

Doc.

Sure.

Lola.

We had awful good times—for a while, didn't we?

Doc.

Yes, Baby.

Lola.

Remember the homecoming dance, when Cheerily Kettlekamp and I won the Charleston Contest?

Doc.

Yah. Please, Honey, I'm trying to read.

Lola.

And you got mad at him cause he thought he should take me home afterwards.

Doc.

I did not.

Lola.

Yes, you did. Charlie was all right, Doc, really he was. You were just jealous.

Doc.

I WASN'T jealous.

Lola.

(She has become very coy and flirtatious now, an old dog playing old tricks) You got jealous. Every time we went out any place and I even looked at another boy. There was never anything between Charlie and me; there never was.

Doc.

That was a long time ago—

Lola.

Lots of other boys called me up for dates—Sammy Knight—Hand Biederman—Dutch McCoy.

Doc.

Sure, Baby. You were the "it" girl.

Lola.

(Pleading for his attention now) But I saved all my dates for you, didn't I, Doc?

Doc.

(Trying to joke) As far as I know, Baby.

Lola.

(Hurt) Daddy, I did. You GOT to believe that. I never took a date with any other boy but you.

Doc.

(A little weary and impatient) That's all forgotten now. (Turns off radio.)

Lola.

How can you talk that way, Doc? That was the happiest time of our lives,

Doc.

(Disapprovingly) Honey!

Lola.

(At the window) That was a nice spring. The trees were so heavy and green and the air smelled so sweet. Remember the walks we used to take, down to the old chapel, where it was so quiet and still? (Sits davenport.)

Doc.

In the spring a young man's fancy turns—pretty fancy.

Lola.

(In the same tone of reverie) I was pretty then, wasn't I, Doc? Remember the first time you kissed me? You were scared as a young girl, I believe, Doc; you trembled so. (She is being very soft and delicate. Caught in the reverie, he chokes a little and cannot answer.) We'd been going together all year and you were always so shy. Then for the first time you grabbed me and kissed me. Tears came to your eyes, Doc, and you said you'd love me forever and ever. Remember? You said—if I didn't marry you, you wanted to die—I remember 'cause it scared me for anyone to say a thing like that.

Doc.

(In a repressed tone) Yes, Baby.

Lola.

And when the evening came on, we stretched out on the cool grass and you kissed me all night long.

Doc.

(Rises. Opens door) Baby, you've got to forget those things. That was twenty years ago.

Lola.

I'll soon be forty. Those years have just vanished—vanished into thin air.

Doc.

Yes.

Lola.

Just disappeared—like Little Sheba. (Pause) Maybe you're sorry you married me now. You didn't know I was going to get old and fat and sloppy—

Doc.

Oh, Baby!

Lola.

It's the truth. That's what I am. But I didn't know it, either. Are you sorry you married me, Doc?

Doc.

Of course not.

Lola.

(Rises; crosses to Doc) I mean, are you sorry you HAD to marry me?

Doc.

(Onto porch) We were never going to talk about that, Baby.

Lola.

(Following Doc out) You WERE the first one, Daddy, the ONLY one. I'd just die if you didn't believe that.

Doc.

(Tenderly) I know, Baby.

Lola.

You were so nice and so proper, Doc: I thought nothing we could do together could ever be wrong—or make us unhappy. Do you think we did wrong, Doc?

Doc.

(Consoling) No, Baby, of course I don't.

Lola.

I don't think anyone knows about it except my folks, do you?

Doc.

(Crossing in to up Right) Of course not, Baby.

Lola.

(Follows in) I wish the baby had lived, Doc. I don't think that woman knew her business, do you, Doc?

Doc.

I guess not.

Lola.

If we'd gone to a doctor, she would have lived, don't you think?

Doc.

Perhaps.

Lola.

A doctor wouldn't have known we'd just got married, Why were we so afraid?

Doc.

(Sits davenport) We were just kids. Kids don't know how to look after things.

Lola.

(Sits davenport) If we'd had the baby she'd be a young girl now; then maybe you'd have SAVED your money, Doc, and she could be going to college—like Marie.

Doc.

Baby, what's done is done.

Lola.

It must make you feel bad at times to think you had to give up being a doctor and to think you don't have any money like you used to.

Doc.

(Takes stage) No—no, Baby. We should never feel bad about what's past. What's in the past can't be helped. You—you've got to forget it and live for the present. If you can't forget the past, you stay in it and never get out. I might be a big M.D. today, instead of a chiropractor; we might have had a family to raise and be with us now; I might still have a lot of money if I'd used my head and invested it carefully, instead of gettin' drunk every night. We might have a nice house, and comforts, and friends. But we don't have any of those things. So what! We gotta keep on living, don't we? I can't stop just 'cause I made a few mistakes. I gotta keep goin'—somehow.

Lola.

Sure, Daddy.

Doc.

(Sighs and wipes brow) I—I wish you wouldn't ask me questions like that, Baby. Let's not talk about it any more. I gotta keep goin', and not let things upset me, or—or—I saw enough at the City Hospital to keep me sober for a long time.

Lola.

I'm sorry, Doc. I didn't mean to upset you.

Doc.

I'm not upset.

Lola.

What time'll you be home tonight?

Doc.

'Bout eleven o'clock.

Lola.

I wish you didn't have to go tonight. I feel kinda lonesome.

Doc.

(Sits davenport) Yah, so do I, Baby, but sometime soon we'll go OUT together. I kinda hate to go to those night clubs and places since I stopped drinking, but some night I'll take you out to dinner.

Lola.

Oh, will you, Daddy?

Doc.

We'll get dressed up and go to the Windermere and have a fine dinner, and dance between courses.

Lola.

(Eagerly) Let's do, Daddy. I got a little money saved up. I got about forty dollars out in the kitchen. We can take that if you need it.

Doc.

I'll have plenty of money the first of the month.

Lola.

(Lola has made a quick response to the change of mood, seeing a future evening of carefree fun) What are we sitting round here so serious for? (To radio) Let's have some music. (Lola gets a lively foxtrot on the radio, dances with Doc. They begin dancing vigorously, as though to dispense with the sadness of the preceding dialogue, but slowly it winds them and leaves Lola panting) We oughta go dancing— all the time, Docky—It'd be good for us. Maybe if I danced more often I'd lose—some of—this fat. I remember—I used to be able to dance like this— all night—and not even notice—it. (Lola breaks into a Charleston routine as of yore) Remember the Charleston, Daddy?

(Doc is clapping his hands in rhythm. Then Marie bursts in through the front door, the personification of the youth that Lola is trying to recapture.)

Doc.

Hi, Marie!

Come Back, Little Sheba

William Inge

It is five-thirty in the morning. Doc has not returned home in time for the dinner party that Lola had planned for Marie and her fiancé. Still in her dinner party dress but completely disheveled, Lola is sleeping on the couch. When she awakens and realizes the situation, she rushes to the telephone and dials a number. For more background on this play, see introduction to the previous scene on page 125.

DOC, LOLA

Lola.

(At telephone. She sounds frantic) Mr. Anderson? Mr. Anderson, this is Mrs. Delaney again. I'm sorry to call you so early, but I just HAD to—Did you find Doc?—No, he's not home yet. I don't suppose he'll come home till he's drunk all he can hold and wants to sleep—I don't know what else to think, Mr. Anderson. I'm scared, Mr. Anderson. I'm awful scared. Will you come right over?—Thanks, Mr. Anderson. (Hangs up and goes to kitchen to make

coffee. She finds some left from the night before, so turns on the fire to warm it up. She wanders around vaguely, trying to get her thoughts in order, jumping at every sound. Pours herself a cup of coffee, then takes it to living room, sits down Right and sips it. Very quietly Doc enters through the back way into the kitchen. He carries a big bottle of whiskey, which he carefully places back in the cabinet, not making a sound—hangs up overcoat, then puts suitcoat on back of chair. Starts to go upstairs. But Lola speaks) Doc? That you, Doc?
(Then Doc quietly walks in from kitchen. He is staggering drunk, but he is managing for a few minutes to appear as though he were perfectly sober and nothing had happened. His steps, however, are not too sure and his eyes are like blurred ink pots. Lola is too frightened to talk. Her mouth is gaping and she is breathless with fear.)

Doc.
Good morning, Honey.

Lola.
Doc! You all right?

Doc.
(Crossing down Right by chair) The morning paper here? I wanta see the morning paper.

Lola.
Doc, we don't get a morning paper. YOU know that.

Doc.
(Sits down Right) Oh, then I suppose I'm drunk or something. That what you're trying to say?

Lola.
No, Doc—

Doc.
Then give me the morning paper.

Lola.
(Scampering to get last night's paper from table Left) Sure, Doc. Here it is. Now you just sit there and be quiet.

Doc.

(Resistance rising) Why shouldn't I be quiet?

Lola.

Nothin', Doc—

Doc.

(Has trouble unfolding paper. He places it before his face in order not to be seen. But he is too blind even to see. Mockingly) Nothing, Doc.

Lola.

(Cautiously, after a few minutes' silence) Doc, are you all right?

Doc.

Of course I'm all right. Why shouldn't I be all right?

Lola.

Where you been?

Doc.

What's it your business where I been? I been to London to see the Queen. What do you think of that? (Apparently she doesn't know what to think of it.) Just let me alone. That's all I ask. I'm all right.

Lola.

(Sits Right end of davenport. Simpering) Doc, what made you do it? You said you'd be home last night—'cause we were having company. Bruce was here and I had a big dinner fixed—and you never came. What was the matter, Doc?

Doc.

(Mockingly) We had a big dinner for BRUCE.

Lola.

Doc, it was for you, too.

Doc.

Well—I don't want it.

Lola.

Don't get mad, Doc.

Doc.

(Threateningly. Rises, crosses up Center) Where's Marie?

Lola.

I don't know, Doc. She didn't come in last night. She was out with Bruce.

Doc.

(Back to audience) I suppose you tucked them in bed together and peeked through the keyhole and applauded.

Lola.

(Sickened) Doc, don't talk that way. Bruce is a nice boy. They're gonna get married.

Doc.

He probably HAS to marry her, the poor bastard. Just 'cause she's pretty and he got amorous one day—Just like I had to marry YOU.

Lola.

Oh, Doc!

Doc.

You and Marie are both a couple of sluts.

Lola.

(Rises, crosses Right) Doc, please don't talk like that.

Doc.

What are you good for? You can't even get up in the morning and cook my breakfast.

Lola.

(Mumbling) I will, Doc. I will after this.

Doc.

You won't even sweep the floors till some bozo comes along to make love to Marie, and then you fix things up like Buckingham Palace or a Chinese whorehouse with perfume on the lampbulbs, and flowers, and the gold-trimmed china MY MOTHER gave us. We're not going to use these any more. My mother didn't buy those dishes for whores to eat off of. (Jerks the cloth off the table, sending the dishes rattling to the floor.)

Lola.

(Breaking Left) Doc! Look what you done.

Doc.

Look what I DID, not DONE. I'm going to get me a drink. (To kitchen.)

Lola.

(Follows to platform) Oh no, Doc! You know what it does to you!

Doc.

You're damn right I know what it does to me. It makes me willing to come home here and look at you, you two-ton old heifer. (Gets bottle. Takes a long swallow) There! And pretty soon I'm going to have another, then another.

Lola.

(With dread) Oh, Doc! (Lola takes phone. Doc sees this, rushes for the butcher-knife in kitchen cabinet drawer. Not finding it, he gets a hatchet from the back porch.) Mr. Anderson? Come quick, Mr. Anderson. He's back. He's BACK! He's got a hatchet!

Doc.

God damn you! Get away from that telephone. (He chases her into living room, where she gets the davenport between them; Lola downstage, Doc up.) That's right, phone! Tell the world I'm drunk. Tell the whole damn world. Scream your head off, you fat slut. Holler till all the neighbors think I'm beatin' hell out of you. Where's Bruce now—under Marie's bed? You got all fresh and pretty for him, didn't you? Combed your hair for once—You even washed the back of your neck, and put on a girdle. You were willing to harness all that fat into one bundle.

Lola.

(About to faint under the weight of the crushing accusation) Doc, don't say any more—I'd rather you hit me with an axe, Doc—Honest I would. But I can't stand to hear you talk like that.

Doc.

I oughta hack off all that fat, and then wait for Marie and chop off those pretty ankles she's always dancing around on—then start lookin' for Turk and fix him, too.

Lola.

Daddy, you're talking crazy!

Doc.

(Moves to above Right end of davenport) I'm making sense for the first time in my life. You didn't know I knew about it, did you? But I saw him coming outa there. I saw him. You knew about it all the time and thought you were hidin' something—

Lola.

(To up Center of davenport) Daddy, I didn't know anything about it at all. Honest, Daddy.

Doc.

Then YOU'RE the one that's crazy, if you think I didn't know. You were running a regular house, weren't you? It's probably been going on for years, ever since we were married. (He lunges for her. She breaks for kitchen. They struggle in front of sink.)

Lola.

Doc, it's not so; it's not so. You gotta believe me, Doc.

Doc.

You're lyin'. But none a that's gonna happen any more. I'm gonna fix you now, once and for all—

Lola.

Doc, don't do that to me. (Lola, in a frenzy of fear, clutches him around the neck, holding arm with axe

by his side) Remember, Doc. It's ME, Lola! You
said I was the prettiest girl you ever saw. Remember, Doc! It's me! Lola!

Doc.

(The memory has overpowered him. He collapses,
slowly mumbling) Lola—my pretty Lola.

(He passes out on the floor. Lola stands, now, as
though in a trance.)

Death of a Salesman

Arthur Miller

This scene is from one of America's most acclaimed, most performed and most loved plays, which has been considered a clas-
sic ever since its first performance in 1949. The set, a relatively
new design at the time, is expressionistic, with a partially trans-
parent house. This scene is the opening scene between Willy
Loman and his wife, Linda. In her bedroom, Linda hears Willy
coming home; he is carrying two large suitcases. He is exhausted. The sound of a flute is heard in the background. Two
lines from the sons in their bedrooms and a stage direction
referring to them are deleted and marked with asterisks.

WILLY, LINDA

Linda.

(Hearing Willy outside the bedroom, calls with some trepidation:) Willy!

Willy.

It's all right. I came back..

Linda.

Why? What happened? (Slight pause.) Did something happen, Willy?

Willy.

No, nothing happened.

Linda.

You didn't smash the car, did you?

Willy.

(With casual irritation:) I said nothing happened. Didn't you hear me?

Linda.

Don't you feel well?

Willy.

I'm tired to the death. (The flute has faded away. He sits on the bed beside her, a little numb.) I couldn't make it. I just couldn't make it, Linda.

Linda.

(Very carefully, delicately:) Where were you all day? You look terrible.

Willy.

I got as far as a little above Yonkers. I stopped for a cup of coffee. Maybe it was the coffee.

Linda.

What?

Willy.

(After a pause:) I suddenly couldn't drive any more. The car kept going off onto the shoulder, y'know?

Linda.

(Helpfully.) Oh. Maybe it was the steering again. I don't think Angelo knows the Studebaker.

Willy.

No, it's me, it's me. Suddenly I realize I'm going sixty miles an hour and I don't remember the last five minutes. I'm—I can't seem to—keep my mind to it.

Linda.

Maybe it's your glasses. You never went for your new glasses.

Willy.

No, I see everything. I came back ten miles an hour. It took me nearly four hours from Yonkers.

Linda.

(Resigned.) Well, you'll just have to take a rest, Willy, you can't continue this way.

Willy.

I just got back from Florida.

Linda.

But you didn't rest your mind. Your mind is over-active, and the mind is what counts, dear.

Willy.

I'll start out in the morning. Maybe I'll feel better in the morning. (She is taking off his shoes.) These goddam arch supports are killing me.

Linda.

Take an aspirin. Should I get you an aspirin? It'll soothe you.

Willy.

(With wonder.) I was driving along, you understand? And I was fine. I was even observing the scenery. You can imagine, me looking at scenery, on the road every week of my life. But it's so beautiful up there, Linda, the trees are so thick, and the sun is warm. I opened the windshield and just let the warm air bathe over me. And then all of a sudden I'm going off the road! I'm tellin' ya. I absolutely forgot I was driving. If I'd've gone the other way over the white line I might've killed somebody. So I went on again—and five minutes later I'm dreamin' again, and I nearly—(He presses two fingers against his eyes.) I have such thoughts, I have such strange thoughts.

Linda.

Willy, dear. Talk to them again. There's no reason why you can't work in New York.

Willy.

They don't need me in New York. I'm the New England man. I'm vital in New England.

Linda.

But you're sixty years old. They can't expect you to keep traveling every week.

Willy.

I'll have to send a wire to Portland. I'm supposed to see Brown and Morrison tomorrow morning at ten o'clock to show the line. Goddammit, I could sell them! (He starts putting on his jacket.)

Linda.

(Taking the jacket from him:) Why don't you go down to the place tomorrow and tell Howard you've simply got to work in New York? You're too accommodating, dear.

Willy.

If old man Wagner was alive I'd been in charge of New York now! That man was a prince, he was a masterful man. But that boy of his, that Howard, he don't appreciate. When I went north the first time, the Wagner Company didn't know where New England was!

Linda.

Why don't you tell those things to Howard, dear?

Willy.

(Encouraged.) I will. I definitely will. Is there any cheese?

Linda.

I'll make you a sandwich.

Willy.

No, go to sleep. I'll take some milk. I'll be up right away. The boys in?

Linda.

They're sleeping. Happy took Biff on a date tonight.

Willy.

(Interested.) That so?

Linda. '

It was so nice to see them shaving together, one behind the other, in the bathroom. And going out together. You notice? The whole house smells of shaving lotion.

Willy.

Figure it out. Work a lifetime to pay off a house. You finally own it, and there's nobody to live in it.

Linda.

Well, dear, life is a casting off. It's always that way.

Willy.

No, no, some people—some people accomplish something. Did Biff say anything after I went this morning?

Linda.

You shouldn't have criticized him, Willy, especially after he just got off the train. You mustn't lose your temper with him.

Willy.

When the hell did I lose my temper? I simply asked him if he was making any money. Is that a criticism?

Linda.

But, dear, how could he make any money?

Willy.

(Worried and angered:) There's such an undercurrent in him. He became a moody man. Did he apologize when I left this morning?

Linda.

He was crestfallen, Willy. You know how he admires you. I think if he finds himself, then you'll
both be happier and not fight any more.

Willy.

How can he find himself on a farm? Is that a life?
A farmhand? In the beginning, when he was young,
I thought, well, a young man, it's good for him to
tramp around, take a lot of different jobs. But it's
more than ten years now and he has yet to make
thirty-five dollars a week!

Linda.

He's finding himself, Willy.

Willy.

Not finding yourself at the age of thirty-four is a
disgrace!

Linda.

Shh!

Willy.

The trouble is he's lazy, goddammit!

Linda.

Willy, please!

Willy.

Biff is a lazy bum!

Linda.

They're sleeping. Get something to eat. Go on
down.

Willy.

Why did he come home? I would like to know what
brought him home.

Linda.

I don't know. I think he's still lost, Willy. I think
he's very lost.

Willy.

Biff Loman is lost. In the greatest country in the
world a young man with such—personal attractive-

ness, gets lost. And such a hard worker. There's one
thing about Biff—he's not lazy.

Linda.

Never.

Willy.

(With pity and resolve:) I'll see him in the morning;
I'll have a nice talk with him. I'll get him a job
selling. He could be big in no time. My God! Remember how they used to follow him around in high
school? When he smiled at one of them their faces
lit up. When he walked down the street . . . (He
loses himself in reminiscences.)

Linda.

(Trying to bring him out of it:) Willy, dear, I got a
new kind of American-type cheese today. It's
whipped.

Willy.

Why do you get American when I like Swiss?

Linda.

I just thought you'd like a change—

Willy.

I don't want a change! I want Swiss cheese. Why
am I always being contradicted?

Linda.

(With a covering laugh.) I thought it would be a
surprise.

Willy.

Why don't you open a window in here, for God's
sake?

Linda.

(With infinite patience:) They're all open, dear.

Willy.

The way they boxed us in here. Bricks and windows, windows and bricks.

Linda.

We should've bought the land next door.

Willy.

The street is lined with cars. There's not a breath of fresh air in the neighborhood. The grass don't grow any more, you can't raise a carrot in the back yard. They should've had a law against apartment houses. Remember those two beautiful elm trees out there? When I and Biff hung the swing between them?

Linda.

Yeah, like being a million miles from the city.

Willy.

They should've arrested the builder for cutting those down. They massacred the neighborhood. Lost: More and more I think of those days, Linda. This time of year it was lilac and wisteria. And then the peonies would come out, and the daffodils. What fragrance in this room!

Linda.

Well, after all, people had to move somewhere.

Willy.

No, there's more people now.

Linda.

I don't think there's more people. I think—

Willy.

There's more people! That's what's ruining this country! Population is getting out of control. The competition is maddening! Smell the stink from that apartment house! And another one on the other side . . . How can they whip cheese?

******

Linda.

Go down, try it. And be quiet.

Willy.

(Turning to Linda, guiltily.) You're not worried about me, are you, sweetheart?

******

Linda.

You've got too much on the ball to worry about.

Willy.

You're my foundation and my support, Linda.

Linda.

Just try to relax, dear. You make mountains out of molehills.

Willy.

I won't fight with him any more. If he wants to go back to Texas, let him go.

Linda.

He'll find his way.

Willy.

Sure. Certain men just don't get started till later in life. Like Thomas Edison, I think. Or B.F. Goodrich. One of them was deaf. (He starts for the bedroom doorway.) I'll put my money on Biff.

Linda.

And Willy—if it's warm Sunday we'll drive in the country. And we'll open the windshield, and take lunch.

Willy.

No, the windshields don't open on the new cars.

Linda.

But you opened it today.

Willy.

Me? I didn't. (He stops.) Now isn't that peculiar! Isn't that a remarkable—(He breaks off in amazement and fright as the flute is heard distantly.)

Linda.

What, darling?

Willy.

That is the most remarkable thing.

Linda.

What, dear?

Willy.

I was thinking of the Chevvy. (Slight pause.) Nineteen twenty-eight . . . when I had that red Chevvy— (Breaks off.) That funny? I coulda sworn I was driving that Chevvy today.

Linda.

Well, that's nothing. Something must've reminded you.

Willy.

Remarkable. Ts. Remember those days? The way Biff used to simonize that car? The dealer refused to believe there was eighty-thousand miles on it. (He shakes his head.) Heh! (To Linda:) Close your eyes, I'll be right up. (He walks out of the bedroom.)

Driving Miss Daisy

Alfred Uhry

∽•∾

First performed in New York in 1987, this play covers a long period of time, starting in 1948 and running to 1973. This scene begins in Atlanta, Georgia, in Daisy Werthan's living room, with the action later moving to a car. As the author states, "The scenery is meant to be simple and evocative. The action shifts frequently." Daisy is a seventy-two-year-old white woman when the play opens. In a previous scene, she has had a very heated argument with her son who insists on hiring a chauffeur for her because she has had a car accident in her own driveway,

*doing considerable damage to the car and to both her and her
neighbor's property. She was not injured, however, and she ve-
hemently disapproves of a chauffeur. However, the son prevails
and hires Hoke, a sixty-year-old black man. This scene opens
with Miss Daisy reading the morning paper. Hoke enters, cap
in hand. "Her concentration on the paper becomes fierce when
she senses Hoke's presence." This is their first scene together.*

DAISY, HOKE

Hoke.
Mornin' Miz Daisy.
Daisy.
Good morning.
Hoke.
Right cool in the night, wasn't it?
Daisy.
I wouldn't know. I was asleep.
Hoke.
Yassum. What yo' plans today?
Daisy.
That's my business.
Hoke.
You right about dat. Idella say we runnin' outta cof-
fee and Dutch Cleanser.
Daisy.
We?
Hoke.
She say we low on silver polish too.
Daisy.
Thank you. I will go to the Piggly Wiggly on the
trolley this afternoon.
Hoke.
Now, Miz Daisy, how come you doan' let me carry
you?
Daisy.
No, thank you.

Hoke.

Ain't that what Mist' Werthan hire me for?

Daisy.

That's his problem.

Hoke.

All right den. I find something to do. I tend yo' zinnias.

Daisy.

Leave my flower bed alone.

Hoke.

Yassum. You got a nice place back beyond the garage ain' doin' nothin' but sittin' there. I could put you in some butter beans and some tomatoes and even some Irish potatoes could we get some ones with good eyes.

Daisy.

If I want a vegetable garden, I'll plant it for myself.

Hoke.

Well, I go out and set in the kitchen then, like I been doin' all week.

Daisy.

Don't talk to Idella. She has work to do!.

Hoke.

Nome. I jes' sit there till five o'clock.

Daisy.

That's your affair.

Hoke.

Seem a shame, do. That fine Oldsmobile settin' out there in the garage. Ain't move a inch from when Mist' Werthan rode it over here from Mitchell Motors. Only got nineteen miles on it. Seem like that insurance company give you a whole new car for nothin'.

Daisy.

That's your opinion.

Hoke.

Yassum. And my other opinion is a fine rich Jewish lady like you doan' b'long draggin' up the steps of no bus, luggin' no grocery-store bags. I come along and carry them fo' you.

Daisy.

I don't need you. I don't want you. And I don't like you saying I'm rich.

Hoke.

I won' say it then.

Daisy.

Is that what you and Idella talk about in the kitchen? Oh, I hate this! I hate being discussed behind my back in my own house! I was born on Forsyth Street and, believe you me, I knew the value of a penny. My brother Manny brought home a white cat one day and Papa said we couldn't keep it because we couldn't afford to feed it. My sisters saved up money so I could go to school and be a teacher. We didn't have anything!

Hoke.

Yassum, but look like you doin' all right now.

Daisy.

And I've ridden the trolley with groceries plenty of times!

Hoke.

Yassum, but I feel bad takin' Mist' Werthan's money for doin' nothin'. You understand?

Daisy.

How much does he pay you?

Hoke.

That between me and him, Miz Daisy.

Daisy.

Anything over seven dollars a week is robbery. Highway robbery!

Hoke.

Specially when I doan' do nothin' but set on a stool in the kitchen all day long. Tell you what, while you goin' on the trolley to the Piggly Wiggly, I hose down you' front steps.

(Daisy is putting on her hat)

Daisy.

All right.

Hoke.

All right I hose yo' steps?

Daisy.

All right the Piggly Wiggly. And then home. Nowhere else.

Hoke.

Yassum.

Daisy.

Wait. You don't know how to run the Oldsmobile!

Hoke.

Miz Daisy, a gearshift like a third arm to me. Anyway, thissun automatic. Any fool can run it.

Daisy.

Any fool but me, apparently.

Hoke.

Ain't no need to be so hard on yo' seff now. You cain' drive but you probably do alotta things I cain' do.

Daisy.

The idea!

Hoke.

It all work out.

Daisy.

(Calling offstage): I'm gone to the market, Idella.

Hoke.

(Also calling): And I right behind her!

(Hoke puts on his cap and helps Daisy into the car.*

_____
*The car is suggested using a few chairs.

He sits at the wheel and backs the car down the driveway. Daisy, in the rear, is in full bristle.)
I love a new car smell. Doan' you?
(Daisy slides over to the other side of the seat.)

Daisy.
I'm nobody's fool, Hoke.

Hoke.
Nome.

Daisy.
I can see the speedometer as well as you can.

Hoke.
I see dat.

Daisy.
My husband taught me how to run a car.

Hoke.
Yassum.

Daisy.
I still remember everything he said. So don't you even think for a second that you can—wait! You're speeding! I see it!

Hoke.
We ain't goin' but nineteen miles an hour.

Daisy.
I like to go under the speed limit.

Hoke.
Speed limit thirty-five here.

Daisy.
The slower you go, the more you save on gas. My husband told me that.

Hoke.
We barely movin'. Might as well walk to the Piggly Wiggly.

Daisy.
Is this your car?

Hoke.

Nome.

Daisy.

Do you pay for the gas?

Hoke.

Nome.

Daisy.

All right then. My fine son may think I'm losing my abilities, but I am still in control of what goes on in my car. Where are you going?

Hoke.

To the grocery store.

Daisy.

Then why didn't you turn on Highland Avenue?

Hoke.

Piggly Wiggly ain' on Highland Avenue. It on Euclid, down there near—

Daisy.

I know where it is and I want to go to it the way I always go. On Highland Avenue.

Hoke.

That three blocks out of the way, Miz' Daisy.

Daisy.

Go back! Go back this minute!

Hoke.

We in the wrong lane! I cain' jes'—

Daisy.

Go back I said! If you don't, I'll get out of this car and walk!

Hoke.

We movin'! You cain' open the do'!

Daisy.

This is wrong! Where are you taking me?

Hoke.

The sto'.

Daisy.
This is wrong. You have to go back to Highland Avenue!

Hoke.
Mmmm-hmmmm.

Daisy.
I've been driving to the Piggly Wiggly since the day they put it up and opened it for business. This isn't the way! Go back! Go back this minute!

Hoke.
Yonder the Piggly Wiggly.

Daisy.
Get ready to turn now.

Hoke.
Yassum.

Daisy.
Look out! There's a little boy behind that shopping cart!

Hoke.
I see dat.

Daisy.
Pull in next to the blue car.

Hoke.
We closer to the do' right here.

Daisy.
Next to the blue car! I don't park in the sun! It fades the upholstery.

Hoke.
Yassum.
(He pulls in, and gets out as Daisy springs out of the back seat.)

Daisy.
Wait a minute. Give me the car keys.

Hoke.
Yassum.

Daisy.

Stay right here by the car. And you don't have to tell everybody my business.

Hoke.

Nome. Doan' forget the Dutch Cleanser now.

(Daisy fixes him with a look meant to kill and exits. Hoke waits by the car for a minute, then hurries to the phone booth at the corner.)

Hoke.

Hello? Miz McClatchey? Hoke Coleburn here. Can I speak to him? (Pause.) Mornin' sir, Mist' Werthan. Guess where I'm at? I'm at dis here phone booth on Euclid Avenue right next to the Piggly Wiggly. I jes' drove you' mama to the market. (Pause.) She flap around some on the way. But she all right. She in the store. Uh-oh. Miz Daisy look out the store window and doan' see me, she liable to throw a fit right there by the checkout. (Pause.) Yassuh, only took six days. Same time it take the Lawd to make the worl'.

(Lights out on Hoke. We hear a choir singing.)

The Father

August Strindberg

⌘

This play, written in 1885, is by August Strindberg, who was one of the world's foremost playwrights and, along with Henrik Ibsen and Anton Chekhov, is considered by many to be one of the founders of modern theatre. The play is set in a remote country district of Sweden in 1886 in the home of the Captain, a cavalry officer. A friend, the Pastor, has just left and the Captain is working at his desk when his wife, Laura, enters. They have been in dispute over the future of their teenage daughter, Bertha. There is a short exchange between Bertha and her parents which has been deleted and marked with asterisks.

CAPTAIN, LAURA

Laura.
(entering from the next room.) Will you please . . .
Captain.
One moment!—Sixty-six, seventy-one, eighty-four, eighty-nine, ninety-two, a hundred. What is it?
Laura.
Am I disturbing you?

Captain.

Not in the least. Housekeeping money, I suppose?

Laura.

Yes, housekeeping money.

Captain.

If you put the accounts down there, I will go through them.

Laura.

Accounts?

Captain.

Yes.

Laura.

Do you expect me to keep accounts now?

Captain.

Of course you must keep accounts. Our position's most precarious, and if we go bankrupt, we must have accounts to show. Otherwise we could be accused of negligence.

Laura.

It's not my fault if we're in debt.

Captain.

That's what the accounts will show.

Laura.

It's not my fault the tenant farmer doesn't pay.

Captain.

Who was it recommended him so strongly? You. Why did you recommend such a—shall we call him a scatterbrain?

Laura.

Why did you take on such a scatterbrain?

Captain.

Because I wasn't allowed to eat in peace, sleep in peace or work in peace till you got him here. You wanted him because your brother wanted to get rid of him; my mother-in-law wanted him because I didn't; and old Margaret because she had known his grandmother as a child. That's why, and if I hadn't taken him I should be in a lunatic asylum by now, or else in the family vault. However, here's the housekeeping allowance and your pin money. You can give me the accounts later.

Laura.

(with an ironic bob.) Thank you so much.—By the way, do you keep accounts yourself—of what you spend outside the household?

Captain.

That's none of your business.

Laura.

True. As little my business as the future of my own child. Did you gentlemen come to any decision at this evening's conference?

Captain.

I had already made my decision, so I merely had to communicate it to the only friend I have in the family. Bertha is going to live in town. She will leave in a fortnight's time.

Laura.

Where, if I may ask, is she going to stay?

Captain.

At Savberg's—the solicitor's.

Laura.

That Freethinker!

Captain.

According to the law as it now stands, children are brought up in their father's faith.

Laura.

And the mother has no say in the matter?

Captain.

None whatever. She sells her birthright by legal contract and surrenders all her rights. In return the husband supports her and her children.

Laura.

So she has no rights over her own child?

Captain.

None at all. When you have sold something, you don't expect to get it back and keep the money too.

Laura.

But supposing the father and mother were to decide things together . . . ?

Captain.

How would that work out? I want her to live in town; you want her to live at home. The mathematical mean would be for her to stop at the railway station, midway between home and town. You see? It's a deadlock.

Laura.

Then the lock must be forced . . . what was Nojd doing here?

Captain.

That's a professional secret.

Laura.

Which the whole kitchen knows.

Captain.

Then doubtless you know it too.

Laura.

I do.

Captain.

And are ready to sit in judgment?

Laura.

The law does that.

Captain.

The law doesn't say who the child's father is.

Laura.

Well, people know that for themselves.

Captain.

Discerning people say that's what one never can know.

Laura.

How extraordinary! Can't one tell who a child's father is?

Captain.

Apparently not.

Laura.

How perfectly extraordinary! Then how can the father have those rights over the mother's child?

Captain.

He only has them when he takes on the responsibility—or has it forced on him. But of course in marriage there is no doubt about the paternity.

Laura.

No doubt?

Captain.

I should hope not.

Laura.

But supposing the wife has been unfaithful?

Captain.

Well, such a supposition has no bearing on our problem. Is there anything else you want to ask me about?

******

Laura.

You are afraid to hear her* opinion because you knew she would agree with me.

Captain.

I know she wants to leave home, but I also know you have the power to make her change her mind.

Laura.

Oh, have I much power?

Captain.

Yes, you have a fiendish power of getting your own way, like all people who are unscrupulous about the means they employ. How, for instance, did you get rid of Dr. Norling? And how did you get hold of the new doctor?

---

*Bertha's

Laura.

Yes, how did I?

Captain.

You ran the old doctor down until he had to leave, and then you got your brother to canvass for this one.

Laura.

Well, that was quite simple and perfectly legal. Then is Bertha to leave home?

Captain.

Yes, in a fortnight's time.

Laura.

I warn you I shall do my best to prevent it.

Captain.

You can't.

Laura.

Can't I? Do you expect me to give up my child to be taught by wicked people that all she has learnt from her mother is nonsense? So that I would be despised by my own daughter for the rest of my life.

Captain.

Do you expect me to allow ignorant and bumptious women to teach my daughter that her father is a charlatan?

Laura.

That shouldn't matter so much to you—now.

Captain.

What on earth do you mean?

Laura.

Well, the mother's closer to the child, since the discovery that no one can tell who the father is.

Captain.

What's that got to do with us?

Laura.

You don't know if you are Bertha's father.

Captain.

Don't know?

Laura.

How can you know what nobody knows?

Captain.

Are you joking?

Laura.

No, I'm simply applying your own theory. How do you know I haven't been unfaithful to you?

Captain.

I can believe a good deal of you, but not that. And if it were so, you wouldn't talk about it.

Laura.

Supposing I were prepared for anything, for being turned out and ostracised, anything to keep my child under my own control. Supposing I am telling the truth now when I say: Bertha is my child but not yours. Supposing . . .

Captain.

Stop it!

Laura.

Just supposing . . . then your power would be over.

Captain.

Not till you had proved I wasn't the father.

Laura.

That wouldn't be difficult. Do you want me to?

Captain.

Stop.

Laura.

I should only have to give the name of the real fa-ther—with particulars of place and time, of course. For that matter—when was Bertha born? In the third year of our marriage . . .

Captain.

Will you stop it now . . .

Laura.

Or what? Very well, let's stop. All the same, I should think twice before you decide anything. And, above all, don't make yourself ridiculous.

Captain.

I find the whole thing tragic.

Laura.

Which makes you still more ridiculous.

Captain.

But not you?

Laura.

No, we're in such a strong position.

Captain.

That's why we can't fight you.

Laura.

Why try to fight a superior enemy?

Captain.

Superior?

Laura.

Yes. It's odd, but I have never been able to look at a man without feeling myself his superior.

Captain.

One day you may meet your master—and you'll never forget it.

Laura.

That will be fascinating.

The Fourposter

Jan de Hartog

❦

In the first five scenes of this play, which was produced on Broadway in 1951, we follow Agnes and Michael through a long marriage starting at the turn of the century and touching upon major events in their lives. All scenes are set in their bedroom. This is the sixth and final scene of the play. They are elderly now and busily packing to move on to an apartment. The room is stripped of pictures and curtains and there are suitcases scattered everywhere. Only the canopied four-poster remains. The scene starts with Michael entering from the bathroom carrying toilet articles. After fumbling through several attenpts at packing these articles, he drops them on the floor, mutters "Damn," and is on his hands and knees when Agnes enters. She sees him and hides a little pillow behind her back. The author refers to them as He and She.

HE, SHE

She.
(At Center) What are you doing?

.e.

(Rises) Packing.

She.

(Picks up knitting bag from floor at foot of bed and puts it Left of suitcases down Center.) Well, hurry up, darling. The car comes at eight and it's almost twenty of. What have you been doing all this time?

He.

Taking down the soap dish in the bathroom.

She.

The soap dish? What on earth for?

He.

I thought it might come in useful.

She.

(Crosses to him) But darling, you mustn't. It's a fixture.

He.

(On dais) Nonsense. Anything that is screwed on isn't a fixture Only things that are nailed.

She.

That's not true at all. The agent explained it most carefully. Anything that's been fixed for more than twenty-five years is a fixture.

He.

(Hands her the soap dish) Then I'm a fixture, too.

She.

(Crosses to bathroom down Left) Don't be witty, darling. There isn't time.

He.

(Seeing little pillow under her arm) Hey! Hey! Hey!
(SHE stops.)
We don't have to take that little horror with us, do we?

She.

No. (Exits into bathroom.)

He.

(Picks up part of his toilet things) What about the bed?

She.

(Off) What?

He.

(Crossing down Center to suitcases) Are you going to unmake the bed or have we sold the blankets and the sheets with it? (Starts packing toilet things.)

She.

(Off) What is it, dear?

He.

Have we only sold the horse or the saddle as well?

She.

(Re-enters, stands down Left holding the little pillow) Horse, what horse?

He.

What's to become of those things? Have we sold the bedclothes or haven't we?

She.

Oh, no dear. Only the spread. I'll pack the rest. (Crosses onto dais. Puts little pillow under arm and strips pillow cases.)

He.

In what? These suitcases are landmines. Why are you nursing that thing?

(SHE mumbles something and tucks little pillow more firmly under her arm. HE crosses up to her) Just what are you planning to do with it?

She.

(On dais) I thought I'd leave it as a surprise.

He.

A surprise?

She.

Yes, for the new tenants. Such a nice young couple. (Places pillow.)

He.

Have you visualized that surprise, may I ask?

She.

Why?

He.

(At Center) Two young people entering the bedroom on their first night of their marriage, uncovering the bed and finding a pillow a foot across with "God Is Love" written on it.

She.

(Picks up rest of toilet articles and newspaper from bed. Puts them down on dais, the newspaper on top) You've got nothing to do with it.

He.

(Crosses up onto dais) Oh, I haven't have I? Well, I have. I've only met those people once, but I'm not going to make a fool of myself.

She.

But, darling—

He.

There's going to be no arguing about it, and that's final. (Snatches pillow, crosses down Right to suitcases and throws it on trunk at Right. Mutters.) God Is Love!

She.

(Stripping blanket and sheets from bed.) All right. Now, why don't you run downstairs and have a look at the cellar.

He.

Why?

She.

(Stuffs bed linen in pillow case.) To see if there's anything left there.

He.

Suppose there is something left there, what do you suggest we do with it? Take it with us? You don't

seem to realize that the apartment won't hold the
stuff from one floor of this house.

She.

Please, darling, don't bicker. We agreed that it was
silly to stay on here with all these empty rooms.

He.

But where are we going to put all this stuff?

She.

Now, I've arranged all that. Why don't you go down
and see if there's anything left in the wine cellar?

He.

Ah, now you're talking! (HE goes out Center.)

(SHE twirls the pillow case tight, crosses down Center and leaves it by the suitcases. Picks up the ''God
Is Love'' pillow, returns to the bed, and places it on
top of the regular bed pillows, then stands back and
admires it. With one hand on bedpost, SHE glances
over the entire bed and smiles fondly. Then straightens the spread, moves around to upstage side,
smooths out the cover, goes to foot of bed, stops,
hears him coming: crosses around to upstage side
again and quickly covers the ''God Is Love'' pillow
with spread.)

He.

(Entering with champagne bottle and crossing down
Center.) Look what I've found!

She.

(Crossing to foot of bed and arranging the cover
there.) What?

He.

Champagne! (Blows dust from bottle.) Must be one
that was left over from Robert's wedding.

She.

Oh.

He.

(Crossing up onto dais.) Have we got any glasses
up here?

She.

Only the tooth glasses.

He.

(Sits on edge of bed.) All right, get them.

She.

You aren't going to drink it now?

He.

Of course. Now, don't tell me this is a fixture! (Tears off foil from bottle.)

She.

But darling, we can't drink champagne at eight o'clock in the morning.

He.

Why not?

She.

We'll be reeling about when we get to that place. That would be a nice first impression to make on the landlady!

He.

I'd be delighted. I'd go up to that female sergeant major and say, "Hiya! Hah! Hah!" (Blows his breath in her face as in the First Act.)

(The memory strikes them both. They stay for a moment motionless. SHE pats his cheek lovingly.)

She.

I'll go get those glasses. (SHE exits into bathroom.)

(HE rises, throws the foil into the wastebasket at foot of bed, crosses down Center to suitcases and puts bottle on floor Right of suitcases. Goes back to bed and looks for the rest of his toilet articles. HE pulls back the spread, picks up the "God is Love" pillow, looks under it, tosses it back, looks under the other pillows, then suddenly realizes that the "God is Love" pillow has been put back in the bed. Picks it up and calls:)

He.

Agnes.

She.

(Off.) What?

He.

Agnes.

She.

(Reenters carrying towel and two glasses.) What? Oh—(SHE is upset when she sees what it is, and very self-conscious.)

He.

Agnes, did you put this back in the bed?

She.

(Standing at bathroom door.) Yes.

He.

(Crossing down to her.) Why, for Heaven's sake?

She.

(Crossing below him to Center.) I told you—I wanted to leave something—friendly for that young couple—a sort of message.

He.

(Crossing down Left of her.) What message?

She.

I'd like to tell them how happy we'd been—and that it was a very good bed—I mean, it's had a very nice history, and that—marriage was a good thing.

He.

Well, believe me, that's not the message they'll read from this pillow. Agnes, we'll do anything you like, we'll write them a letter, or carve our initials in the bed, but I won't let you do this to that boy—

She.

Why not? (SHE puts glasses and towel on floor beside knitting bag, takes little pillow from him and crosses up to bed. HE crosses up Center.) When I found this very same little pillow in this very same

bed on the first night of our marriage, I nearly burst
into tears!

He.

(Crosses up to Right of her.) Oh, you did, did you?
Well, so did I! And it's time you heard about it!
When, on that night, at that moment, I first saw that
pillow, I suddenly felt as if I'd been caught in a
world of women. Yes, women! I suddenly saw loom
up behind you the biggest trade union in existence,
and if I hadn't been a coward in long woolen underwear with my shoes off, I would have made a
dive for freedom.

She.

That's a fine thing to say! After all these years—

He.

Now, we'll have none of that. You can burst into
tears, you can stand on your head, you can divorce
me, but I'm not going to let you paralyze that boy
at a crucial moment.

She.

But it isn't a crucial moment!

He.

It is THE crucial moment!

She.

It is not! She would find it before, when she made
the bed. That's why I put it there. It is meant for
her, not for him, not for you, for her from me! (Puts
little pillow on bed as before.)

He.

Whomever it's for, the answer is NO. (HE takes the
little pillow, crosses down Right Center and puts it
on the trunk again. She pulls the spread up over the
bed pillows.) Whatever did I do with the rest of my
toilet things? (SHE picks them up from floor by bed,
crosses to him, hands them to him, puts newspaper
in wastebasket, sets basket Left of arch and crosses

down Center to him. HE is very carefully packing his things. When he is finished, he closes the lid to the suitcase.) You'll have to sit on this with me. I'll never get it shut alone. (SHE sits down beside him.) Now, get hold of the lock and when I say "Yes," we'll both do—that. (HE bounces on the suitcase) Ready? Yes! (They bounce.) (HE fastens his lock.) Is it shut?

She.

(Trying to fix catch.) Not quite.

He.

What do you mean, not quite? Either it's shut or it isn't.

She.

It isn't.

He.

All right. Here we go again. Ready? Yes! (They bounce again.) All right?

She.

Yes.

He.

(Picks up champagne bottle.) Now, do we drink this champagne or don't we?

She.

(Picks up glasses, towel, packs them in knitting bag.) No.

He.

All right. I just thought it would be a nice idea. Sort of round things off. (Puts champagne bottle back on floor.) Well, what do we do? Sit here on the suitcase till the car comes, or go downstairs and wait in the hall?

She.

I don't know.

He.

(Looks at her, then at the little pillow on trunk, then smiles at her anger.) It's odd, you know, how after you have lived in a place for so long, a room gets full of echoes. Almost everything we've said this morning we have said before. It's the bed—(SHE lays her head on his shoulder.) It's the bed, really, that I regret most. Pity it wouldn't fit. I wonder how the next couple will get along. Do you know what he does?

She.

He's a salesman.

He.

A salesman, eh? Well, why not? So was I. Only I realized it too late. The nights that I lay awake in that bed thinking how I'd beat Shakespeare at the game—

She.

Never mind, darling, you've given a lot of invalids a very nice time.

There follows some stage business with the pillow put on the bed by Agnes, taken off by the husband, etc. but finally, HE puts it back on the bed, kisses her, then carries her out of the room.

CURTAIN

Foxfire

Susan Cooper and Hume Cronyn

This play, first produced in 1982, is set in southern Appalachia in the 1980s and is based on materials from the Foxfire *books. The following is the first scene from the play and takes place on a porch of a cabin. Annie sits in her porch rocker, mending a quilt. She is a mountain woman of seventy-nine, wearing steel-rimmed spectacles and an apron over her long dark dress. Hector leans against a porch, upright, removed, lost in the view. He is seventy-seven, dressed in the worn and patched work clothes of a mountain farmer. Their son, Dillard, is a folk singer and his music opens the play.*

ANNIE, HECTOR

Annie.
  You there, Hector?
Hector.
  I'm always here.
Annie.
  Y'know what day it is?

Hector.

Nope.

Annie.

Friday the 29th—Labor Day comin' up.

Hector.

Signs is in the bowels. I wouldn't cook that meat if I was you.

Annie.

Now how'd you know about that?

Hector.

Well, y'got water on the stove, an' a hog's head sittin' in the bucket.

Annie.

I ain't worryin' s'much about the cookin' as the fixin'. Don't know as I've got m' strength f'r that.

Hector.

You ain't worryin' 'bout cookin' or fixin'—you're worryin' about Dillard.

Annie.

Sometimes I wish I could keep m'thoughts to m'self.

(Hector moves downstage, but she does not look at him.)

Hector.

You think it—I know it. Besides, y's always said I knew everythin'.

Annie.

Y' read his letter?

Hector.

Nope.

(Annie takes letter from her apron pocket.)

Annie.

Starts off about his concert. Says he's got a date this week-end at Hiawassee Fairground—

Hector.

Hiawassee! That's thirty miles from here—you ain't goin'.

Annie.

Don't have t'—he says he'll stop by. Goes on—
(She reads.) "Guess Cheryl ain't wrote in quite a
while. She got promoted. We moved agin." (She
sighs.) That must be the fifth time. (She reads again.
Hector mumbles.) "Kids send their love. I do what
I can with 'em when I'm home. I know I'm a poor
hand at letter-writing', but don't worry, everythin's
fine, an' I'll see you on the 30th even if I can't stay
long—" (She breaks off.) The 30th! That's tomorrow—I want that hog's head outa the way.

Hector.

What's chewin' on y'?

Annie.

Don't rightly know. Wish he'd told more 'bout the
children. I ain't heared from Cheryl since last
Christmas.

Hector.

I never wrote a letter in m'life, 'cept t' President
Hoover—an' he never answered that.

Annie.

It ain't hardly the same.

Hector.

Well, he says everythin's fine.

Annie.

No, he says "Don't worry, everythin's fine." Makes
me uneasy.

Hector.

Dillard always done that.

Annie.

He's a good boy.

Hector.

He's a grown man! Traipsin' round the country with
a guitar—what kinda work's that?

Annie.

Now, Hector.

Hector.
Well, this land woulda took care a'him.
Annie.
He weren't cut out.
Hector.
And of his family.
Annie.
Cheryl neither.
Hector.
Agh—Cheryl! What d' we know 'bout Cheryl?
Annie.
She loves Dillard, an' she give him two beautiful kids.
Hector.
She give him! Where was he?
Annie.
You know what I mean.
Hector.
Yeah—m'grandchildren. Wouldn't know 'em if I fell over 'em.
Annie.
'Cause you always took off. Most times they bin here, you jus' up an' disappeared.
Hector.
Do it agin, too. What with her cackle an' his strummin' muddies up the air.
Annie.
He has t'practice—it's his job.
Hector.
Never practiced farmin', an' that's a job as counts. Set him ploughin' a straight furrow, it looked like the mule got into m'liquor.
Annie.
Cheryl never did take t'these mountains. She told me direckly one time—she said the name a' this place was too well suited.

Hector.

Well, she weren't the first. When m'pa first brought m'ma up here, he says—

Annie.

I KNOW, Hector. I'm goin' back t'that hog's head. Got mosta the hair off, but I dunno what I'm gonna do 'bout them eyes. (She goes indoors. Undeterred, Hector tells his story, as if thinkin' aloud.)

Hector.

When m'pa first brought m'ma up here, he says to her, "Sarah, y're standin' tip-top a'Georgia. The Blue Ridge. Some folks says it's the most beautiful place in America. What d'y' make of it?" So she looks—an' she were bad f'r speakin' out—an' she says, "It's stony." Then she listens t'the quiet, an' she says, "It's lonesome." An' he says, "Well, it's all yours, so y'c'n call it that!" (He grins at the audience.) An' she did, too. Stony Lonesome. But she raised nine kids here. Nine—an' Cheryl's got two. Seems like the crop's fallin' off. When Dillard got married we give him the old family crib— Cheryl planted geraniums in it. My ma took what the Lord handed her, an' she made the best of it— made it work. Now that's the trick. But Dillard ain't learned it.

Ghosts

Henrik Ibsen

❧

This play, written in 1881, infuriated the public because it deals with syphilis, although in deference to Victorian audiences the disease is never named. The play opens with some exposition that tells us that Osvald, the sickly son, has just returned home to Norway after spending several years in Paris as an artist. While he is resting upstairs, Pastor Manders comes to visit Mrs. Alving. She has had an orphanage built and is dedicating it the next day. In the following scene, Osvald has just shocked Manders by his criticism of the so-called morality of the time, and then left the room.

MRS. ALVING, PASTOR MANDERS

Mrs. Alving.

Poor boy!

Manders.

You may well say so!—that he should have sunk to this! (Mrs. Alving looks at him in silence. Manders paces up and down.) He called himself the Prodigal Son—Tragic!—Tragic! (Mrs. Alving continues to

look at him silently.) And what do you say to all
this?

Mrs. Alving.

I saw Osvald was right in every word he said.

Manders.

(Stops pacing.) Right?—You mean you agree to
such principles?

Mrs. Alving.

Living here alone all these years, I've come to the
same conclusions—but I've never put my thoughts
into words—Well—now my boy can speak for me.

Manders.

You are greatly to be pitied, Mrs. Alving!—I have
always had your best interests at heart; for many
years I have advised you in business matters; for
many years I have been your friend and your late
husband's friend; as your spiritual adviser I once
saved you from a reckless and foolhardy action; and
it is as your spiritual adviser that I now feel it my
duty to talk to you with the utmost solemnity.

Mrs. Alving.

And what have you to say to me, as my "spiritual
adviser," Mr. Manders?

Manders.

Look back over the years—it's appropriate that you
should do so today, for tomorrow is the tenth anniversary of your husband's death and his Memorial
will be unveiled; tomorrow I shall speak to the
crowd assembled in his honor—but today I must
speak to you alone.

Mrs. Alving.

I'm listening.

Manders.

You had been married scarcely a year when you
took the step that might have wrecked your life: You
left house and home and ran away from your hus-

band—yes, Mrs. Alving, ran away—and refused to go back to him in spite of all his entreaties.

Mrs. Alving.

I was miserably unhappy that first year—don't forget that.

Manders.

What right have we to expect happiness in this life? It is the sign of a rebellious spirit—No! Mrs. Alving, we are here to do our duty, and it was your duty to stay with the man you had chosen and to whom you were bound in Holy Matrimony.

Mrs. Alving.

You know the kind of life Alving led in those days, his dissipation—his excesses—

Manders.

It's true, I heard many rumors about him—and had those rumors been true, I should have been the first to condemn his conduct at that time; but it is not a wife's place to judge her husband; your duty was to resign yourself and bear your cross with true humility. But you rebelled against it and instead of giving your husband the help—and support he needed, you deserted him, and by so doing jeopardized your own good name and reputation—and that of others too.

Mrs. Alving.

Of "others"? Of ONE, you mean.

Manders.

It was highly imprudent to come to me, of all people, for help.

Mrs. Alving.

But why? Weren't you our "spiritual adviser" as well as our friend?

Manders.

All the more reason. You should go down on your knees and thank God that I found the necessary strength of mind to dissuade you from your reckless purpose, to guide you back to the path of duty, and home to your husband.

Mrs. Alving.

Yes, Mr. Manders—that was certainly your doing.

Manders.

I was merely an instrument in God's hand. And, as I had foreseen—once you had returned to your duties, and humbled your spirit in obedience—you were repaid a hundredfold. Alving reformed entirely, and remained a good and loving husband to the end of his days. He became a real benefactor to this whole community, and he allowed you to share, as his fellow-worker too—I am aware of that, Mrs. Alving—I must pay you that tribute; but now I come to the second great error of your life.

Mrs. Alving.

What do you mean by that?

Manders.

You first betrayed your duty as a wife—you later betrayed your duty as a mother.

Mrs. Alving.

Ah—!

Manders.

All your life you have been possessed by a willful, rebellious spirit. Your natural inclinations always led you toward the undisciplined and lawless. You could never tolerate the slightest restraint; you have always disregarded any responsibility—carelessly and unscrupulously—as though it were a burden you had a right to cast aside. It no longer suited you to be a wife—so you left your husband. The cares of motherhood were too much for you—so you sent your child away to be brought up by strangers.

Mrs. Alving.

That's true—I did do that.

Manders.

And for that reason you are now a stranger to him.

Mrs. Alving.

No! No! I'm not!

Manders.

Of course you are! How could you be otherwise? And now you see the result of your conduct. You have much to atone for; you were guilty as a wife, Mrs. Alving, you failed your husband miserably— you are seeking to atone for that by raising this Memorial in his honor; how are you going to atone for your failure toward your son? It may not be too late to save him: by redeeming yourself—you may still help him to redemption! I warned you! (With raised forefinger.) You are guilty as a mother, Mrs. Alving. I felt it my duty to tell you this.

(Pause.)

Mrs. Alving.

(Slowly, with great control.) I have listened to you talk, Mr. Manders. Tomorrow you will be making speeches in my husband's honor; I shall not make any speeches tomorrow; but now I intend to talk to you—just as frankly—just as brutally—as you have talked to me!

Manders.

Of course—it's natural that you should try and justify your conduct.

Mrs. Alving.

No—I only want to make a few things clear to you.

Manders.

Well?

Mrs. Alving.

You've just talked a great deal about my married life after you—as you put it—"led me back to the path of duty." What do you really know about it?

From that day on you never set foot inside our house—you who had been our closest friend—

Manders.

But you and your husband left town, immediately afterwards—

Mrs. Alving.

And you never once came out here to see us during my husband's lifetime. It wasn't until this Orphanage business, that you felt compelled to visit me.

Manders.

(In a low uncertain tone.) If that is meant as a reproach, my dear Helene, I beg you to consider—

Mrs. Alving.

—that in your position you had to protect your reputation! After all—I was a wife who had tried to leave her husband! One can't be too careful with such disreputable women!

Manders.

My dear! Mrs. Alving—what a gross exaggeration!

Mrs. Alving.

Well—never mind about that—the point is this: your opinions of my married life are based on nothing but hearsay.

Manders.

That may be so—what then?

Mrs. Alving.

Just this: that now, Manders, I am going to tell you the truth! I swore to myself that one day I would tell it to you—to you alone!

Manders.

Well? And what is the truth?

Mrs. Alving.

The truth is this: My husband continued to be a depraved profligate to the day of his death.

Manders.

(Feeling for a chair.) What did you say?

Mrs. Alving.

After nineteen years of marriage—just as depraved, just as dissolute—as he was the day you married us.

Manders.

How can you use such words—?

Mrs. Alving.

They are the words our doctor used.

Manders.

I don't understand you.

Mrs. Alving.

It's not necessary that you should.

Manders.

I can't take it in. You mean—that this seemingly happy marriage—those long years of comradeship—all that was only a pretense—to cover up this hideous abyss?

Mrs. Alving.

That is just exactly what it was—nothing else.

Manders.

But—it's inconceivable—I can't grasp it! How was it possible to—? How could the truth remain concealed?

Mrs. Alving.

My life became one long fight to that end: After Osvald was born, Alving seemed to me a little better—but it didn't last long! And then I had to fight for my son as well: I was determined that no living soul should ever know the kind of father my boy had—As a matter of fact, you know how charming Alving could be—it was hard for people to think ill of him. He was one of those fortunate men whose private lives never seem to damage their public reputation. But then, Manders—I want you to know the whole story—then the most horrible thing of all happened.

Manders.

How could anything be worse than—?

Mrs. Alving.

I knew well enough all that was going on—and I put up with it as long as I didn't have to see it—but, when I was faced with it here—in my own home—!

Manders.

Here?

Mrs. Alving.

Yes—in this very house. The first time I became aware of it, I was in there—(Points to the downstage door right.) in the dining room—I was busy with something, and the door was ajar—then I heard the maid come up from the garden with water for the plants—

Manders.

Yes?

Mrs. Alving.

In a few moments, I heard Alving come in after her—he said something to her in a low voice—and then I heard—(With a short laugh.) it still rings in my ears—it was so horrible, and yet somehow so ludicrous—I heard my own servant-girl whisper: "Let me go, Mr. Alving! Leave me alone!"

Manders.

But he couldn't have meant anything by it, Mrs. Alving—believe me—I'm sure he didn't—

Mrs. Alving.

I soon found out what to believe: My husband had his way with the girl, and there were—consequences, Mr. Manders.

Manders.

(As though turned to stone.) To think—that in this house—!

Mrs. Alving.

I had been through a lot in this house! I sat up in his study with him—pretending to join him in his private drinking-bouts. I sat there alone with him for hours on end listening to his obscene, senseless talk—I had to struggle with him—fight with sheer brute force—in order to drag him to his bed.

Manders.

(Shaken.) How were you able to endure all this?

Mrs. Alving.

I had to endure it—I had my little boy to think of. But when I discovered this final outrage—with a servant—in our own house—! That was the end. From that day on I became master here. I took full control—over him and over everything. Alving didn't say a word—he knew he was in my power. It was then I decided to send Osvald away. He was nearly seven and was beginning to notice things and ask questions, as children do. This I could not endure, Manders. I felt the child would be poisoned in this sordid, degraded home. That's why I sent him away. Now perhaps you understand why I never let him set foot in this house as long as his father was alive. What you could never understand—is what agony it was to have to do it!

Manders.

To think of all you have been through—!

Mrs. Alving.

I could never have stood it if I hadn't had my work. For I can honestly say I have worked! Alving received all the praise—all the credit—but don't imagine he had anything to do with it. The increase in the value of our property—the improvements— all those fine enterprises you spoke of—all that was MY work. All he did was to sprawl on the sofa in his study reading old newspapers. In his few lucid moments I did try to spur him to some effort—but it was no use. He sank back again into his old habits and spent days in a maudlin state of penitence and self-pity.

Manders.

And you're building a Memorial to such a man!?

Mrs. Alving.

That's what comes of having a bad conscience.

Manders.

A bad—? What do you mean?

Mrs. Alving.

It seemed to me inevitable that the truth must come out, and that people would believe it; so I decided to dedicate this Orphanage to Alving—in order to dispel once and for all any possible rumors—any possible doubts.

Manders.

You've fully succeeded in that.

Mrs. Alving.

But I had another reason: I didn't want my son to inherit anything whatsoever from his father.

Manders.

I see—so you used Alving's money to—?

Mrs. Alving.

Precisely. The money that has gone into the Orphanage amounts to the exact sum—I've calculated it very carefully—to the exact sum of the fortune, that once made people consider Lt. Alving a good match.

Manders.

I understand you.

Mrs. Alving.

I sold myself for that sum. I don't want Osvald to touch a penny of it. Everything he has will come from me—everything!

(Osvald enters.)

The Gin Game

D. L. Coburn

❦

This is a two-character play which opened on Broadway in 1977 and features a man and woman of similar age who have not known each other prior to becoming residents in a home for the aged. Weller Martin, who has always fancied himself an expert gin player, has taught the game to Fonsia Dorsey but so far she has won every game. In the previous scene, Weller, getting progressively frustrated and angry, loses control and in a rage overturns the card table and storms off. This scene opens with Weller on the sunporch and Fonsia just outside in the garden.

There are many other interesting scenes in this play with these two characters for those actors who would like more. The scene just preceding this one is exceptionally fine.

WELLER, FONSIA

Weller.

Fonsie. Fonsie, is that you out there?

Fonsia.

(She is in the House Left Aisle.) What is it, Weller?

Weller.

(Having crossed onto the flagstone apron.) I wanted

194

to talk to you. It's getting pretty dark out there. You'd better come in.

Fonsia.

I'll be in, in a little while. (Weller sits Stage Right on the step.) Why don't you just go on.

Weller.

I'll just sit here until you're ready to come in.

Fonsia.

Weller, I want to be alone for awhile—out here . . . not in my room.

Weller.

I didn't mean to disturb you, Fonsia. Honestly, I don't mind sitting here . . . waiting.

Fonsia.

(Beginning to cross toward the stage.) No. You're right. It is dark out there now. It was so pretty before, with all the spring flowers.

Weller.

(Rises and crosses to Fonsia who now stands Stage Right on the apron. Fonsia is wearing a navy blue dress with white polka-dots, the same rose-colored sweater and the same sandals.) Fonsia, I'll get right to the point. I owe you an apology.

Fonsia.

Yes, you do.

Weller.

Alright, Fonsia, I am embarrassed by my own behavior yesterday and I sincerely apologize. (Weller bows to Fonsia.)

Fonsia.

(Passing Weller and crossing up the step.) I can't tell whether you're joking or whether you really mean it.

Weller.

Of course I mean it. What do you want me to say?

That I behaved like a complete ass? I'm sorry that
I upset you, and . . . I'm just sorry, that's all.

Fonsia.

You frightened me. I don't think you realize how
much your temper affects people.

Weller.

(Crossing Center on the step.) I'm sure it can be
rather awesome at times—but, it's nothing to be
afraid of.

Fonsia.

(Crossing Right of Center.) I don't think I'm so
much afraid of what you're going to do to me. I just
don't know what's going to happen next. When you
threw that table . . .

Weller.

(Crossing Center, onto the stage.) Oh, that was nothing. It wasn't directed at you, anyway.

Fonsia.

(Sitting Stage Right on the glide.) It still frightened
me.

Weller.

(Crosses and sits Stage Left on the glider.) Fonsie,
let's be realistic about this. Except for the couple of
times that I lost my temper, I think we've thoroughly enjoyed each other's company.

Fonsia.

I enjoy your company, Weller . . . but you can't play
Gin.

Weller.

What? What do you mean I can't play Gin. Lord,
woman, I was playing Gin . . .

Fonsia.

No, no. No, Weller. I didn't mean you can't PLAY
Gin. I mean you can't play without losing your temper.

Weller.

Jesus. Next thing you know, you'll be thinking you're some sort of expert, for Christsake.

Fonsia.

My lands, no. Lord knows I'm no expert. I just play like an expert.

Weller.

(Rising and crossing to the bookcase.) Oh God. Now she's done it.

Fonsia.

Oh, Weller. I was only teasing.

Weller.

(At the bookcase.) Goddamnit, where are those cards. (He finds a deck of cards and crosses to the cardtable.)

Fonsia.

As the Lord is my savior, Weller, I was only teasing you.

Weller.

Lots of people tease like that. They say exactly what the hell they mean—then they say, "I was only kidding." (Weller pulls the table to Center—under the light fixture.) Where's my scorepad? You can't keep anything around this place. (Weller puts the cards on the table and crosses Stage Left to get a chair.)

Fonsia.

Now, Weller. I'm not going to play any Gin with you.

Weller.

(Crossing with a chair and placing it Stage Left at the table.) Oh, come on, Fonsie, for God's sake.

Fonsia.

I mean it.

Weller.

(Crossing Stage Left to get the second chair.) Alright, don't play. Go back in there with all those

glassy-eyed bastards. (He places this chair Stage
Right on the table.)

Fonsia.

You shouldn't talk about them that way. You're part
of this thing here too, you know.

Weller.

Yeah, well, in that case, I'm the part of it that's
breathing. (He crosses to the light switch on the
Stage Right wall.) Don't kid yourself that this is
anything more than a warehouse for the intellectu-
ally and emotionally dead. (He switches on the light
and crosses to Stage Right of the table.) Nothing
more than a place to store them until their bodies
quit.

Fonsia.

God, you're cynical.

Weller.

(Sitting in the Stage Right chair.) It isn't cynical.
It's a fact, that's all.

Fonsia.

Well, I'm sure glad I don't look at life that way.
It's just the mercy of God that we're able to get
around a little better than they are. They're just sick,
that's all.

Weller.

(Shuffling the cards.) They're not half as sick as the
ones who put them here. And they're not a third as
sick as this bunch that's supposed to be taking care
of them.

Fonsia.

Which side of this thing are you on, anyway? Sometimes I think you're just looking for a fight.

Weller.

(Dealing out a game of solitaire.) I'm just looking
to mind my own business.

Fonsia.

And you've got a horrible temper . . . and a sarcastic streak.

Weller.

(Turning to look at Fonsia.) So what. If I were you, I wouldn't be talking about anybody's else's shortcomings. (He turns back to the table.)

Fonsia.

What's that supposed to mean?

Weller.

Well, neither one of us is winning any popularity contest out here on Visitors' Day.

Fonsia.

Oh, I see. No one visits me, so I'm an evil person.

Weller.

(Turns toward Fonsia.) Did you ever hear of Ty Cobb?

Fonsia.

He played baseball.

Weller.

(Returning to game.) That's right. Ty Cobb played baseball. He played baseball for 24 years. You know how many of his team-mates showed up for his funeral? Three! Kinda makes you think that Ty Cobb may have been something less than a warm, loving human being, doesn't it.

Fonsia.

Maybe.

Weller.

Well, sir. He's three ahead of us on visitors.

Fonsia.

Just what are you driving at, Weller?

Weller.

(Turning to Fonsia.) Why doesn't your son come to visit you?

Fonsia.

I told you. He lives in Denver. I thought you understood that.

Weller.

Then why aren't you in an old age home in Denver? Or you'd think at least he'd come to see that you're comfortable and that it's a decent place . . .

Fonsia.

I don't want to talk about this anymore. (Weller turns back to the table.) The Sunshine Ladies are going to be here tonight. I think I'll go in and talk to them for awhile.

Weller.

Help yourself.

Fonsia.

I suppose you think they're just so many jerks, too.

Weller.

Now, I never said anything like that. They're a damn sight more sincere than some that come out here. Like that group that came looking for substitute Grandparents. What was that called?

Fonsia.

Extension Family.

Weller.

That's it, Extension Family. No, it wasn't extension . . .

Fonsia.

Extended!

Weller.

Extended! That's it! Unitarians. Wanted to psychoanalyze everything for Christsake.

Fonsia.

Weller, I wish you wouldn't take the Lord's name so much.

Weller.

What's it going to be? Gin or the Sunshine Ladies.

Fonsia.

Oh, I think I should go in.

Weller.

Hell, they're not going to be here for an hour or more.

Fonsia.

Still, . . . I think I'd better. (She rises and slowly starts to cross to the Stage Right door.)

Weller.

Alright, Goddamnit! Go ahead. I don't see how you can stand it in there. The same damn empty look on face after face. You ought to see them the day they change the bed linens. Maybe you have. All lined up in their wheelchairs. all up and down the hall . . . like rows of wrinkled pumpkin heads.

Fonsia.

(At the Stage Right door, she turns and crosses back to center.) Maybe we could play a few hands. You're just going to pester me 'til I play anyway. (She crosses to the piano to get her pillow.)

Weller.

Well, what the hell else is there to do?

Fonsia.

(Crossing to the table.) Not much, I guess.

Weller.

Would you see if you can find my scorepad? Thank you.

Fonsia.

(Leaves the pillow on the chair and crosses to the bookcase to get the pad and pencil.) I'm so tired of the TV. And all Mrs. Leala wants to talk about is her funeral arrangements. (She crosses to the table and puts the pad and pencil down.)

Weller.

You won't find a hotter topic of conversation—I don't care who you talk to. Not around here. (He marks the lines on the pad.)

Fonsia.

(Sitting in the Stage Left chair.) My mother was that way. As far as I can remember, funerals were the only social life she had. Well, if this isn't the pot calling the kettle black. Here I sit talking about the same thing they are. (She puts on her glasses.)

Weller.

That's what happens when you get too far away from playing Gin. Atrophy. Next thing you know, you'll be staring out of the window all day long.

Fonsia.

Weller, you're impos . . .

Weller.

(Dealing.) One, one. Two, two. Three, three. Four, four. Five, five. Six, six. Seven, seven. Eight, eight. Nine, nine. Ten, ten. And eleven for you. (They pick up their cards.)

Fonsia.

Now, if I win, don't you shout at me.

Weller.

Fonsia, I fully expect you to win, and I promise to do my level best not to rant and rave about it.

Fonsia.

Well, now. I'm going to hold you to that.

Weller.

I swear, Fonsie, you get yourself upset about the silliest things.

Fonsia.

Well . . .

Weller.

Well, you do.

Fonsia.

Sometimes, I guess. (They begin to play.)

Juno and the Paycock

Sean O'Casey

This play was produced at the Abbey Theatre in Ireland in 1923. It is a realistic tragedy by one of the great Irish playwrights and takes place in a very modest apartment in Ireland in 1922. "Captain" Jack Boyle, sixty, has a flamboyant, self-centered persona, the "paycock" of the title. He drinks too much and is often unemployed as a result. His wife, Juno Boyle, is forty-five years old and "twenty years ago must have been a pretty woman; but her face has now assumed that look which ultimately settles down upon the faces of the women of the working-class, a look of listless monotony and harassed anxiety, blending with an expression of mechanical resistance." In the time and place of the setting, it was not unusual for wives to be considerably younger than their husbands. Juno and Jack have been expecting a small inheritance from a relative which would alleviate their poverty. They have two grown children, Johnny and Mary. Boyle has just been talking to his son as the scene opens.

"CAPTAIN" JACK BOYLE, JUNO BOYLE

(Mrs. Boyle enters; it is apparent from the serious look on her face that something has happened. She takes off her hat and coat without a word and puts them by. She then sits down near the fire, and there is a few moments' pause.)

Boyle.

Well, what did the doctor say about Mary?

Mrs. Boyle.

(In an earnest manner and with suppressed agitation.) Sit down here, Jack; I've something to say to you . . . about Mary.

Boyle.

(Awed by her manner.) About . . . Mary?

Mrs. Boyle.

Close that door there and sit down here.

Boyle.

(Closing the door.) More throuble in our native land, is it? (He sits down.) Well, what is it?

Mrs. Boyle.

It's about Mary.

Boyle.

Well, what about Mary—there's nothin' wrong with her, is there?

Mrs. Boyle.

I'm sorry to say there's a gradle wrong with her.

Boyle.

A gradle wrong with her! (Peevishly.) First Johnny an' now Mary is the whole house goin' to become an hospital! It's not consumption, is it?

Mrs. Boyle.

No . . . it's not consumption . . . it's worse.

Mrs. Boyle.

We'll all have to mind her now. You might as well know now, as another time. D'ye know what the doctor said to me about her, Jack?

Boyle.

How ud I know—I wasn't there, was I?

Mrs. Boyle.

He told me to get her married at wanst.

Boyle.

Married at wanst! An' why did he say the like o' that?

Mrs. Boyle.

Because Mary's goin' to have a baby in a short time.

Boyle.

Goin' to have a baby! My God, what'll Bentham say when he hears that?

Mrs. Boyle.

Are you blind, man, that you can't see that it was Bentham that has done this wrong to her?

Boyle.

(Passionately.) Then he'll marry her, he'll have to marry her!

Mrs. Boyle.

You know he's gone to England, an' God knows where he is now.

Boyle.

I'll folley him, I'll folley him, an' bring him back, an' make him do her justice. The scoundrel, I might ha' known what he was, with his yogees an' his prawna!

Mrs. Boyle.

We'll have to keep it quiet till we see what we can do.

Boyle.

Oh, isn't this a nice thing to come on top o' me, an' the state I'm in. A pretty show I'll be to Joxer an' to that oul' wan, Madigan. Amn't I affther goin' through enough without havin' to go through this!

Mrs. Boyle.

What you an' I'll have to go through'll be nothing to what poor Mary'll have to go through; for you

an' me is middlin' old, an' most of our years is
spent' but Mary'll have maybe forty years to face
an' handle, an' every wan of them'll be tainted with
a bitther memory.

Boyle.

Where is she? Where is she till I tell her off? I'm
tellin' you when I'm done with her she'll be a sorry
girl!

Mrs. Boyle.

I left her in me sisther's till I came to speak to you.
You'll say nothin' to her, Jack; ever since she left
school she's earned her livin', an' your fatherly care
never throubled the poor girl.

Boyle.

Gwan, take her part agen her father! But I'll let you
see whether I'll say nothin' to her or no! Her an'
her readin'! That's more o' th' blasted nonsense that
has the house fallin' down on top of us! What did
th' likes of her, born in a tenement house, want with
readin'? Her readin's afther bringin' her to a nice
pass—oh, it's madnin', madnin', madnin'!

Mrs. Boyle.

When she comes back say nothin' to her, Jack, or
she'll leave this place.

Boyle.

Leave this place! Ay, she'll leave this place, an'
quick too!

Mrs. Boyle.

If Mary goes, I'll go with her.

Boyle.

Well, go with her! Well, go, th' pair o' yous! I lived
before I seen yous, an' I can live when yous are
gone. Isn't this a nice thing to come rollin' in on
top o' me afther all your prayin' to St. Anthony an'
The Little Flower. An' she's a Child o' Mary, too—
I wonder what'll the nuns think of her now? An'
it'll be bellows'd all over the disthrict before you

could say Jack Robinson; an' whenever I'm seen they'll whisper, ''That th' father of Mary Boyle that had th' kid by th' swank she used to go with; d'ye know, d'ye know?'' To be sure they'll know—more about it than I will meself!

Mrs. Boyle.

We needn't let it be bellows'd all over the place; all we've got to do is to leave this place quietly an' go somewhere where we're not known, an' nobody'll be the wiser.

Boyle.

You're talkin' like a two-year-oul' woman. Where'll we get a place ou' o' this?—places aren't that easily got.

Mrs. Boyle.

But, Jack, when we get the money . . .

Boyle.

Money—what money?

Mrs. Boyle.

Why, oul' Ellison's money, of course.

Boyle.

There's no money comin' from oul' Ellison, or any-one else. Since you hears of wan throuble, you might as well hear of another. There's no money comin' to us at all—the Will's a wash-out!

Mrs. Boyle.

What are you sayin', man—no money?

Boyle.

The boyo that's afther doin' it to Mary done it to me as well. The thick made out the Will wrong; he said in th' Will, only first cousin an' second cousin, instead of mentionin' our names, an' now any one that thinks he's a first cousin or second cousin t'oul' Ellison can claim the money as well as me, an' they're spring' up in hundreds, an' comin' from America an' Australia, thinkin' to get their whack

out of it, while all the time the lawyers is gobblin'
it up, till there's not as much as ud buy a stockin'
for your lovely daughter's baby!

Mrs. Boyle.

I don't believe it, I don't believe it, I don't believe
it! You're not serious, Jack! You're not serious!

Boyle.

I'm tellin' you the scholar, Bentham, made a banjax
o' th' Will instead o' sayin', ''th' rest o' me property to be divided between me first cousin, Jack
Boyle, an' me second cousin, Mick Finnegan, o'
Santhry,'' he writ down only, ''me first an' second
cousins,'' and the world an' his wife are afther th'
property now.

Mrs. Boyle.

Now, I know why Bentham left poor Mary in th'
lurch; I can see it all now—oh, is there not even a
middlin' honest man left in th' world?

Boyle.

. . . Go an' get Bentham if you want satisfaction for
all that's afther happenin' to us. I'm goin' out now
to have a few drinks with th' last few mates I have,
an' tell that lassie o' yours not to be here when I
come back' for if I lay me eyes on her, I'll lay me
han's on her, an' if I lay me han's on her, I won't
be accountable for me actions! (Exits.)

The Kingfisher

William Douglas Home

This comedy, which opened in England in 1978, is set in Sir Cecil's garden in England of the late 1970s. At the opening of the play, Cecil, a sophisticated bachelor and man-about-town, as well as a successful writer, has admitted to his butler, Hawkins, that he feels he has missed something in his life. He hopes, at this late date, to remedy that. A woman is coming to visit with whom he had a flirtation fifty years before. She is coming from her husband's funeral. Hawkins has just been sent off with instructions not to come back until Cecil rings because he wants to be alone with his visitor. There is a short exchange with Hawkins in which he brings in a tea service which is deleted and marked with asterisks.

CECIL, EVELYN

(Evelyn comes through from the house.)
Evelyn.
  Cecil.
Cecil.
  Evelyn. Everything go off alright?

Evelyn.

Yes, thank you. What do you mean, Cecil? Wouldn't it have been surprising if it hadn't! Actually, someone did tell me once that they'd been to a country funeral where the bell ringers got tight and thought it was the harvest festival and the bells kept pealing all though the service.

Cecil.

You needn't make jokes like that, Evelyn. Let yourself go. Have a good cry. (He moves away—tactfully—then starts eyeing her.)

Evelyn.

I'm alright, Cecil.

Cecil.

You've still got your figure.

Evelyn.

Thank you, Cecil.

Cecil.

Evelyn, look at me. (She does.) You've changed.

Evelyn.

So have you.

Cecil.

You've lost something.

Evelyn.

That's right. I've lost Reggie, Cecil.

Cecil.

No, I don't mean that. You're not the girl I held in my arms here in 1927.

Evelyn.

Here?

Cecil.

Yes. Underneath this beech tree. It's the same one, Evelyn.

Evelyn.

So it is, and there's the stream.

Cecil.

As you say, there's the stream.

Evelyn.

How too extraordinary.

Cecil.

It isn't really. I bought up the land when my first book was a success, and built the house.

Evelyn.

Why did you choose here?

Cecil.

Why not? It's a very nice place.

Evelyn.

True enough. And so, I'm not the girl that I was fifty years ago. Is that surprising?

Cecil.

I suppose not. No.

Evelyn.

And you're not the man who held me, if it comes to that.

Cecil.

It always does, they say.

Evelyn.

In what way do you find me different?

Cecil.

You're tougher.

Evelyn.

So's the beech tree, I imagine. So are you, I shouldn't wonder.

******

Evelyn.

Shall I pour?

Cecil.

Why not?

Evelyn.

Milk?

Cecil.

Yes, please.

Evelyn.

Sugar?

Cecil.

No, thanks.

Evelyn.

Don't tell me you're slimming, Cecil.

Cecil.

I'm not slimming. I just don't like sugar.

Evelyn.

Reggie loved it.

Cecil.

So I should imagine.

Evelyn.

What does that mean?

Cecil.

Well, he liked the good things of life, obviously. What hole did it happen on?

Evelyn.

The seventeenth.

Cecil.

Oh, nearly made it. Was he doing a good round?

Evelyn.

Twelve over. Not bad, for him. And his tee shot was pin high. It's quite a short hole.

Cecil.

Were you playing with him?

Evelyn.

No, no. I was playing bridge back in the Clubhouse with the other wives. I'd just gone six No Trumps when the Pro rushed in.

Cecil.

Did you make it?

Evelyn.

Cecil, you've not changed at all. I'm glad it happened at St. Enedoc because he used to play there as a boy.

Cecil.

Did you love Reggie?

Evelyn.

What a question!

Cecil.

Never mind the question. What's the answer?

Evelyn.

Have a scone. You know the answer quite well. Butter?

Cecil.

Thank you.

Evelyn.

Jam?

Cecil.

No, thank you. Don't keep asking silly questions.

Evelyn.

You began it.

Cecil.

Fifty years with someone that you didn't love.
You've weathered it well, Evelyn.

Evelyn.

Thank you.

Cecil.

Better than the same without someone that you did.

Evelyn.

Sorry, I don't follow.

Cecil.

Fifty years with someone that one didn't love, like
you with Reggie, judging from your general appearance, may be less wearing than fifty years without someone one does love—like me without you.

Evelyn.

You're telling me you loved me, Cecil?

Cecil.

Yes.

Evelyn.

You had a funny way of showing it.

Cecil.

Not funny-natural.

Evelyn.

For animals, I daresay, but not human beings.

Cecil.

Both.

Evelyn.

Not if you wanted marriage. You lacked all restraint. You frightened me.

Cecil.

I see that, now.

Evelyn.

That's why I ran back to the Suttons.

Cecil.

I know, and I'm sorry. Jim's still living there, you know—at Sutton Place.

Evelyn.

I know—he wired when Reggie died.

Cecil.

Oh, did he? Good for Jim.

Evelyn.

When did you realize you loved me, Cecil?

Cecil.

Following you back to the Suttons.

Evelyn.

But you never said so.

Cecil.

No, I never got the chance. We played that awful game all evening. Then you went to bed. Then, the next morning—

Evelyn.

I'd gone back to London.

Cecil.

You'd gone to Reggie.

Evelyn.

Yes. We got engaged that evening.

Cecil.

On the rebound?

Evelyn.

Cake?

Cecil.

Please. Answer, Evelyn.

Evelyn.

I have answered.

Cecil.

In a thoroughly facetious manner. Was it on the rebound?

Evelyn.

Does it matter—now?

Cecil.

To me, yes—very much.

Evelyn.

Why?

Cecil.

Because all my life's been spent on the assumption that it was. That's why I never married. That's why I played fast and loose with women—why I'm where I am now.

Evelyn.

Sitting pretty.

Cecil.

Sitting lonely—standing by for death, without the least experience of life.

Evelyn.

You, Cecil—don't be silly! You—without experience of life! You're the best selling, the most famous author in the British Isles—and you say, without experience of life—

Cecil.

Of living, then.

Evelyn.

Ah, that's a different thing.

Cecil.

Wouldn't Reggie let you see me?

Evelyn.

No, I promised.

Cecil.

Or write to me?

Evelyn.

No, I promised that, too.

Cecil.

That explains it. I wrote every day for three years.

Evelyn.

Don't I know it.

Cecil.

And did Reggie?

Evelyn.

Yes. He used to burn them. Wait until he had enough to make a good-sized bonfire in the garden— and then burn them.

Cecil.

All unopened?

Evelyn.

All except one.

Cecil.

And who opened that one?

Evelyn.

I did.

Cecil.

What did it say?

Evelyn.

That you wanted me to run away with you.

Cecil.

They all said that.

Evelyn.

I think this must have been the first one.

Cecil.

Why?

Evelyn.
Because it gave the time and place and date.
Cecil.
Victoria—the boat train platform—9:15 a.m. on May 10th.
Evelyn.
That's right.
Cecil.
It was the first one.
Evelyn.
Were you there?
Cecil.
Yes, I was. Where were you?
Evelyn.
In Ullapool.
Cecil.
Where's that?
Evelyn.
In Scotland. We were fishing. At least Reggie was. And I was walking through the heather, thinking.
Cecil.
Of what?
Evelyn.
You. How long did you wait?
Cecil.
Till the train went.
Evelyn.
Then what did you do?
Cecil.
I got a refund on the tickets.
Evelyn.
More tea?
Cecil.
No, thanks. Then you started breeding.
Evelyn.
Yes.

Cecil.

How many did you notch up?

Evelyn.

Two. To make sure of security of tenure. And to stop you tempting me away from Reggie.

Cecil.

Did he ever talk about me?

Evelyn.

Not if he could help it. Only when your first book came out.

Cecil.

What did he say then?

Evelyn.

He said that it confirmed his worst opinions of you.

Cecil.

Literally speaking?

Evelyn.

No, no. He conceded that the style was quite good. But he didn't like the content.

Cecil.

I don't blame him.

Evelyn.

He assumed the bore that she rebounded onto in the second chapter was himself.

Cecil.

He was quite right.

Evelyn.

And that the young man who seduced her was yourself.

Cecil.

With licence.

Evelyn.

I should hope so. Underneath a beech tree, near a stream, of all the cheek. Just think of the discomfort! Beech mast, sticks and baby thistles.

Cecil.

Don't forget they had a rug.

Evelyn.

We didn't.

Cecil.

What a lot we missed!

Evelyn.

You're just a dirty old man! I've heard the expression often, but I've never seen it in the flesh before.

Cecil.

I'm just a dreamer, Evelyn.

Evelyn.

Nonsense.

Cecil.

Dreaming of what might have been, if I'd played my cards right.

Evelyn.

If you'd played them right, you would have married me.

Cecil.

That's what I wanted.

Evelyn.

Nonsense. What you wanted was a good affair. The only thing I'd guess that ever meant a thing to you as far as women are concerned. And you didn't want marriage, so please don't pretend you did.

Cecil.

I did. And I'll prove it to you.

Evelyn.

How?

Cecil.

By asking you to marry me now.

Evelyn.

That proves nothing.

Cecil.

It proves everything.

Evelyn.

It doesn't. It's the only thing you can ask now.

Cecil.

Don't you believe it.

Evelyn.

Don't be silly, Cecil. Be your age. It's out of reach, that aspect of the matter. Gone beyond recall. So we're down to second best. And I'm not playing.

Cecil.

Second best?

Evelyn.

Yes. What's the use of asking me to marry you now? It's like giving somebody an empty boiled-eggshell for breakfast, it's a favorite joke with children— But not very popular with grown-ups.

Cecil.

I thought you loved me.

Evelyn.

So I did. But not enough to put your slippers out, and knit your pullovers. That isn't what I dreamed about for fifty years.

Cecil.

You can't have really loved me, then.

Evelyn.

I did. I loved you day in, day out, till it nearly drove me mad.

Cecil.

I loved you in the same way.

Evelyn.

Well, you should have shown more self-control.

Cecil.

Please don't rebuke me, Evelyn. I can't bear it.

Evelyn.

I think I'd better go.

Cecil.

No, don't go, Evelyn. Please don't go. Stay here the night—a few days. Stay and see if you could bear

to stay here always. You could have a free hand in
the garden and the house. You could refurnish it,
according to your taste—re-do it altogether. I'm
well off. Extremely well off. I'd give you a free
hand.

Evelyn.

No, thank you, Cecil. It's too late. I'm sorry but it's
fifty years too late. The young man who was lying
underneath this beech tree fifty years ago, was quite
a marriageable proposition. Well, comparatively
speaking. You were arrogant, of course, and cynical
and irresponsible. But you were honest, at least.
Flora was the trouble, wasn't she?

Cecil.

That was before I met you.

Evelyn.

She was most attractive wasn't she? I'm surprised
she didn't come and see you when her husband died.

Cecil.

She did.

Evelyn.

Did you ask her to marry you?

Cecil.

Yes.

Evelyn.

And you say you've always loved me!

Cecil.

I thought Reggie was immortal.

Evelyn.

What was her excuse?

Cecil.

The same as yours. That it was fifty years too late.

Evelyn.

And what about the Paris woman?

Cecil.

So you know about her?

Evelyn.

It was in the papers.

Cecil.

So it was.

Evelyn.

She shot herself.

Cecil.

She missed.

Evelyn.

What was her name?

Cecil.

You tell me.

Evelyn.

Yvette—Yvette something.

Cecil.

That's right.

Evelyn.

A bit of luck for you, that—wasn't it?

Cecil.

You mean that she missed me as well?

Evelyn.

No, that she didn't kill herself. You would have been in trouble.

Cecil.

Not at all. I thought so at the time, I must admit. I panicked for a moment, but if women go round shooting themselves just because they fall in love, it's really up to them—one can't be held responsible.

Evelyn.

Have you seen Yvette since then?

Cecil.

Yes. She came here seven years ago. Her husband had just died.

Evelyn.

You seem to do a thriving line in widows. Did she turn you down, too?

Cecil.

Yes, indeed she did.

Evelyn.

The same excuse?

Cecil.

Precisely.

Evelyn.

I'm not sorry. Yvette rather shocked me, if you must know. Not herself, I mean, the melodrama.

Cecil.

And the bullet only missed me by a bee's wing. Hawkins told me—he worked out the angles. You're not armed, are you? Except with integrity!

Evelyn.

You're still as irresponsible as ever, Cecil. You're still prepared to pay a compliment, and carry on outrageously at the same time.

Cecil.

I haven't been outrageous.

Evelyn.

No! You sit there asking me to marry you, and then, without a blush, you tell me that you've done the same thing to two other women when their husbands died.

Cecil.

What's that but honesty?

Evelyn.

For one thing, it's bad manners.

Cecil.

Not at all. You must remember that I'm getting on. I have to take my chances when they come. For all I know, old Reggie might have gone on playing golf till Kingdom come. Well, he did, didn't he? So, you can't blame me, can you?

Evelyn.

I'm not blaming you. I'm merely telling you it isn't any use.

Cecil.

Because it's fifty years too late?

Evelyn.

Yes.

Cecil.

Not because you don't still love me.

Evelyn.

I must go.

Cecil.

Go? Why the devil did you come here then?

Evelyn.

(Gets up.) To have a cup of tea. How do we get hold of the chauffeur?

Cecil.

I'll ring for Hawkins. (He rings a hut bell.) It was sex in fact, on your side. And once that was over, well, it wouldn't have worked anyway.

Evelyn.

What makes you think so?

Cecil.

Well, your present attitude. If you'd really loved me, then you would have married me.

Evelyn.

You never asked me.

Cecil.

Yes, I did. Just now.

Evelyn.

Oh, Cecil—can't you understand—don't go on so.
                    (Hawkins enters. ******)

Cecil.

Perhaps we'll meet at Wimbledon, or somewhere, Evelyn.

Evelyn.

Perhaps.

Cecil.
  Anyway, I'll write to you. The chances are they might get read, now.
Evelyn.
  They might, Cecil. (She goes.)

The Kingfisher

William Douglas Home

This scene follows the previous one. Though Evelyn has rejected Cecil's proposal of marriage and departed, she has come back almost immediately. We have learned that Evelyn and Cecil had a sexual encounter fifty years ago. For more background on the play, see introduction to previous scene on page 209. The brief entrance of the butler, Hawkins, has been deleted and marked with asterisks. Cecil has just thought his slippers were misplaced only to find them on his feet.

CECIL, EVELYN

Cecil.
  Do you get like that, Evelyn?
Evelyn.
  No.
Cecil.
  You will. You've got it coming to you. Everybody does, when they start going back.

Evelyn.

What an expression.

Cecil.

I find it descriptive.

Evelyn.

I find it depressing.

Cecil.

Why? It's natural. They issued us with return tickets when we came into this world, remember? Now we're on the way back. And, soon, we'll hit the buffers, crash-bang—

Evelyn.

Don't!

Cecil.

Why not? One may as well face facts. The only truth in life is death.

Evelyn.

You might as well say that the only truth in death is life.

******

Cecil.

(After a pause.) To your blue eyes, Evelyn.

Evelyn.

(Raising her glass.) ''To my darling Sheila with undying love from Cecil.''

Cecil.

So he told you about that, too?

Evelyn.

He did.

Cecil.

Poor girl. You could say she was my Reggie.

Evelyn.

Not as Hawkins just described her.

Cecil.

On the rebound, I mean. Sheila was my attempt to scotch the disappointment and frustration of your not being at Victoria Station.

Evelyn.

And Countess von Hornstein!

Cecil.

Who told you about her?

Evelyn.

Hawkins.

Cecil.

I don't know why I keep that fellow.

Evelyn.

I do. No one else would stand your bestial behaviour!

Cecil.

Bestial!

Evelyn.

Yes, there's no other word for it. Just like a badger killing for the fun of it. Hen feathers flying everywhere—then silence in the morning, and no eggs.

Cecil.

I didn't kill the countess—we just fell apart. I wish there had been silence in the morning, Evelyn, and at night. I never knew a woman talk so much, that's why I left her.

Evelyn.

Then you went to Cairo.

Cecil.

Did I?

Evelyn.

Hawkins said you did.

Cecil.

That's right. We both did.

Evelyn.

You and Hawkins?

Cecil.

That's right. We went up the Nile. Another sidecar?

Evelyn.

Thank you, Cecil. Where you met the belly dancer?

Cecil.

(Stopping.) Belly dancer! Fatima, you mean.

Evelyn.

I wouldn't know. And how long did you stay with her?

Cecil.

Till custom staled her infinite variety. And so it went on. But I didn't love them—any of them.

Evelyn.

But you loved me.

Cecil.

Passionately.

Evelyn.

Then why didn't you propose?

Cecil.

I did.

Evelyn.

Not marriage, Cecil. Why not marriage?

Cecil.

I was young, and not quite certain of myself.

Evelyn.

You didn't seem that way to me.

Cecil.

Evelyn, you know that weekend we first met at Sutton Place. (He changes the subject, and gets away with it.)

Evelyn.

Yes.

Cecil.

Do you know I didn't want to go.

Evelyn.

You were quite right for Prudence, I suppose.

Cecil.

Quite right. A sweet girl but she never would've launched a 1,000 ships. She'd've sunk the lot.

Evelyn.

I didn't want to go because I wanted to play golf with Reggie.

Cecil.

Well, why didn't you?

Evelyn.

Because my mother didn't want me staying the weekend with him because his parents were away.

Cecil.

And Mother didn't trust you?

Evelyn.

Evidently not.

Cecil.

You mean to say you found Reggie attractive?

Evelyn.

He was kind.

Cecil.

That's not an answer.

Evelyn.

It's the only one you're going to get.

Cecil.

(After a pause.) I didn't want to come because I wanted to go sailing.

Evelyn.

Who with?

Cecil.

Flora.

Evelyn.

What did she know about sailing?

Cecil.

Nothing.

Evelyn.

Still she cooked the dinner, I suppose, and made the bed?

Cecil.

Precisely.

Evelyn.

So you came down to the tennis court at Sutton Place and saw me being beaten six love by Jim.

Cecil.

And I fell in love with you on the spot. Then I asked you to walk up the river, after tea. We found a moorhen's nest, remember?

Evelyn.

That's right. It was floating. And you told me that they almost always made them like that in case of a flood. It had five eggs.

Cecil.

That's right. And then we saw a kingfisher.

Evelyn.

Yes, I remember. It flew out from under the bank.

Cecil.

Then we both climbed down to see if we could find its nest.

Evelyn.

You did. I jumped and landed in your arms, and nearly knocked you over backwards.

Cecil.

That was when I kissed you for the first time.

Evelyn.

And we didn't find the nest.

Cecil.

The bank was too hard. They like sand. They can't dig in it, otherwise. They bore a hole with their beaks you know.

Evelyn.

So you told me.

Cecil.

I've heard people say they kick off from the other bank, and hit the sand head first.

Evelyn.

You told me that, as well.

Cecil.

That's why they need it soft.

Evelyn.

Yes, I can understand that.

Cecil.

Otherwise, if it was hard mud, or stones, they'd break their necks.

Evelyn.

Yes, Cecil.

Cecil.

A damned risky business. Thank God I'm not a kingfisher! I saw it just before you came this afternoon.

Evelyn.

I know, you told me.

Cecil.

Lovely little creature! Say they breed their first year—barring accidents, of course—it ought to be the forty-ninth descendant of the one that we saw. That's a thought, eh?

Evelyn.

Isn't it indeed!

Cecil.

Another sidecar?

Evelyn.

Well, a very little one.

Cecil.

(Over by the tray.) And then we took our shoes and stockings off, and paddled upstream.

Evelyn.

And I hit my toe against a pebble.

Cecil.

Yes.

Evelyn.

And you took out your handkerchief and dried it. And then kissed it better. Then we paddled on again.

Until we got here. Then you said, "Let's climb out and sit underneath that tree." And we did. Then you dried my feet again.

Cecil.

They were the smallest feet I ever saw.

Evelyn.

They're bigger now.

Cecil.

Not much.

Evelyn.

Of course they are. Colossal—Reggie always used to say how big they were.

Cecil.

Oh, good for Reggie! (Pouring.) Say when.

Evelyn.

When.

Cecil.

And you had a mole behind your left knee.

Evelyn.

That's right.

Cecil.

Is it still there?

Evelyn.

I believe so. I've not looked for thirty years.

Cecil.

May I look, Evelyn?

Evelyn.

No.

Cecil.

How long did we stay under that tree?

Evelyn.

Nearly three hours. We were late for dinner. Then we played a dreadful word game, after dinner—

Cecil.

Then you went to bed and all we dared to do was shake hands.

Evelyn.

Prudence came up with me.

Cecil.

Don't I know it. I could hear you talking through the wall for hours. What did you tell her?

Evelyn.

Everything. Girls do, you know. They like second opinions.

Cecil.

And what was your joint conclusion?

Evelyn.

That you didn't love me. Prudence said you wouldn't have done what you did, if you had.

Cecil.

She was dead wrong, Evelyn.

Evelyn.

So you say.

Cecil.

How could you listen to her?

Evelyn.

Easily. Because she'd had experience.

Cecil.

I don't believe it. Who was the shortsighted fellow?

Evelyn.

Reggie.

Cecil.

Reggie!!

Evelyn.

Yes. He'd done the same to her.

Cecil.

Good heavens—when?

Evelyn.

The week before, at Swinley Forest—in the heather. At the 12th hole. They were looking for his ball.

Cecil.

And did they find it?

Evelyn.

Don't be flippant, Cecil. That's what made me marry Reggie.

Cecil.

I don't get you.

Evelyn.

Well, he hadn't done it to me.

Cecil.

What chance had he had, good heavens!

Evelyn.

Quite a lot, at dances, and at weekends and in people's gardens.

Cecil.

Gardens don't have heather. If you'd gone to Swinley Forest with him, he'd have had a go all right.

Evelyn.

I lay awake all night.

Cecil.

Why?

Evelyn.

Thinking about you, and hoping you'd come in. Then I got up early the next morning, and went up to London. And went straight to Reggie's house. His parents were away and he was still in bed. Like you were, I imagine.

Cecil.

No, I wasn't. I came down to breakfast early, specially to see you, but you'd gone.

Evelyn.

You could have followed me.

Cecil.

I didn't know you'd gone, then, I thought you were breakfasting in bed.

Evelyn.

No, not me. Reggie was though. So I went up to his bedroom and I said ''Now look here, Reggie.

What's all this that Prudence Sutton told me last night?" "What did Prudence tell you?" he asked, blushing like a beetroot. "About Swinley Forest" I said. "Oh, that," he said, getting even redder. "Listen, Reggie," I said, "If I'd come to Swinley Forest with you this weekend would you have done the same to me?" "Of course not, Evelyn," he said.

Cecil.

Bloody liar.

Evelyn.

"Why not?" I said. "Because I respect you," he said.

Cecil.

Sanctimonious prig!

Evelyn.

Cecil, be quiet. Now I've forgotten where I'd got to.

Cecil.

Reggie was respecting you.

Evelyn.

Yes, that's right. Then I said "Prove it." "How the devil can I?" he said. "Easily," I said, "I'm getting into bed with you right now." "Good God!" he said, "I haven't had my egg yet." "Never mind that," I said. "Give me that tray." Then I put it on the bedside table.

Cecil.

Wait a minute, Evelyn. How the devil did you manage that?

Evelyn.

Manage what, Cecil?

Cecil.

Putting the tray on the bedside table. When I try that lark, it's always cluttered up with telephones and books and lamps and ashtrays and alarm-clocks.

Not the tray, old girl, the bedside table—don't misunderstand me.

Evelyn.

Do you want to hear the story of my life or don't you, Cecil?

Cecil.

Yes, please.

Evelyn.

Well, shut up about the tray then. Take it from me—it was on the bedside table.

Cecil.

Right.

Evelyn.

And then I started to undress.

Cecil.

Good heavens!

Evelyn.

That's what Reggie said. Then I went on undressing.

Cecil.

Bless my soul!

Evelyn.

Then Reggie said, "I'd rather marry you, old girl, to tell the truth." "I don't believe you," I said. "It's the truth," he said. And so we got engaged. And then I ate his egg.

******

Evelyn.

What are you thinking, Cecil?

Cecil.

Nothing.

Evelyn.

Come along, I'm your guest and I want to know.

Cecil.

When you ate Reggie's egg—where were you? In bed?

Evelyn.
No, of course not.
Cecil.
Why not?
Evelyn.
Because Reggie was a gentleman.
Cecil.
(Put out by this.) Straight up the steps and through
the hall and just right.
(They exit.)

The Little Foxes

Lillian Hellman

*This play, first produced in 1939, is one of many Hellman plays
which hit their peak in popularity before the mid-century mark.
Today, we may find some of her characters a little less than
complex, limited to outright villains or people of integrity, who
are usually victimized by the villains. This play is set in the
living room of a well-appointed house in the South in the spring
of 1900. In this charming setting, the Hubbards appear: Ben,
Oscar, Leo, and Regina. They are anything but charming, a
possessive, scheming, despotic, and unprincipled family, both as
a group and individually. Regina, the sister, is married to Horace Giddens and this is their home. Horace has had a heart
attack and was hospitalized. Oscar, Ben, and Leo, anticipating*

*Horace's imminent demise, have stolen a large sum of money
from Horace's strongbox for a new venture concerning a cotton
mill. The following scene is between Regina and Horace and
takes place shortly after Horace's return from the hospital.*

REGINA, HORACE

(Regina comes in from hall. Horace's chair is now so
placed that he is in front of table with the medicine.
Regina stands in the hall, shakes umbrella, stands it in
U.R. corner, takes off her cloak and throws it over
bannister. She stares at Horace.)
Regina.
 (As she takes off her gloves, crossing to C.) We had
 agreed that you were to stay in your part of this
 house and I in mine. This room is MY part of the
 house. Please don't come down here again.
Horace.
 I won't.
Regina.
 (Crossing D.R. toward bell-cord below mantel.) I'll
 get Cal to take you upstairs.
Horace.
 (Smiles.) Before you do I want to tell you that after
 all, we have invested our money in Hubbard, Sons
 and Marshall, Cotton Manufacturers.
Regina.
 (Stops, turns, stares at him.) What are you talking
 about? You haven't seen Ben—When did you
 change your mind?
Horace.
 I didn't change my mind. I didn't invest the money.
 (Smiles at the expression on her face.) It was in-
 vested for me.
Regina.
 (Angrily.) What—?

Horace.

I had eighty-eight thousand dollars' worth of Union Pacific bonds in that safe deposit box. They are not there now. Go and look. (As she stares at him. Points to box.) Go and look, Regina. (She crosses quickly to box, opens it. He speaks when she is at table.) Those bonds are as negotiable as money. (She closes box.)

Regina.

(Turns back to him.) What kind of joke are you playing now? Is this for my benefit?

Horace.

I don't look in that box very often, but three days ago, on Wednesday it was, because I had made a decision—

Regina.

I want to know what you are talking about.

Horace.

(Sharply.) Don't interrupt me again. (Regina stiffens.) Because I had made a decision, I sent for the box. The bonds were gone. Eighty-eight thousand dollars gone. (He smiles at her.)

Regina.

(After a moment's silence, quietly crossing U.C.) Do you think I'm crazy enough to believe what you're saying?

Horace.

(Shrugs.) Believe anything you like.

Regina.

(Stares at him, slowly.) Where did they go to?

Horace.

They are in Chicago. With Mr. Marshall, I should guess.

Regina.

(Crossing D. to chair L.C.) What did they do? Walk to Chicago? Have you really gone crazy?

Horace.

Leo took the bonds.

Regina.

(Turns sharply then speaks softly, without conviction.) I don't believe it.

Horace.

(Leans forward.) I wasn't there but I can guess what happened. (Regina sits chair L.C.) This fine gentleman, to whom you were willing to marry your daughter, took the keys and opened the box. You remember that the day of the fight, Oscar went to Chicago? Well, he went with my bonds that his son Leo had stolen for him. (Pleasantly.) And for Ben, of course, too.

Regina.

(Slowly, nods.) When did you find out the bonds were gone?

Horace.

Wednesday night.

Regina.

I thought that's what you said. Why have you waited three days to do anything? (Suddenly laughs.) This WILL make a fine story.

Horace.

(Nods.) Couldn't it?

Regina.

(Still laughing. Rises, crosses U.L.—takes off hat.) A fine story to hold over their heads. How could they be such fools? (Turns to him back of settee.)

Horace.

But I'm not going to hold it over their heads.

Regina.

(The laugh stops.) What?

Horace.

(Turns his chair to face L.) I'm going to let them keep the bonds—as a loan from you. An eighty-eight thousand dollar loan; they should be grateful to you. They will be, I think.

Regina.

(Slowly, smiles.) I see. You are punishing me. But I won't let you punish me. If you won't do anything, I will. Now. (She starts for door.)

Horace.

You won't do anything. Because you can't. (Regina stops above chair R.C.) It won't do you any good to make trouble because I shall simply say that I lent them the bonds.

Regina.

(Slowly.) You would do that?

Horace.

Yes. (Regina crosses D. to chair L.C.) For once in your life I am tying your hands. There is nothing for you to do. (There is silence. Then she sits down.)

Regina.

I see. You are going to lend them the bonds and let them keep all the profit they make on them, and there is nothing I can do about it. Is that right?

Horace.

Yes.

Regina.

(Softly.) Why did you say that I was making this gift?

Horace.

I was coming to that. I am going to make a new will, Regina, leaving you eighty-eight thousand dollars in Union Pacific bonds. The rest will go to Zan. It's true that your brothers have borrowed your share for a little while. After my death I advise you to talk to Ben and Oscar. They won't admit anything and Ben, I think, will be smart enough to see that he's SAFE. Because I knew about the theft and said nothing. Nor WILL I say anything as long as I live. Is that clear to you?

Regina.

(Nods, softly, without looking at him.) You will not say anything as long as you live.

Horace.

That's right. And by that time they will probably have replaced your bonds, and then they'll belong to you and nobody but us will ever know what happened. (Stops, smiles.) They'll be around any minute to see what I am going to do. I took good care to see that word reached Leo. They'll be mighty relieved to know I'm going to do nothing and Ben will think it all a capital joke on you. And that will be the end of that. There's nothing you can do to them, nothing you can do to me.

Regina.

You hate me very much.

Horace.

No.

Regina.

Oh, I think you do. (Puts her head back, sighs.) Well, we haven't been very good together. Anyway, I don't hate you either. I have only contempt for you. I've always had.

Horace.

From the very first?

Regina.

I think so.

Horace.

I was in love with YOU. But why did YOU marry ME?

Regina.

I was lonely when I was young.

Horace.

YOU were lonely?

Regina.

Not the way people usually mean. Lonely for all the things I wasn't going to get. Everything in this house was so busy and there was so little place for what I wanted. I wanted the world. Then, and then— (Smiles.) Papa died and left the money to Ben and Oscar.

Horace.

And you married me?

Regina.

Yes, I thought—but I was wrong. You were a small-town clerk then. You haven't changed.

Horace.

(Nods, smiles.) And that wasn't what you wanted.

Regina.

No, No, it wasn't what I wanted. (Pauses, leans back, pleasantly.) It took me a little while to find out I had made a mistake. As for you—I don't know. It was almost as if I couldn't stand the kind of man you were— (Smiles, softly.) I used to lie there at night, praying you wouldn't come near—

Horace.

Really? It was as bad as that?

Regina.

(Nods.) Remember when I went to Doctor Sloan and I told you he said there was something the matter with me and that you shouldn't touch me any more?

Horace.

I remember.

Regina.

But you believed it? I couldn't understand that. I couldn't understand that anybody could be such a soft fool. That was when I began to despise you.

Horace.

(Puts his hand to his throat, glances around at bottle of medicine on table, then to her.) Why didn't you leave me?

Regina.

I told you I married you FOR something. It turned out it was only for this. (Carefully.) This wasn't what I wanted, but it was something. I never thought about it much, but if I had, (Horace puts his hand to his throat.) I'd have known that you would die before I would. But I couldn't have known that you would get heart trouble so early and so bad. I'm lucky, Horace. I've always been lucky. (Horace turns slowly to medicine.) I'll be lucky again. (Horace looks at her. Then he puts his hand to his throat. Because he cannot reach the bottle he moves the chair closer. He reaches for medicine, takes out cork, picks up spoon, tries to pour some in the spoon, the bottle slips out of his shaking fingers, and crashes on the table. He draws in his breath, gasps.)

Horace.

Please. Tell Addie—the other bottle is upstairs. (She has not moved. She does not move now. He stares at her. Then, suddenly as if he understood, he raises his voice. It is a panic-stricken whisper, too small to be heard outside the room.) Addie! Addie! Come— (Stops as he hears the softness of his voice. He makes a sudden, furious spring from the chair to the stairs, taking the first few steps as if he were a desperate runner. On the fourth step he slips, gasps, grasps the rail, makes a great effort to reach the landing. When he reaches the landing, he is on his knees. His knees give way, he falls on the landing, out of view. Regina has not turned during his climb up the stairs. Now she waits a second. Then she goes below the landing, speaks up.)

Regina.

Horace. (When there is no answer, she turns, crosses to door L., opens door, calls.) Addie! Cal! Come in here. (Crosses R. Starts up the steps.) He's had an attack. Come up here.

The Master Builder

Henrik Ibsen

❧

This play was produced in Norway in 1892 and deals with an aging architect who is worried about what he perceives as threats to his career by a younger man. He also has marital problems. The following scene reflects the tension between Halvard Solness, the middle-aged master builder, and his slightly younger wife. The scene takes place in his office in Norway at the end of the nineteenth century. Kaja, a young woman who works for Solness, has just left the room and has demonstrated an interest toward Solness as he has toward her. For more background, see the introduction to the previous scene from this play on page 31.

SOLNESS, MRS. SOLNESS

Solness.
Aline dear, don't you think you should go out and get a little fresh air?
Mrs. Solness.
Yes, I should, shouldn't I? (Continues attending to the flowers.)

Solness.

(Bent over the drawings.) Is she still asleep?

Mrs. Solness.

(Looks at him.) Is it Miss Wangel you're sitting there thinking about?

Solness.

(Indifferently.) Just happened to think of her.

Mrs. Solness.

Miss Wangel's been up a long time.

Solness.

Oh, has she?

Mrs. Solness.

When I looked in she was seeing to her clothes. (She goes to the mirror and begins slowly to put on her hat.)

Solness.

(After a short pause.) Well, we've found a use for one of the nurseries after all, haven't we, Aline?

Mrs. Solness.

Yes, we have.

Solness.

I think that's better than that they should all stand empty.

Mrs. Solness.

Yes, that emptiness is horrible. You're right there.

Solness.

(Closes the portfolio, gets up, and goes over to her.) From now on things will be better, Aline. You'll see. Much more satisfactory. Life will be easier to bear. Especially for you.

Mrs. Solness.

(Looks at him.) From now on?

Solness.

Yes, Aline, believe me—

Mrs. Solness.

You mean—because she's come?

Solness.

(Controls himself.) I mean, of course, once we've moved into the new house.

Mrs. Solness.

(Takes her overcoat.) Do you really think so, Halvard? Things will be better?

Solness.

I'm sure they will. You believe that too, don't you?

Mrs. Solness.

I don't believe anything where that new house is concerned.

Solness.

(Vexed.) I'm sorry to hear that, my dear. It was mainly for your sake I built it. (Tries to help her on with her coat.

Mrs. Solness.

(Moves away.) You do much too much for me.

Solness.

(Almost violently.) No, no, you mustn't talk like that, Aline. I can't bear to hear you say such things.

Mrs. Solness.

Very well, Halvard, I won't say them.

Solness.

I'm right, though. You'll be happy in that new house—you'll see.

Mrs. Solness.

God! I—happy—?

Solness.

Yes! Yes! I promise you! Don't you see, there'll be so much there that'll remind you of your own home—

Mrs. Solness.

Father's and Mother's home. And it was burnt. All burnt.

Solness.

(Subdued.) Yes, my poor Aline. That was a horrible blow for you.

Mrs. Solness.

You can build as much as you like, Halvard—you'll never be able to build a real home for me again.

Solness.

(Turns and walks away across the room.) Well, in that case, for God's sake let's not talk about it any more.

Mrs. Solness.

Well, we don't usually talk about it, anyway. You always avoid the subject—

Solness.

(Stops abruptly and looks at her.) I do? And why should I avoid the subject?

Mrs. Solness.

Oh, I understand you so well, Halvard. You want to spare me. And stop me feeling guilty. As far as you can.

Solness.

(Stares amazed.) Stop YOU feeling guilty? Are you—are you talking about yourself, Aline?

Mrs. Solness.

Yes, who else would I be talking about?

Solness.

(Involuntarily, to himself.) That too!

Mrs. Solness.

It's not so much what happened to the old house. I think I could resign myself to that. After all, that was an accident—

Solness.

Yes, you're right. Accidents will happen, and it's no use blaming oneself for them.

Mrs. Solness.

But the dreadful thing that happened after the fire! That's what I can't forget. I can't, I can't, I can't!

Solness.

(Violently.) Don't think about it, Aline.

Mrs. Solness.

I have to think about it. And I must talk about it some time. I don't think I can endure it any longer. And I never can forgive myself—

Solness.

Forgive YOURSELF—?

Mrs. Solness.

Yes, because I had a duty to all of you. To you, and the children. I should have hardened myself, I shouldn't have let fear weaken me. Or grief for my burnt home. Oh, if only I'd had the strength, Halvard.

Solness.

(Quiet, shaken, comes towards her.) Aline, you must promise me you'll never let these thoughts enter your head again. Promise me that, my dear.

Mrs. Solness.

God—promise, promise! It's easy to promise anything—

Solness.

(Walks across the room.) Oh, this is hopeless, hopeless! Not a ray of light ever enters this home. Not a glimmer.

Mrs. Solness.

This is no home, Halvard.

Solness.

No, you're so right. And, God knows, you may be right, too, when you say it won't be any better in the new house.

Mrs. Solness.

Never. It'll be just as empty and just as desolate there as it is here.

Solness.

(Violently.) Why in God's name have we built it then? Can you tell me that?

Mrs. Solness.

No, that you must answer yourself.

Solness.

(Looks at her suspiciously.) What do you mean by that, Aline?

Mrs. Solness.

What do I mean?

Solness.

Yes, damn it! You said it so strangely. As though you meant something else.

Mrs. Solness.

No, I assure you—

Solness.

(Goes closer.) Oh, thank you very much—I know what I know. I've got eyes and ears, Aline. You can be sure of that.

Mrs. Solness.

What do you mean? What do you mean?

Solness.

(Stands in front of her.) You find some cunning, hidden meaning in every harmless little thing I say, don't you, eh?

Mrs. Solness.

I, Halvard? Do I do that?

Solness.

(Laughs.) Oh, it's very understandable, Aline. When you've a sick man on your hands, well—

Mrs. Solness.

(Alarmed.) Sick? Are you sick, Halvard?

Solness.

An idiot, then! a lunatic! Call me what you like.

Mrs. Solness.

(Gropes for the back of the chair and sits down.) Halvard—for God's sake—

Solness.

But you're wrong, both of you. You and your doctor. There's nothing the matter with me. (He walks up and down the room. Mrs. Solness watches him

anxiously. At length he comes over to her. Calmly.)
There's nothing the matter with me at all.

Mrs. Solness.

No, of course not. But—what's worrying you, then?

Solness.

It's this dreadful burden of debt that's crushing me—

Mrs. Solness.

Debt? But you're not in debt to anyone, Halvard.

Solness.

(Quietly.) I owe a boundless debt to you. To you,
Aline.

Mrs. Solness.

(Rises slowly.) What is behind all this?

Solness.

There's nothing behind it. I've never done you any
harm. Not wittingly, anyway. And yet—it feels as
though a huge stone of guilt lay on me, weighing
me down, crushing me.

Mrs. Solness.

Guilt? Towards me, you mean? Then you really
are—sick, Halvard.

Solness.

I suppose I must be. Sick—or something. (Glances
toward the door on the right, as it is opened.)

The Middle Ages

A. R. Gurney

❦

This play, which opened in 1977, is set in the trophy room of
an exclusive men's club in a large American city. It moves both
back and forth in time from the mid-forties to the early seventies. During the first part of this scene a wedding is taking
place. The scene is between Charles, the father of the groom,
and Myra, the mother of the bride. References are made to
Barney, the brother of the groom, who has always been in love
with Eleanor, the bride. Asterisks denote a movement forward
in time.

MYRA, CHARLES

Myra.
Oh Charles, guess what just arrived.
Charles.
What?
Myra.
A wedding present. Special delivery to the club.
Charles.
From Barney?

Myra.
From your elder son.

Charles.
I'm delighted he finally sent one.

Myra.
You won't say that when you hear what it was. I took the liberty of opening it.

Charles.
Go on. (Myra sits at the desk, D.R. Charles follows.)

Myra.
It was a picture frame.

Charles.
What's wrong with that?

Myra.
A silver picture frame. From Gump's.

Charles.
What's wrong with Gump's?

Myra.
Nothing's wrong with Gump's. Gump's is one of the finest stores in San Francisco. It's what was IN the frame that's wrong.

Charles.
Well what was, Myra?

Myra.
His picture.

Charles.
Barney's picture?

Myra.
Barney's picture was in that frame.

Charles.
Well I think that's rather touching. I should have a picture of Barney in his sailor suit. I'll put it on the piano.

Myra.
He wasn't in his sailor suit.

Charles.
Oh?

Myra.
He was in his birthday suit.

Charles.
(Exploding.) Barney sent, as a wedding present, a picture of himself in the NUDE?

Myra.
Full front. Eleven by thirteen. In kodacolor.

Charles.
Oh good Lord! (He sits on couch, D.R. Myra follows him.)

Myra.
And . . .

Charles.
And?

Myra.
How do I say this?

Charles.
How do you say what?

Myra.
He had this great big white bow tied around his— dingy. (She sits beside him on the couch.) Oh, oh, oh.

Charles.
Oh, oh, oh.

Myra.
And . . .

Charles.
(Anguished) AND? AND?

Myra.
There was a note.

Charles.
SAYING WHAT?

Myra.
Saying "wish we could be there."

Charles.
Oh God, oh God, oh God.

Myra.

Thank heavens he's a million miles away, Charles

Charles.

That's what I told Eleanor.

Myra.

Absolutely. And that's what I told those two sailors downstairs.

Charles.

(Looking at her.) Sailors?

Myra.

Yes. Sailors. I think they were sailors. Except they wore leggings and armbands and carried nightsticks, like policemen.

Charles.

(Jumping up, grabbing her.) Shore Patrol! What the hell did they want?

Myra.

They wanted Barney. So I said he was on his ship for the Far East. They asked if they could wait outside. I said there was no point, but they could. And I sent them each down a glass of champagne. Because they're defending us all against communism.

Charles.

I'd better talk to them.

Myra.

All right Charles. (Indicates bathroom.) I'm going to powder my nose. The downstairs ladies room has been occupée all afternoon with tipsy bridesmaids. I'll see you on the dance floor.

******

(He crosses the stage, getting older by the step. The lights come up as Myra comes on in a pantsuit, also looking older. Her costume suggests the late sixties.)

Myra.

(Hesitantly.) Charlie. . . . (He turns to her.) There was a telephone message at the desk. I told them I'd give it to you.

Charles.

Yes?

Myra.

Long distance. From California. From you-know-who.

Charles.

Go on.

Myra.

He needs money again.

Charles.

Why?

Myra.

For bail. Again.

Charles.

What did he do this time?

Myra.

What difference does it make? Marching without a permit, lying down in front of troop trains, picketing against poor Mr. Nixon, it's all the same.

Charles.

How much does he need?

Myra.

It's higher this time.

Charles.

How much?

Myra.

A thousand. (Pause.)

Charles.

What time do the banks close these days?

Myra.

Oh Charlie, you're not going to keep DOING this.

Charles.

He hasn't got a dime.

Myra.

Whose fault is that? He lost a perfectly good teaching job. Because he STOLE, Charles.

Charles.

He didn't STEAL, Myra.

Myra.

He stole private property, Charles.

Charles.

It was public property.

Myra.

He stole the university president's CAR. and drove it AROUND.

Charles.

He didn't keep it. He gave it to the poor.

Myra.

He gave it to Angela Davis.

Charles.

Well Angela Davis is poor, Myra. Quite poor. I don't believe Angela Davis has a net worth of more than—

Myra.

Charlie, honestly!

Charles.

(With a sigh.) Oh Myra, I'm suddenly very tired.

Myra.

So am I, Charlie. So am I. Tired of seeing you tear yourself apart over that boy. Charlie, he is simply *de trop*. Now you've got a wonderful, hard-working son and a lovely daughter-in-law, and three marvelous grandchildren—

Charles.

They tire me too.

Myra.

Charlie!

Charles.

They do. I don't like it out there. Those noisy meals, the television blaring away, the endless chatter about schools. I don't like it out there much.

Myra.

Why Charlie: you're getting old.

Charles.

That's it. Old. And I want to be with people my own age. (He looks at her.) Let's get married, Myra.

Myra.

Charlie!

Charles.

Why not?

Myra.

I thought you were tired.

Charles.

I am. Let's lean on each other in our autumn years.

Myra.

But Charlie . . .

Charles.

Think about it. Take your time. I'll go see about that boy. (He goes off. Myra looks after him, looks at audience, ponders very briefly, clears her throat.)

Myra.

After long and careful thought, I have decided to marry Mr. Charles Rusher, of this city. It will be a small, sober ceremony, family only, I probably won't even wear a hat. Then a few friends back here afterward for a quiet drink. A glass of champagne, maybe, French champagne, and I hope someone will get on his feet and make a toast. There might be music. I could bring in that accordian player from the Park Plaza who plays nothing but Fred Astaire. Which means someone might want to dance. . . . (She begins to sing, dance.) "Heaven . . . I'm in Heaven . . ." (Stops.) And let there be food.

Chicken in patties and peas. Oh hell, let's have a party! Let's have a biggie! Let's have the most spectacular get-together since the Cerebral Palsy Ball! (Charles appears at the door.)

Charles.

Myra . . .

Myra.

(Swirling to him.) Oh Charlie, yes, yes, YES!

Charles.

(Patting her hand.) That's fine, dear. You make the arrangements. I've got to rush to the bank before they close. (He goes out. She stands looking after him, then comes slowly D.)

Myra.

Make the arrangements, make the arrangements, Myra . . . Strange . . . my first husband used to say the same thing. Wouldn't drive, wouldn't carve, wouldn't . . . never mind what he wouldn't do. Oh why do I seem to attract such exhausted men? Or are they only exhausted when they get to me? (She sits down.) Why can't I be exhausted once in a while? What if I said No. I refuse. I am hereby *hors de combat.* (She leans back, closes her eyes.) Oh this is marvellous. (She opens her eyes, sits up.) But then who will move him out of that great barn of a house and into a nice apartment? And who will remind him to take his pills? And who will get him to think about his will, and the college education of three grandchildren? (She stands up, squares her shoulders.) Me! I'll do it! Myra Rusher will make the arrangements! I'll plan the trips and manage the meals and send out the Christmas cards year after year! And when things fall apart, I'll hold them together with Scotch Tape and Elmer's Glue and Gilbey's Gin! Somebody has to do these things! On my head be it! *Apres moi, le deluge!* I'll arrange things until the day I die! Then I'll arrrange my own funeral! Nobody else will bother, that's for sure! (The lights come up on the trophy room. She defiantly takes a tape measure out of her pocket and begins to measure a chair, getting older with each move. . . .)

Mixed Emotions

Richard Baer

This play received its Broadway premiere in 1993. It takes place in the living room of Christine's apartment in Manhattan in the early 1990s. There are cartons, boxes, and other items indicating that Christine is in the midst of moving. Christine is described as age sixty-one, "gorgeous, sensible, unpretentious" and dressed smartly but casually. She is alone in the room when the door chimes sound. On the way to the door, she notices three sample carpet swatches. She hides them behind a cushion and opens the door to Herman. He is sixty-five and is a "shrewd, blunt, self-made man who can be simultaneously exasperating and endearing."

CHRISTINE, HERMAN

Christine.
Hello, Herman. What an unexpected surprise.

Herman.
Where were you?

Christine.
Where was I when?

Herman.
This afternoon. At three o'clock.

Christine.
I was in my kitchen, packing my dishes.

Herman.
Why weren't you in Long Island, at your husband's cemetery?

Christine.
What for?

Herman.
To pay your respects to him.

Christine.
I did that yesterday.

Herman.
Yesterday. Why yesterday?

Christine.
Because a year ago yesterday was when he died.

Herman.
Wrong. He died a year ago today.

Christine.
He died a year ago yesterday.

Herman.
Then why did you call me last Sunday and invite me to join you at your husband's grave at three o'clock this Thursday?

Christine.
I invited you to join me at three o'clock this Wednesday.

Herman.
You said Thursday. I wrote it down in my date book.

Christine.

I don't care where you wrote it—I said Wednesday.

Herman.

You said Thursday. Today. When for a fifty-six dollar round trip cab fare I had the pleasure of grieving all alone, in a blinding snowstorm.

Christine.

Herman, I said, slowly and clearly, Wednesday, February fourth.

Herman.

Aha! You just trapped yourself. Moe died on February fifth.

Christine.

No he didn't. He died on February fourth.

Herman.

Christine, are you telling me I don't know when my best friend died?

Christine.

Are you telling me I don't know when my husband died?

Herman.

Yes, I am. Go check the certificate. I'll wait. (He descends to living room, sits on sofa, as Christine closes front door, then descends to living room.)

Christine.

If you don't believe me, ask my daughters, both of whom, and their husbands, were with me at the cemetery, yesterday, Wednesday, February fourth.

Herman.

Oh. How much did the cab cost?

Christine.

We went in Joan and Larry's car. Because last Sunday I told you to meet us at their apartment so we could all drive out together. Then when you didn't show up I called your secretary to find out where you were, and she said you were on the way to a major fight with your accountant.

Herman.

Did you try to reach me at his office?

Christine.

No. I was very hurt that fighting with your account-ant took precedence over honoring the memory of your best friend. (Crossing to shelves) Herman, ex-cuse me, but I have a lot of packing to do, so with your kind permission I'll do it. (She proceeds to pack books, while Herman fans his forehead.)

Herman.

Why do you keep this room so hot?

Christine.

I'm sorry. I can either turn on the air conditioner, or you can take off your snowsuit.

Herman.

I forgot I had it on. (He rises, removes gloves, coat, hat, and muffler, puts them on ottoman.) Christine, permit me to point out that by the same token that YOU were hurt, I'M hurt that you thought anything could stop me from being at that cemetery unless, as the evidence seems to indicate, I was at the right place at the wrong time. (He sits on sofa, removes galoshes.) I'm also hurt that you didn't call to find out why I failed to appear. For all you knew I could've suddenly followed in your husband's foot-steps.

Christine.

I DID call. Last night. Your line was busy.

Herman.

It could've been the paramedics, calling the coroner.

Christine.

Would that tie up the phone for two hours?

Herman.

No. I was continuing my fight with my accountant. But you could've told the operator to cut in for an emergency.

Christine.

I had her verify there was conversation—from which I cleverly deduced that if you were on the phone you were alive.

Herman.

Let me know when you're tired of picking on me. Getting picked on is not the reason I came here.

Christine.

What is?

Herman.

I came to cheer you up. To take your mind off the horrible tragedy of Moe's death.

Christine.

That's very thoughtful of you.

Herman.

Especially in a blinding snowstorm.

Christine.

However, I don't need cheering up. I'm not depressed.

Herman.

Why not? Don't you miss him?

Christine.

Of course I do. And yesterday I was depressed. But last night I went out to dinner with my family . . . we toasted Moe's memory . . . we went around the table, each of us describing one of his fine qualities . . . we all realized how much he meant to us . . . but life must go on . . . and I got over my depression.

Herman.

Completely?

ould've paid.

the cemetery you'd've been
use, wistfully.) You know what

send a check to Paul and Larry?

Christine.
No. If last night, up there . . . Moe and Miriam had
dinner together.

Herman.
Well, if they did, let's hope it wasn't at her apartment, so he didn't have to eat her cooking.

Christine.
Herman, with all due respect, that's a rotten thing
to say.

Herman.
It's true. My wife had many virtues—but two things
she never was noted for were parachute jumping and
cooking.

Christine.

(Upon reflection.) Bro█

Herman.

Possibly. Anything else?

Christine.

(More reflection, then.) She █
meatloaf.

Herman.

The topic is "edible," not "interesting."

Christine.

Then let's change the topic! Why can't you let Miriam's cooking, and Miriam, rest in peace?

Herman.

I can, and I will.

Christine.

Thank you.

Herman.

Except to say that I strongly doubt that Miriam and Moe even SEE each other (Pointing upward.) up there. Because I strongly doubt that up there even exists. In case you never noticed, I'm not a devout Catholic.

Christine.

Neither am I. As I told you about nine thousand times you teased me about it, I quit being devout when I got married.

Herman.

But every now and then doesn't it sneak up on you? Like when you're walking up Fifth Avenue, on route to Sak's or Bergdorf's and you come to St. Patrick's Cathedral. Don't you ever duck inside and light a candle? (Christine picks up the candy dish.)

Christine.

Would you care for a chocolate?

Herman.

No thanks, all I'd care for is an answer to my question. (She takes a piece of candy, eats it, sets down dish.) Do you or don't you ever duck inside and light a candle?

Christine.

I do. But very infrequently.

Herman.

How infrequently?

Christine.

Two or three times a year.

Herman.

Closer to two, or closer to three?

Christine.

Closer to three. But only since Moe died.

Herman.

And each time, how many candles do you light?

Christine.

Four. One for my mother, one for my father, one for Moe, and one for Miriam.

Herman.

So counting each candle as a separate religious experience . . . four candles three times per year adds

up to twelve candles per year, or one candle per
month. And the total should really be doubled.

Christine.

Why?

Herman.

Because lighting Catholic candles for Jews is burning the candle at both ends.

Christine.

(Wearily.) Herman, go home. It's been nice chatting
with you, but I'm very, very, very busy, so thanks
for coming and go home.

Herman.

Aren't you even going to offer me a glass of water?

Christine.

No. I offered you chocolate, and you rejected me.
(Herman reaches over, takes a chocolate, eats it.)

Herman.

There. Now if only I had something to wash it
down.

Christine.

Herman, may I offer you a glass of water?

Herman.

I accept. (Christine ascends to entry hall. Herman
calls.) Unless you happen to have Diet Pepsi.
(Christine returns, crosses to bar's refrigerator, takes
out a beverage bottle, opens it.)

Christine.

Do you take your Diet Pepsi with ice or without?

Herman.

Was it in the refrigerator?

Christine.

Yes.

Herman.

How long?

Christine.

A week, two weeks—I don't keep formal inventory.

Herman.

If you store soft drinks too long they lose their fizz. (Christine pours cola, into a glass, and reports.)

Christine.

It didn't lose its fizz. It's fizzing superbly.

Herman.

Then why weaken its flavor with ice? (She sets down the bottle, shuts refrigerator, carries glass to Herman, gives it to him.) Thanks.

Christine.

You're welcome. (He sets glass on table.) Aren't you going to drink it?

Herman.

First I let it breathe. (Christine packs more books.) Well, are you excited?

Christine.

About what?

Herman.

Moving to Florida, and sharing a condominium with a wonderful woman like Beverly Siegel.

Christine.

Yes, I'm excited. So is she. I'm lonely without Moe; she's lonely without Arnold. (Stops packing.) Herman, will you please do me a favor?

Herman.

What?

Christine.

(Re: his cola.) Drink. If it loses its fizz I'll never forgive myself. (Herman takes a sip, then springs to his feet.)

Herman.

Hold everything!

Christine.

What's wrong?

Herman.

This isn't Diet Pepsi. It's Diet Coke.

Christine.

(Feigning dread.) Oh my God, he caught me! (He strides to bar, sets down glass, picks up empty bottle, displays it.)

Herman.

See? It doesn't say Diet Pepsi; it says Diet Coke.

Christine.

Fool that I am, I thought I could get away with it.

Herman.

No chance. Most people can't tell the difference, but I can. I have very sensitive taste buds.

Christine.

I'm sorry. Can you ever forgive me, or did I seal my doom?

Herman.

That depends on what other diet beverages you've got. (Christine crosses, opens refrigerator, looks inside.)

Christine.

I have club soda . . . and club soda.

Herman.

Club soda. (Christine extracts the bottle, closes refrigerator, gets a clean glass.) Nobody ever accused me of being difficult. (She opens can, fills glass.)

Christine.

Yippee! It's fizzing like hotcakes. To celebrate, I'll drink the Diet Coke. (She sets down bottle, gives him the soda, picks up the cola, and they exchange toasts.)

Herman.

To the memory of Moe Millman.

Christine.

And the memory of Miriam Lewis. (They clink glasses, sip their drinks then Christine goes to bookcase, sets glass on a shelf, packs more books.)

Herman.

Last night, at the restaurant, when everybody described Moe's fine qualities, what'd YOU say?

Christine.

I said he was kind, gentle, and considerate.

Herman.

If I was there, I would've said his finest quality was something else.

Christine.

What?

Herman.

His warmth. He had more warmth than any coat he ever sold. I loved him like a brother.

Christine.

He loved you too. And he loved Miriam. And so did I. (She resumes packing; he crosses to her.)

Herman.

So it looks like you're moving to Florida.

Christine.

Yep, that's what it looks like.

Herman.

When do the movers come?

Christine.

They're already here.

Herman.

They're here? Where?

Christine.

In the kitchen. They're supposed to be packing my books, but they can't, because I'm having company. (She packs more books.)

Herman.

When do the movers with the moving van show up?

Christine.

Tomorrow morning, eight A.M. But they're the same movers. If you'd like to meet them before you leave, I'll call them in right now.

.man.

Don't bother. You're paying them to work, not to socialize. (Beat.) So in other words, the movers leave tomorrow and you leave Saturday.

Christine.

Half right, half wrong. The movers leave tomorrow, and so do I. From Kennedy Airport, at five-fifteen P.M.

Herman.

Tomorrow? You told me you leave Saturday.

Christine.

No I didn't.

Herman.

Christine, explain something to me. Unless Beverly has two living rooms and two dining rooms and six bedrooms, how can all the furniture in your apartment fit in her apartment?

Christine.

It can't. That's why I'm putting my furniture in storage, and all I'm sending to Florida is clothes, books, records, and prized possessions.

Herman.

I didn't know that.

Christine.

I told you the last time I saw you in person, January first, at Joan and Larry's New Year's party.

Herman.

All you said at that party was you were thinking of selling your apartment.

Christine.

I said I sold it. I said I was thinking of selling the NEXT to last time I saw you. At Paul and Barbara's. On Thanksgiving. (Carton full, she packs another.)

Herman.

Won't you miss the furniture that you and Moe invested so much sentimental value in?

Christine.

I'm being practical. Bev's apartment is furnished fully and magnificently. She used a magnificent decorator. Me.

Herman.

Is her carpeting equally magnificent?

Christine.

Almost.

Herman.

And THAT, if memory serves, you got from me. At cost.

Christine.

Plus twelve percent.

Herman.

Eleven. (After sipping his drink.) I presume Bev lined up lots of clients for you.

Christine.

She's trying.

Herman.

She'll succeed. When she throws her two hundred pounds around, she can do anything.

Christine.

Two hundred? She's one fifteen, or tops, one twenty.

Herman.

I added the weight of her makeup and jewelry.

Christine.

Untrue, and unkind. She may be slightly . . . overstated, but she's more fun to be with than anyone I know—present company excluded.

Herman.

She's also the world's leading non-stop talker. Rumor has it that when Arnold wisely died, Beverly talked to him five days before she noticed he wasn't showing any interest. (He sits on sofa, puts glass on coffee table. Christine takes an art book from its shelf, looks at its title.)

Christine.

ART TREASURES OF THE LOUVRE MUSEUM. Remember where this came from?

Herman.

No. Where?

Christine.

From the Louvre Museum. Miriam bought it for me on the last vacation the four of us took together. (She sits beside him, flips pages, and waxes nostalgic.) Twenty-six glorious days. In England . . . Ireland . . . Scotland . . . France . . . Italy . . . Spain . . . Portugal . . . Norway . . . Denmark . . . Sweden . . .Switzerland . . . and Israel.

Herman.

And I thought we were spreading ourselves too thin.

Christine.

But we weren't, thanks to Miriam She studied guide books, she planned each day in advance, so we saw everything worth seeing and did everything worth doing.

Herman.

Remember that time in Rome? At the Vatican? When the four of us stood in the parking lot waiting for the Pope to come out on his balcony and wave hello.

Christine.

It wasn't a parking lot, it was St. Peter's Square. There must've been ten thousand people.

Herman.

You, of course, were in your element. But Moe and Miriam and me were like three misplaced matzoh balls.

Christine.

Then the Pope came out on the balcony and went like this. (She makes three arm gestures, to her left, her center, and her right.) Miriam said, "Christine, what does that mean?" And before I could answer, you said it means: (Repeating arm gestures.) "I want the three Jewish people to get off my private property." (Nostalgia ended, Christine rises, puts book in carton, packs others. Herman rises, crosses to her.)

Herman.

Let's say you DO find clients in Florida. What about your business sources? All of them are here.

Christine.

And I'll order from them. And I'll develop sources there.

Herman.

Including for carpeting?

Christine.

No. I promise all my carpeting will come from you.

Herman.

Good. Then I guess all you'll have to worry about is how happy you can be living two thousand miles away from your children and grandchildren.

Christine.

The distance from New York City to Miami is one thousand and ninety miles. The flying time is two hours and thirty-eight minutes. I'll still be able to visit my family, and they'll still be able to visit me.

Herman.

I hope you have the energy to show them a good time.

Christine.

Why shouldn't I have the energy?

Herman.

You'll be exhausted from floundering like a fish out of water. You're a native New Yorker. Once a native New Yorker, always a native New Yorker.

Christine.
Bev was a native New Yorker. She's not floundering.

Herman.
You're not Bev. Bev can swim anywhere. She's a barracuda.

Christine.
Your son was a native New Yorker Is he floundering?

Herman.
He's not in Florida; he's in California.

Christine.
And is he happy or unhappy?

Herman.
He's happy. He's got everything he ever wanted. A house with a tennis court . . . a Mercedes-Benz convertible . . . two beautiful children . . . two beautiful ex-wives.

Christine.
You omitted his thriving practice.

Herman.
All orthopedic surgeons thrive in California. Between the tennis and the skiing and the surfing and the drunken driving, the whole state is a mass of broken bones. (Christine gets her glass, sips cola, then.)

Christine.
Herman, I have a question for you.

Herman.
If it's can I stay for dinner, the answer is yes.

Christine.
I'm sorry, but the movers are working until eight o'clock, and I'll probably be working till at least ten.

Herman.
Don't over-exert yourself. Every few minutes take a break to look at the majestic New York skyline.

(Pointing toward windows.) You'll never see a sight like that anyplace else on earth.

Christine.

That leads me to my question.

Herman.

And at night, it's a glittering diamond necklace that not even Beverly Siegel could afford.

Christine.

I'll try again. That leads me to my question.

Herman.

As always, you have my undivided attention. (He sits on sofa. Christine sets her glass on coffee table.)

Christine.

Since there's about to be a big change in my life, and since I made it clear I hope it's a change for the better, and since you and I have known each other more than thirty years, and although we don't always see eye to eye, I like to believe you have a certain degree of respect for my ability, for my RIGHT to make my own decisions, and since my decision is to move to Florida . . . and here comes the question . . . Don't you think it might be appropriate for you to SUPPORT my decision, and wish me luck and stop being such a kvetch?

Herman.

I'm glad you asked that, because I have an excellent answer. (He reaches toward his inner jacket pocket, and knocks over the cushion behind which Christine put the three carpet swatches. He picks them up.) What are these?

Christine.

Cocktail napkins.

Herman.

To me, they look like carpet samples. (Reading their identification tags.) They ARE carpet samples. And according to the tag, this one is from a dealer named

Gotham Carpets. And so is this one. And so is this one.

Christine.

Are you trying to make me feel guilty?

Herman.

Guilty? Why? Merely because none of the tags on none of the samples happen to say Herman Lewis Floor Coverings, Incorporated? (Receiving no reply, he rises, and ''supportively'' assures.) Christine, it's a free country. You've got every right to trade with firms who haven't known you practically all of your adult life and who weren't your husband's best friend, so please, under no circumstances, don't feel guilty.

Christine.

I don't.

Herman.

(Brandishing samples.) Then why did you hide them from me?

Christine.

I didn't hide them. I just put them where I hoped you wouldn't find them.

Herman.

Why?

Christine.

To avoid bruising your delicate ego.

Herman.

You didn't. You only amused it, because these are three of the most laughable samples I've ever seen. (He tosses them on coffee table.)

Christine.

Then the laugh is on you, because, for your information, Herman Lewis Floor Coverings carries the exact same lines.

Herman.

Only two of them. The apricot we discontinued.

Christine.

And ha ha ha—the apricot is what Bev chose. (She realizes she blundered, and she pays the price.)

Herman.

Bev? Bev Siegel? You're buying carpet from Gotham Carpets for a condominium that YOU'RE going to live in?

Christine.

It's only for the powder room. She insists I order it from Gotham in tribute to Arnold. His nephew works there.

Herman.

So when you promised you'd buy all your carpeting from me . . .

Christine.

I lied. (Picking up her glass.) I also lied about the Diet Pepsi. I gave you Diet Coke on purpose—and to trick your taste buds, I slipped in arsenic. (She drinks what's left of the cola chug-a-lug.) Farewell, Herman. I no longer deserve to live. (She sets down glass, falls into the armchair, rigidly thrusts out her legs, closes her eyes, plays dead.)

Herman.

Christine.

Christine.

Too late. I'm already up there. (Darting one arm upward.) Hi, Moe. Hi, Miriam. (She lowers arm, sits inert.)

Herman.

Christine. (She doesn't respond. He inquires.) Christine, will you marry me? (Christine opens her eyes, otherwise not moving.)

Christine.

Will I what?

Herman.

Will you marry me? (She sits normally.)

Christine.

Congratulations, Herman. You really know how to wake the dead.

Herman.

I was looking for a way to lead into it a bit more gracefully, but I couldn't find one. So will you marry me?

Christine.

(Incredulously.) Will I marry you? Will I marry you?

Herman.

That's the general drift of the question, yes.

Christine.

Herman, be serious. You're not serious. Are you serious?

Herman.

If I wasn't, would I come here in a blinding snowstorm, and run the risk of not finding a taxi when I leave?

Christine.

Oh my God, you're serious!

Herman.

I think it's the logical move for both of us.

Christine.

Why? (From his inner jacket pocket Herman takes reading glasses and a folded sheet of paper. He puts on glasses, unfolds paper, and refers to what he wrote on it.)

Herman.

Number one:

Christine.

You made a list?

Herman.

That's correct. Four reasons why we should get married.

Christine.

When did you make a list?

Herman.

Last night, after I surrendered to my accountant. But I've been toying with the concept for the past three months.

Christine.

Why didn't you tell me? You had plenty of opportunity. In the past three months we've been constant companions. Once in November and once in January.

Herman.

I was keeping a low profile. Until I was totally positive that my logic has no flaws in it. Which it doesn't. For the following reasons. (Looking at list.) Number one:

Christine.

Herman, don't do this! Please, don't do this. I'm very flattered—but not only would it not be logical for us to get married, it would be insane.

Herman.

At least do me the courtesy of listening with an open mind.

Christine.

But my answer will still be no.

Herman.

Then do me the courtesy of listening with a closed mind. (She sighs in resignation. He looks at list, speaks as if proposing a business deal.) Number one: The economic factor. Two can live cheaper than one. If you live with me, in my apartment, I won't charge you any rent. Plus there'll only be one phone bill, one electric bill, and one gas bill. We'll also save money on things like cereal and toothpaste by buying the large economy family size.

Christine.

Am I allowed to ask questions, or make comments?

Herman.

Certainly.

Christine.

Number one on SOME lists is: "I'm madly in love with you."

Herman.

I cover that aspect of the situation under . . . (Consulting list.) Number three. Also under number four.

Christine.

When Moe proposed to me, love was number one. Wasn't it number one when you proposed to Miriam?

Herman.

I don't remember.

Christine.

I bet it was.

Herman.

You might very well be right. But when I proposed to Miriam I didn't have a nickel to my name, so I placed the economic factor way down at the bottom.

Christine.

(To get on with it.) What's number two?

Herman.

(Consulting list.) Number two: The age factor. That covers the point that neither of us is a spring chicken. I'm sixty-five; you're sixty-three.

Christine.

(Taken aback.) No I'm not.

Herman.

(Surprised.) You're not? How old are you?

Christine.

Sixty-one. Who told you I'm sixty-three?

Herman.

Nobody. But if Miriam was alive that's what she'd be—and I always thought you were the same age.

Christine.

Well, we weren't. I was two years younger.

Herman.

(Not fully convinced.) Be that as it may . . . (Reading from notes.) Anyone who's sixty-three or older—

Christine.

(Interrupting.) Sixty-one.

Herman.

Excuse me. I wrote sixty-three.

Christine.

Erase it.

Herman.

(Revising his "text.") Anyone who's sixty-one or older has no way of knowing how much time the future holds in store. So it's to our mutual benefit to grab each other while the grabbing's good.

Christine.

What's number three?

Herman.

Number three: The period of adjustment factor. You and I have known each other for more than thirty years—so we won't be newlyweds who only know each other on the surface, and after the wedding it takes them months, or years, to learn what really makes the other (After turning to back of page, where the sentence is completed.) person tick. (Beat.) Number four:

Christine.

Not so fast! You said number three discusses love.

Herman.

It does My specific note to myself is: (Reading.) When two people have held warm affection for each other for as long as we have, warm affection can blossom into love. (Looking at her.) But due to your negative attitude I left that out. (She rises, crosses to him.)

Christine.

I DO hold warm affection for you. But there's a large leap from holding affection and . . . and . . .

Herman.

Desiring to share my bed?

Christine.

Yes. To be perfectly honest . . . (She sits on sofa, touches the empty cola glass.) I even felt squeamish about drinking from your glass. (Undaunted, he sits beside her.)

Herman.

Number four: The physical factor. By that I mean that I possess normal biological urges in the area of sex.

Christine.

Herman, if I may be so bold, at your age—define "normal."

Herman.

I want more than I get.

Christine.

That's a very clear definition.

Herman.

I used it before I got married. And after.

Christine.

I know. Miriam told me.

Herman.

She told you what?

Christine.

She said you were always . . . strongly motivated.

Herman.

I was, and I'm proud to say, I am. (Beat.) What else did she say?

Christine.

She said you were an excellent dancer. And you were. I wished Moe could dance like you. I often

said ''Moe, if you could dance like Herman, the
world would be your oyster.''

Herman.

I meant what else did she say about her sex life?

Christine.

(After a pause.) Nothing.

Herman.

I don't believe you. I think you think she can hear
us . . . (Pointing upward.) up there . . . and you don't
want to embarrass her.

Christine.

Embarrass HER? I don't want to embarrass YOU.

Herman.

Try. The odds are all against you, but try.

Christine.

All right, if you insist . . . the only other thing she
said about her sex life was . . . each and every time
that you were in the mood . . . you said: (In macho
tones.) ''Sweetheart, are you ready for a visit from
the big guy?''

Herman.

I can't believe she told you.

Christine.

Are you embarrassed?

Herman.

Slightly.

Christine.

Why only slightly?

Herman.

I never said it in that tone of voice. I always said it
much more romantically.

Christine.

Miriam must've been afraid it might ruin my marriage, because I couldn't make her tell me how big
the big guy really is.

Herman.

Look it up. It's in the *GUINNESS BOOK OF RECORDS*.

Christine.

I guess Moe saw it, in men's rooms all over the world, but when I asked him if there was anything about you that he was jealous of, he said yes, your dancing.

Herman.

Christine, can we kindly not pursue this? At the moment all I'm offering you is my hand. (Consulting list.) I assume that you have normal biological urges too, and that your urges, like mine, currently find themselves all dressed up with no place to go. Therefore . . . this part I memorized. (Taking her hand.) Christine, I think you're a terrific person, and I'd be grateful and honored if you would be my wife. (Releasing her hand.) That concludes my formal sales pitch. (He folds the paper, removes his glasses, pockets both. Christine leans over, kisses his cheek.) Should I take that as a sign of being sold?

Christine.

(Softly, earnestly.) It's a sign that I'm grateful and honored to be—and I hope to stay—your friend.

Herman.

But you won't marry me.

Christine.

I can't. (Herman rises, starts to put on his muffler, overcoat, and hat.)

Herman.

I'll be out of here in less than fifteen seconds.

(Christine rises, crosses to him, reasons.)

Christine.

Herman, how can I marry you? How can you marry me? (He gets his galoshes, starts to put them on, but doesn't fasten them.) It wouldn't work. I'd always think of you as Miriam's husband; you'd always think of me as Moe's wife. (He puts on his gloves.) Isn't that true? Wouldn't both our minds be full of memories of all the years the four of us were together?

Herman.

Goodbye, Christine. Good luck in Florida, and please give my warm regards to Beverly. (He ascends to entry hall. Christine runs past him, blocks his path to door.)

Christine.

I won't let you leave like this.

Herman.

Like what?

Christine.

Hurt, and angry.

Herman.

I'm not either one. The only way I'm leaving is with my few remaining shreds of human dignity. (He tries to move past her, galoshes flapping, but she thwarts him.)

Christine.

Herman, can't you see? You and I can't even agree on how you're leaving an apartment. We could never agree on anything. From the day we met we were always needling each other. Most of the time it was only PLAYFUL needling, but if we were married we wouldn't use needles, we'd use knives, and we'd play for blood.

Herman.

(Archly.) Perhaps. Now, in whatever fashion, may I leave? (She steps aside. Believing he's un-bolting the door, he bolts it, tries to open it, can't. Christine unbolts door, opens it. Herman exits, closing door. Christine walks toward kitchen, as door chimes sound. She comes back, opens door, in comes Herman.)

Christine.

Hi there. Long time no see.

Herman.

I can't let you do this to yourself.

Christine.

Do what?

Herman.

Make a snap decision which you may later regret. You owe it to your future peace-of-mind to mull it over.

Christine.

How long?

Herman.

(Checking his wristwatch.) Three hours. Then I'll pick you up, take you out to dinner, and whatever your non-snap decision is I promise to accept it.

Christine.

Herman, I can't go out on my last night in town.

Herman.

Christine, please. Just a fast bite. One fast bite in honor of more than thirty years of friendship.

Christine.

(After a pause, grimly.) Okay. It's a date. I'd be delighted.

Herman.

Well, I better not overstay my welcome. (He exits, closing door. As Christine starts to bolt it, chimes sound. She opens door, revealing Herman.) I just thought of another item for my list. Number five: The religious factor. (A generous "concession.") If we have children, you can raise them Catholic. (He exits, closing door.)

BLACKOUT

Moon Over Buffalo

Ken Ludwig

❧

This is a broad comedy which opened on Broadway in 1995. It takes place backstage at the Erlanger Theater in Buffalo, New York, in 1953 during the run of a touring company. The two principal characters of this touring company are George and Charlotte Hay, who are in their fifties and apparently have seen better days. In this scene, they have just completed a performance of Cyrano de Bergerac and are in the process of getting out of their costumes.

GEORGE, CHARLOTTE

George.
Ow! God, my neck! Am I getting old, Charlotte?
Charlotte.
No, dear, you're just falling apart.
George.
(Bitterly.) No wonder they didn't want me for the Pimpernel movie.

Charlotte.

Us, dear, they didn't want us.

George.

It would have put us right back on top. George and Charlotte Hay in the new Frank Capra production, "The Twilight of the Scarlet Pimpernel."

Charlotte.

There will be other movies.

George.

We were this close, Charlotte. I could taste it! (Beat.) No wonder Hollywood is such a cesspool. I mean, please. Frank Capra directs "The Twilight of the Scarlet Pimpernel."

Charlotte.

I didn't even get to meet him.

George.

Nor did I. Nor do I care to, may he rot in hell.

Charlotte.

I can see it now. "Mr. Pimpernel Goes to Washington."

George.

Exactly! Ow! My neck. . . . !

Charlotte.

Get down, George. I'll work on it.

(During the following, George sits next to the chaise and Charlotte massages his neck and shoulders.)

George.

You do realize they started filming yesterday. At this very moment, the cameras are rolling and Ronald Colman is wearing MY TIGHTS.

Charlotte.

(Calmly, as the massage continues.) Oh, George, let them have their Ronald Colman and their Greer Garson. Who gives a damn.

George.

You're right.

Charlotte.

I'm sure that Miss Garson will do a perfectly adequate job.

George.

You're right.

Charlotte.

If that's what they want.

George.

I agree entirely.

Charlotte.

. . . Stupid little bitch. (George laughs.) I met her once. Did you know that? She was filming ''Pride and Prejudice'' and I was next door filming ''Apache Woman.'' (With increasing bitterness.) She was cutting the crusts off little tea sandwiches, and I was boiling a pig in a teepee.

George.

Charlotte—

Charlotte.

She was making love to Laurence Olivier, and I was sacrificing a chicken with Chief Chunkachook. (She starts chanting an Indian war chant, beating on his shoulders with the edges of her hands:) Hiya hiya hiya hiya . . .

George.

(Overlapping.) Charlotte . . . Charlotte!

(Charlotte stops.)

Charlotte.

How's your neck?

George.

Better. But don't stop.

(The massage continues. George is relaxing. He's almost asleep.)

Charlotte.

George?

George.

Hm?

Charlotte.

Can I ask you a question?

George.

Mm.

Charlotte.

Did you sleep with Eileen?

George.

(Sitting up with a start.) Charlotte! How can you say such a thing?!

Charlotte.

I've seen how you look at her.

George.

She's a pretty girl. I'm not dead.

Charlotte.

Not yet. I know exactly when it happened, George. We were in the middle of that terrible fight.

George.

And whose fault was that?

Charlotte.

It was your fault, dear. You called me the world's oldest living ingenue.

George.

I merely mentioned that a woman in her fifties should not try to play Saint Joan. It's like watching Eleanor Roosevelt play Peter Pan.

Charlotte.

I happen to admire Eleanor Roosevelt.

George.

So do I, but I don't want to watch her fly out the window.

Charlotte.

You're changing the subject.

George.

For heaven's sake, Eileen barely knows I exist.

Charlotte.

Oh please. When you walk into the room she starts to glow. I could use her for a reading lamp.

George.

You are off your rocker. It's extraordinary. It is unkind.

Charlotte.

George, I don't mind as long as you tell me the truth! Did you sleep with her or didn't you?! Yes or no?!

George.

NO!!! All right?! The answer is no!!

Charlotte.

(Skeptically.) Really?

George.

Oh, it's killing you about the film, isn't it.

Charlotte.

Don't be silly, that has nothing to do with it.

George.

Scarlet Pimpernel, Scarlet Pimpernel.

Charlotte.

Oh, stop it.

George.

GREER GARSON!

Charlotte.

Don't be an idiot!

George.

I'm sure it's slaying you to be stuck out here in Siberia while Miss Garson swans around the set in Hollywood like the Queen of Sheba.

Charlotte.

George—

George.

I'm sure you had fantastical visions of being slobbered over by a legion of toadies, having your ears powdered.

Charlotte.

All right, George. I'm sorry!

George.

(The injured husband.) WELL, IT'S TOO LATE
NOW, ISN'T IT?! You have hurt my feelings!
(George turns away and sits down, rolling his eyes,
thinking that she can't see him.)

Charlotte.

. . . I saw that.

George.

Saw what?

Charlotte.

You big faker.

George.

I don't know what you're talking about.
(Charlotte sits on George's lap and starts to tickle
him.)

Charlotte.

Faker, faker, faker, faker . . .

George.

(Overlapping.) Stop it! Charlotte! I'm warning
you—!

Oh Dad, Poor Dad, Mama's Hung You in the Closet and I'm Feelin' So Sad

Arthur Kopit

❧

This very funny and bizarre play, which first premiered in 1962, is set in the Caribbean in the 1950s. The setting is a lavish hotel suite where Madame Rosepettle, an eccentric, is staying. The scene opens with her waltzing into the room with the Commodore after a night on the town. The Commodore is a very wealthy man with a luxurious yacht anchored in the harbor. He has been looking forward to this rendezvous for some time and apparently has designs on Madame Rosepettle.

MADAME ROSEPETTLE, THE COMMODORE

The Commodore.
   How lovely it was this evening, madame, don't you think? (She laughs softly and demurely and discreetly lowers her eyes. They waltz about the floor.) How gentle the wind was, madame. And the stars,

295

how clear and bright they were, don't you think? (She turns her face away and smiles softly. They begin to whirl about the floor.) Ah, the waltz. How exquisite it is, madame, don't you think? ONE-two-three. ONE-two-three. ONE-two three. Ahhh, madame, how classically simple. How stark; how strong—how romantic—how sublime. (She giggles girlishly. They whirl madly about the floor.) Oh, if only madame knew how I've waited for this moment. If only madame knew how I've waited for this moment. If only madame knew how long. How this week, these nights, the nights we shared together on my yacht; the warm, wonderful nights, the almost-perfect nights, the would-have-been-perfect nights had it not been for the crew peeking through the portholes. Ah, those nights, madame, those nights; almost alone but never quite, but now, tonight, at last, we are alone. And now, madame, now we are ready for romance. For the night was made for love. And tonight, madame—we will love.

Madame Rosepettle.
(With the blush of innocence.) Oh, Commodore, how you do talk.
(They whirl about the room as the lilting rhythm of the waltz grows and sweeps on and on.)

The Commodore.
(Suavely.) Madame, may I kiss you?

Madame Rosepettle.
Why?

The Commodore.
(After recovering from the abruptness of the question. With forced suaveness.) Your lips . . . are a thing of beauty.

Madame Rosepettle.
My lips, Commodore, are the color of blood. (She smiles at him. He stares blankly ahead. They dance

on.) I must say, you dance exceptionally well, Commodore—for a man your age.

The Commodore.

(Bristling.) I dance with YOU, madame. That is why I dance well. For to dance with you, madame—is to hold you.

Madame Rosepettle.

Well, I don't mind your holding me, Commodore, but at the moment you happen to be holding me too tight.

The Commodore.

I hold you too dear to hold you too tight, madame. I hold you close, that is all. And I hold you close in the hope that my heart may feel your heart beating.

Madame Rosepettle.

ONE-two-three, ONE-two-three. You're not paying enough attention to the music, Commodore. I'm afraid you've fallen out of step.

The Commodore.

Then lead me, madame. Take my hand and lead me where you wish. For I would much rather think of my words than my feet.

Madame Rosepettle.

(With great sweetness.) Why certainly, Commodore. Certainly. If that is what you want—it will be my pleasure to oblige. (They switch hands and she begins to lead him about the floor. They whirl wildly about, spinning faster than they had when the Commodore led.) Beautiful, isn't it, Commodore? The waltz. The Dance of Lovers. I'm so glad you enjoy it so much. (With a gay laugh she whirls him around the floor. Suddenly he puts his arms about her shoulders and leans close to kiss her. She pulls back.) Commodore! You were supposed to spin just then. When I squeeze you in the side it means SPIN!

The Commodore.
> (Flustered.) I—I thought it was a sign of affection.
> > (She laughs.)

Madame Rosepettle.
> You'll learn. (She squeezes him in the side. He spins
> about under her arm.) Ah, you're learning.
> (He continues to spin, around and around, faster and
> faster like a runaway top while Madame Rosepettle,
> not spinning at all, leads him about the floor, a wild
> smile of ecstasy spreading over her face.)

The Commodore.
> Ho-ho, ho-ho. Stop I'm dizzy. Dizzy. Stop, please.
> Stop. Ho-ho. Stop. Dizzy. Ho-ho. Stop. Too fast.
> Slow. Slower. Stop. Ho-ho. Dizzy. Too dizzy.
> Weeeeeee! (And then without any warning at all,
> she grabs him in the middle of a spin and kisses
> him. Her back is to the audience, so the Commo-
> dore's face is visible. At first he is too dizzy to re-
> alize that his motion has been stopped. But shortly
> he does, and his first expression is that of shock.
> But the kiss is long and the shock turns into per-
> plexity and then, finally, into panic; into fear. He
> struggles desperately and breaks free from her arms,
> gasping wildly for air. He points weakly to his chest,
> gasping.) Asthma. (His chest heaves as he gulps in
> air.) Couldn't breathe. Asthmatic. Couldn't get any
> air. (He gasps for air. She starts to walk toward him,
> slowly.) Couldn't get any . . . air. (She nears him.
> Instinctively he backs away.) You—you surprised
> me—you know. Out—of breath. Wasn't ready for
> that. Didn't—expect you to kiss me.

Madame Rosepettle.
> I know. That's why I did it. (She laughs and puts
> her arm tenderly about his waist.) Perhaps you'd
> prefer to sit down for a while, Commodore? Catch
> your breath, so to speak. Dancing can be so terribly
> tiring—when you're growing old. Well, if you like,

Commodore, we could just sit and talk. And perhaps—sip some pink champagne, eh? Champagne?

The Commodore.

Ah, champagne.

Madame Rosepettle.

(She begins to walk with him toward the table.) And
just for the two of us.

The Commodore.

Yes. The two of us. Alone.

Madame Rosepettle.

(With a laugh.) Yes. All alone.

The Commodore.

At last.

Madame Rosepettle.

With music in the distance.

The Commodore.

A waltz.

Madame Rosepettle.

A VIENNESE waltz.

The Commodore.

The Dance of Lovers.

Madame Rosepettle.

(She takes his hand, tenderly.) Yes, Commodore.
The Dance of Lovers. (They look at each other in
silence.)

The Commodore.

Madame, you have won my heart. And easily.

Madame Rosepettle.

No, Commodore. You have lost it. Easily. (She
smiles seductively. The room darkens till only a single spot of light falls upon the table set in the middle
of the room. The waltz plays on. Madame Rosepettle nods to the Commodore and he goes to sit. But
before he can pull his chair out, it slides out under
its own power. He places himself and the chair
slides back in, as if some invisible waiter had been
holding it in his invisible hands. Madame Rosepettle

smiles sweetly and pulling out her chair herself, sits.
They stare at each other in silence. The waltz plays
softly. The Commodore reaches across the table and
touches her hand. A thin smile spreads across her
lips. When finally they speak, their words are soft,
the whispered thoughts of lovers.) Champagne?

The Commodore.
Champagne.

Madame Rosepettle.
Pour?

The Commodore.
Please.
(She lifts the bottle out of the ice bucket and pours
with her right hand, her left being clasped firmly in
the Commodore's passionate hands. They smile se-
renely at each other. She lifts her glass. He lifts his.
The music swells.)

Madame Rosepettle.
A toast?

The Commodore.
To you.

Madame Rosepettle.·
No, Commodore, to you.

The Commodore.
No, madame. To us.

Madame Rosepettle and the Commodore.
(Together.) To us. (They raise their glasses. They
gaze wistfully into each other's eyes. The music
builds to brilliance. The Commodore clicks his glass
against Madame Rosepettle's glass. The glasses
break.)

The Commodore.
(Furiously mopping up the mess.) Pardon, madame!
Pardon!

Madame Rosepettle.
(Flicking some glass off her bodice.) *Pas de quoi,
monsieur.*

The Commodore.

J'etais emport par l'enthousiasme du moment.

Madame Rosepettle.

(Extracting pieces of glass from her lap, Madame Rosepettle lifts the bottle of champagne out of the ice bucket.) *Encore?*

The Commodore.

S'il vous plait. (She pours. They lift their glasses in toast. The music swells again.) To us.

Madame Rosepettle.

To us, Monsieur—Commodore. (They clink their glasses lightly. The Commodore closes his eyes and sips. Madame Rosepettle holds her glass before her lips, poised but not touching, waiting. She watches him. Softly.) Tell me about yourself.

The Commodore.

My heart is speaking, madame. Doesn't it tell you enough?

Madame Rosepettle.

Your heart, monsieur, is growing old. It speaks with a murmur. Its words are too weak to understand.

The Commodore.

But the feeling, madame, is still strong.

Madame Rosepettle.

Feelings are for animals, monsieur. Words are the specialty of Man. Tell me what your heart has to say.

The Commodore.

My heart says it loves you.

Madame Rosepettle.

And how many others, monsieur, has your heart said this to?

The Commodore.

None but you, madame. None but you.

Madame Rosepettle.

And pray, monsieur, just what is it that I've done to make you love me so?

The Commodore.

Nothing, madame. And that is why. You are a strange woman, you see. You go out with me and you know how I feel. Yet, I know nothing of you. You disregard me, madame, but never discourage. You treat my love with indifference—but never disdain. You've led me on, madame. That is what I mean to say.

Madame Rosepettle.

I've led you to my room, monsieur. That is all.

The Commodore.

To me, that is enough.

Madame Rosepettle.

I know. That's why I did it.

(The music swells. She smiles distantly. There is a momentary silence.)

The Commodore.

(With desperation.) Madame, I must ask you something. Why are you here? (Short pause.)

Madame Rosepettle.

Well, I have to be somewhere, don't I?

The Commodore.

But why here, where I am? Why in Port Royale?

Madame Rosepettle.

You flatter yourself, Monsieur. I am in Port Royale only because Port Royale was in my way . . . I think I'll move on tomorrow.

The Commodore.

For—home?

Madame Rosepettle.

(Laughing slightly.) Only the very young and the very old have homes. I am neither. So I have none.

The Commodore.

But—surely you must come from somewhere.

Madame Rosepettle.

Nowhere you've ever been.

The Commodore.

I've been many places.

Madame Rosepettle.

(Softly.) But not many enough. (She picks up her glass of champagne and sips, a distant smile on her lips.)

The Commodore.

(With sudden, overwhelming and soul-rending passion.) Madame, don't go tomorrow. Stay. My heart is yours.

Madame Rosepettle.

How much is it worth?

The Commodore.

A fortune, madame.

Madame Rosepettle.

Good. I'll take it in cash.

The Commodore.

But the heart goes with it, madame.

Madame Rosepettle.

And you with the heart, I suppose?

The Commodore.

Forever.

Madame Rosepettle.

Sorry, monsieur. The money's enticing and the heart would have been nice, but you, I'm afraid, are a bit too bulky to make it all worth while.

The Commodore.

You jest, madame.

Madame Rosepettle.

I never jest, monsieur. There isn't enough time.

The Commodore.

Then you make fun of my passion, madame, which is just as bad.

Madame Rosepettle.

But, monsieur, I've never taken your passion seriously enough to make fun of it.

The Commodore.

(There is a short pause. The Commodore sinks
slowly back in his seat. Weakly, sadly.) Then why
have you gone out with me?

Madame Rosepettle.

So that I might drink champagne with you tonight.

The Commodore.

That makes no sense.

Madame Rosepettle.

It makes PERFECT sense.

The Commodore.

Not to me.

Madame Rosepettle.

It does to me.

The Commodore.

But I don't understand. And I WANT to understand.

Madame Rosepettle.

Don't worry, Commodore. You will.

The Commodore.

When?

Madame Rosepettle.

Soon.

The Commodore.

How soon?

Madame Rosepettle.

Very soon. (He stares at her in submissive confusion. Suddenly, with final desperation, he grabs her
hands in his and, leaning across the table, kisses
them passionately, sobbingly. In a scarcely audible
whisper.) NOW.

The Commodore.

Madame—I love you. Forever. Don't you understand? (He kisses her hands again. A smile of
triumph spreads across his face.) Oh, your husband—He must have been—a wonderful man—to

have deserved a woman such as you. (He sobs and kisses her hands again.)

Madame Rosepettle.

(Nonchalantly.) Would you like to see him?

The Commodore.

A snapshot?

Madame Rosepettle.

No. My husband. He's inside in the closet. I had him stuffed. Wonderful taxidermist I know. H'm? What do you say, Commodore? Wanna peek? He's my favorite trophy. I take him with me wherever I go.

The Commodore.

(Shaken. Not knowing what to make of it.) Hah-hah, hah-hah. Yes. Very good. Very funny. Sort of a—WHITE ELEPHANT, you might say.

Madame Rosepettle.

YOU might say.

The Commodore.

Well, it's certainly very—courageous of you, a—a woman still in mourning, to—to be able to laugh at what most other women wouldn't find—well, shall we say—funny.

Madame Rosepettle.

Life, my dear Commodore, is never funny. It's grim. It's there every morning breathing in your face the moment you open your red baggy eyes. Life, Commodore, is a husband hanging from a hook in the closet. Open the door too quickly and your whole day's shot to hell. But open the door just a little way, sneak your hand in, pull out your dress and your day is made. Yet he's still there, and waiting—and sooner or later the moth balls are gone and you have to clean house. Oh, it's a bad day, Commodore, when you have to stare Life in the face, and

you find he doesn't smile at all; just hangs there—
with his tongue sticking out.

The Commodore.

I—don't find this—very funny.

Madame Rosepettle.

Sorry. I was hoping it would give you a laugh.

The Commodore.

I don't think it's funny at all. And the reason that I
don't think it's funny at all is that it's not my kind
of joke. One must respect the dead.

Madame Rosepettle.

Then tell me, Commodore—why not the living,
too? (Pause. She lifts out the bottle of champagne
and pours herself some more.)

The Commodore.

(Weakly, with a trace of fear.) How—how did he
die?

Madame Rosepettle.

Why, I killed him, of course. Champagne? (She
smiles sweetly and fills his glass. She raises hers in
toast.) To your continued good health. (He stares at
her blankly. The music swells in the background.)
Ah, the waltz, monsieur. Listen. The waltz. The
Dance of Lovers. Beautiful—DON'T YOU
THINK?

(She laughs and sips some more champagne. The
music grows to brilliance. The Commodore starts to
rise from his chair.)

The Commodore.

Forgive me, madame. But—I find I must leave. Urgent business calls. Good evening. (He tries to push
his chair back, but for some reason it will not move.
He looks about in panic. He pushes frantically. It
does not move. It is as if the invisible waiter who
had come and slid the chair out when he went to sit

down, now stood behind the chair and held it in so
he could not get up. And as there are arms on the
chair, the Commodore cannot slide out at the sides.
Madame Rosepettle smiles.)

On Golden Pond

Ernest Thompson

*This play, which opened on Broadway in 1979, is set in the
living room of Norman and Ethel Thayer's summer house on
Golden Pond, Maine. It is an old house, but comfortable, and
the place where the Thayers have spent many summers. It is
the middle of September and they are getting ready to close
up the house for the winter. The scene opens on an empty cluttered room with a humorous description of stage business. Ethel
enters carrying a box. She sets it down on a table and goes back
into the kitchen. Norman comes in, sees the box and picks it
up. He holds it, looking about the room, wanders up to the
platform, and sets the box down. He examines his fishing gear
quickly, and then walks up the stairs. Ethel comes back into the
room with another box. She begins to set it down, realizes the
first is gone, looks for it. She sees it on the platform and stares
at it, puzzled. She sets down the second box and then goes up
the steps for the first, which she carries back down, and then
exits. Norman comes down the stairs, carrying a fishing pole.
He leans it against the couch. He picks up the box Ethel left*

and begins to carry it to door, thinks of something, crosses back to the platform, and sets it down. He goes to the hat rack and studies the collection. Ethel comes in, looks for the box, sees it on the platform.

The references are to Chelsea, their daughter; Bill, her new husband; and Billy, their grandson who has recently spent some time with them at Golden Pond.

ETHEL, NORMAN

Ethel.

Norman, what in the world are you doing with the boxes?

Norman.

Nothing. Which one of these hats is your favorite?

Ethel.

You moved this box and you moved the other box, too. Are we moving out or in?

Norman.

Oh. This box. I'm carrying this box to the car. I'm helping you.

Ethel.

You certainly have a roundabout way of doing it. The car is in the back, you know.

Norman.

I know. Which hat is your favorite?

Ethel.

I dislike them all equally. (She carries the box D.)

Norman.

I was going to take that box.

Ethel.

Yes. It's where you were going to take it that had me concerned, so I'm taking it myself. (Stopping by the fireplace.) What is your old fish pole doing here?

Norman.

I fixed it. I fixed the reel, and I retied the splints.

Ethel.

What's it doing here?

Norman.

It's waiting to go to the car. I'm going to mail it to Billy.

Ethel.

What? You can't mail a fish pole.

Norman.

Of course I can. I'm a taxpayer. He may want to go fishing. I assume they have fish in California.

Ethel.

Well. (She looks up. Norman is now wearing one of the floppy hats.) What are you doing with that terrible hat?

Norman.

(Crossing down.) I'm mailing it to Billy with the fish pole. You can't fish without a hat.

Ethel.

He tries fishing with that thing on his head anywhere outside of Golden Pond, he'll probably be arrested.

Norman.

Not in California he won't.

Ethel.

Well, bring it then. There's barely room. (Norman opens the door. Ethel steps out, but he lingers. He wanders across to the bookshelves and studies them. He pulls down a book. The phone rings. Norman looks up, startled. Ethel comes back in.) Did you get lost?

Norman.

No, I'm over here. (The phone rings again.) The phone's ringing.

Ethel.

Well, what do you know? I suppose we'd better answer it.

Norman.

Yes. (She steps to the phone and picks it up.)

Ethel.

Hello?. . . . Hello? . . . Oh, hello. . . . I'm fine, thank you. How are you?. . . . Good . . . We're leaving right now . . . thank you . . .

Norman.

Who is it?

Ethel.

(Covering the receiver.) I have no idea. (Into the phone.) Who is this? . . . Oh, Bill! How are you? . . . Good. (To Norman.) It's Bill.

Norman.

Bill? Oh, Bill!

Ethel.

Thank you, Bill . . . Well, we'd love to. . . . Yes . . . Of course, put her on. I know this is costing a fortune.

Norman.

I'm surprised he didn't reverse the charges. Chelsea's first husband always used to. (He sits in his covered chair and begins to read.)

Ethel.

Hi, darling. . . . Yes. We're just leaving. Two more boxes and say goodbye to the lake, and that will be that . . . Oh, no. Everyone else is gone practically. . . . Your house sounds wonderful. Send us some pictures. We would love to, dear. Maybe in January. . . . Instead of Florida, yes. We'll discuss it . . . If I can get Norman to accept the fact that Los Angeles is part of the United States, it shouldn't be too much trouble. He's still convinced you need a passport to get out there, and yellow-fever shots and everything . . . Well, bless you. . . . Of course, I'll get him. Norman, she wants to talk to you.

Norman.

(Looking up from his book.) Tsk. I've just started my book.

Ethel.

Norman, she wants to talk to you.

Norman.

Why would she want to talk to me?

Ethel.

Get it in gear, Norman. (He stands. Ethel speaks into the phone.) He's coming, dear. Give my love to Billy. We hope to see you soon. Yes. Bye. (Norman flings his book onto the couch and Ethel hands him the phone.)

Norman.

What will I say to her?

Ethel.

You'll think of something.

Norman.

(Into the phone.) Hello . . . Um. How's the weather? . . . . Oh. No earthquakes? (Ethel shakes her head. She picks up the fishing pole, and takes the hat off Norman's head. She carries them both outside.) . . . Good . . . Oh, I don't know if we'll be able to come way out there. Ethel's health isn't what it could be, you know. . . . No, nothing serious. She's just more ornery than usual. . . . Oh, no, I'm in great form myself. Just a lot of pain. Nothing to worry about . . . Well, we'll certainly consider it . . . Oh, thank you. . . . Oh, well. I love you, too. (He's embarrassed.) Yes. (Brightly.) Billy there? . . . Good. Could I speak to him? . . . Yes, we will. You have fun, too—the three of you . . . Okay, Chelsea. Bye! (He stares off while waiting for Billy.) . . . Hello, cool breeze. How's the chicks? . . . No, the fish are all gone, somewhere . . . I don't know. They go to sleep, I believe. . . . No, I don't think it would be right for me to wake them . . . How's your reading? . . . Don't tell me! How wonderful . . . Yes, I know, but it's pronounced Doo-ma . . . Say that. Doo-ma

... *Tres bien* ... That's okay, run along. I expect you'll want to do a little cruising on your way to school. I'll tell her ... Yes, Billy ... Well, I miss you, too ... Listen, Ethel and I are coming out to visit, you know ... Oh, yes. In the winter ... I'm NOT bullshitting you ... Yes. Me, too. Bye! Adieu, mon vieux. (He hangs up, feeling quite chipper. Ethel enters.) I talked to Billy.

Ethel.

How nice.

Norman.

He said he wants you to mail him some tollhouse cookies.

Ethel.

Oh, he does, does he?

Norman.

Yes. Says Chelsea makes them but they're not as good.

Ethel.

Huh. Well, that's the way it is with us grandmothers, you know. Chelsea mention us going out there for a visit?

Norman.

I think she did.

Ethel.

I guess we could, don't you think?

Norman.

Well. . . . I guess so.

Ethel.

I think they're going to make a go of it.

Norman.

What do you mean?

Ethel.

The marriage. I think it's a success.

Norman.

It's lasted over a month already.

Ethel.

It makes me feel so good to think that Chelsea is finally settling down.

Norman.

Yes. Want to play a quick game of Parcheesi before we go? Loser drives.

Ethel.

No. Haven't you been humiliated enough? You owe me four million dollars.

Norman.

Double or nothing?

Ethel.

When we get home, Norman. We've got the whole winter ahead of us.

Norman.

Yes.

Ethel.

Come on, let's get the other boxes, and be gone. (She heads into the kitchen. Norman stays where he is, looking about. Ethel calls from offstage.) Norman! Would you come here? (He crosses to the kitchen door.)

Norman.

What is it? (He exits.)

Ethel.

(Offstage.) Get the last box if it's not too heavy. (She enters.)

Norman.

Of course it's not too heavy. Good God, this is heavy!

Ethel.

Tsk. Well, wait and I'll help you with it then.

Norman.

(Offstage.) You're trying to kill me.

Ethel.

I've thought about it. (She carries her box D. as he comes out with his.)

Norman.

Good God! (He crosses to the platform. She waits for him at the door. He moves slowly.) Whatever have you got in here?

Ethel.

My mother's china. I've decided to take it to Wilmington and use it there. (Norman is feeling his way down the steps.) We hardly ever eat off it here. Are you all right?

Norman.

Yes. Your mother never liked me.

Ethel.

Oh, stop. She loved you.

Norman.

Then why did she have such heavy china? Oh, my God.

Ethel.

Set it down if it's too much trouble. Norman! (He is in pain. He leans against the couch, still holding the box.) Norman! Put the box down!

Norman.

(He groans.) Unh. I don't want to break your mother's china. Ouch.

Ethel.

Norman! (She drops her box with a tremendous crash. She runs to Norman. He drops his box.)

Norman.

Whoops. (He sags against the couch, clutching his chest. She tries to hold him.)

Ethel.

Sit down, you fool. (She helps him to couch. He slumps.) Where's your medicine?

Norman.

I don't know. You packed.

Ethel.

Oh, God! What did I do with it? I'm afraid it's in the car. (She runs to the door and exits, her speech continuing outside.) Which suitcase? WHICH SUITCASE? (Norman grimaces, clutches his chest. He glances around the room, spots the book on the couch beside him. He reaches for it, opens it, grimaces again. Ethel runs back in with a little jar.) What are you doing, you nitwit? Give me that book! (She grabs it and throws it onto the floor.)

Norman.

What are you doing?

Ethel.

I'm trying to save your life, damn you. Whoever designed these caps is a madman. There, take this and put it under your tongue. (She holds out a pill.)

Norman.

What is it?

Ethel.

Nitroglycerin. Put it under your tongue.

Norman.

You must be mad. I'll blow up.

Ethel.

Do it! (Norman takes the pill. She kneels beside him, watching. He breathes deeply and leans his head back, his eyes closed. Ethel begins to weep.) Oh, dear God, don't take him now. You don't want him, he's a poop. Norman? Norman!

Norman.

(His eyes closed.) Maybe you should call a doctor. We can afford it.

Ethel.

Oh, yes! (She jumps up.) Of course. I should have done that. Dear God. (She rushes to the phone and dials "O".) Hello, hello. Dear God. How are you feeling, Norman?

Norman.

Oh, pretty good. How are you?

Ethel.

Norman, how's the angina?

Norman.

The what?

Ethel.

The pain, dammit!

Norman.

Oh, it's pretty good, as pain goes.

Ethel.

Is the medicine doing anything?

Norman.

No.

Ethel.

Why don't they answer the phone?

Norman.

Who'd you call?

Ethel.

The stupid operator. (Into the receiver.)   Hello??
. . . Hello? (Getting   frantic.)   Hello,hello,hello,
hello,hello,hello! Whatever is the matter with her?

Norman.

She's slow.

Ethel.

How do you feel now?

Norman.

I don't know.

Ethel.

Are you planning to die? Is that what you're up to?
Well, while I'm waiting for this moron to answer
the phone, let me just say something to you, Norman Thayer, Junior. I would rather you didn't.

Norman.

Really?

Ethel.

Yes! This stupid, stupid woman. I'm going to have
to call a hospital directly. (She slams down the

phone and pulls out the phone book.) Where do you look for hospitals? Yellow pages. Hospital, hospital. They're not listed. Oh, wait.. . . .

Norman.

Ethel.

Ethel.

(Fearing the worst.) Yes! What is it!?

Norman.

Come here.

Ethel.

Oh, God. (She rushes over and kneels by his side.) Yes, Norman. My darling.

Norman.

Ethel.

Ethel.

(Crying.) Yes, I'm here. Oh, Norman.

Norman.

Ethel.

Ethel.

Yes, yes, yes.

Norman.

Ethel.

Ethel.

What is it?

Norman.

Ethel, I think I feel all right now.

Ethel.

Are you serious?

Norman.

I think so. My heart's stopped hurting. Maybe I'm dead.

Ethel.

It really doesn't hurt?

Norman.

Really doesn't. Shall I dance to prove it?

Ethel.

(Falling against him.) Oh, Norman. Oh, thank God.
I love you so much. (A moment passes. She cries.
Norman puts his arm around her.)

Norman.

Now my heart's starting to hurt again. (He holds her
close.) Sorry about your mother's china. (He pulls
himself forward to look at it.)

Ethel.

You're such a poop. Sit still and don't move.

Norman.

Are you mad at me?

Ethel.

Yes. Why did you strain yourself? You know better.

Norman.

I was showing off. Trying to turn you on.

Ethel.

Well, you succeeded. There's no need for you to try
that sort of thing again.

Norman.

Good. (For a long moment they sit without moving.
She stares at him as though she's trying to memorize
him. He smiles down at her. The moment passes
and she glances away.)

Ethel.

This is my favorite time of year on Golden Pond.
No bugs.

Norman.

Nope.

Ethel.

Except for that spider up there.

Norman.

(Looking up.) Good God. He's a biggie.

Ethel.

Yes. Well, I'd like to do him in, but I'm afraid I
don't have the energy.

Norman.

Get him the first thing next year.

Ethel.

Right. (Pause.) Norman. (A pause.) This was the first time I've really felt we're going to die.

Norman.

I've known it all along.

Ethel.

Yes, I know. But when I looked at you across the room, I could really see you dead. I could see you in your blue suit and a white starched shirt, lying in Thomas's Funeral Parlor on Bradshaw Street, your hands folded on your stomach, a little smile on your face.

Norman.

How did I look?

Ethel.

Not good, Norman.

Norman.

Which tie was I wearing?

Ethel.

I don't know.

Norman.

How about the one with the picture of the man fishing? Did you pack that one?

Ethel.

Shut up, Norman. (Pause.) You've been talking about dying ever since I met you. It's been your favorite topic of conversation. And I've HAD to think about it. Our parents, my sister and brother, your brother, their wives, our dearest friends, practically everyone from the old days on Golden Pond, all dead. I've seen death, and touched death, and feared it. But today was the first time I've felt it.

Norman.

How's it feel?

Ethel.

It feels . . . odd. Cold, I guess. But not that bad, re-ally. Almost comforting, not so frightening, not such a bad place to go. I don't know.

Norman.

(He holds her head for a moment.) Want to see if you can find my book?

Ethel.

Here it is. (She picks it up from the floor.) Going to take it?

Norman.

Nope. It belongs here. Put it on the shelf. (She crosses and returns the book to its place.) I'll read it next year.

Ethel.

Yes. Next year. (She wanders around behind the couch.) We'll have the whole summer to read and pick berries and play Monopoly, and Billy can come for as long as he likes, and you two can fish and I'll make cookies, and life will go on, won't it?

Norman.

I hope so.

Ethel.

I guess I'll go down and say goodbye to the lake. Feel like coming?

Norman.

Yes. (He rises slowly.)

Ethel.

You sure you're strong enough?

Norman.

I think so. If I fall over face first in the water you'll know I wasn't.

Ethel.

(Waiting for him.) Well, go easy, for God's sake. I'm only good for one near miss a day.

Norman.

(Getting to her slowly.) Hello there.

Ethel.

Hi.

Norman.

(Taking her in his arms.) Want to dance? Or would you rather just suck face?

Ethel.

You really are a case, you know. (Call of a loon.)

Norman.

Yes.

Ethel.

My word, Norman, the loons. They've come round to say goodbye.

Norman.

How nice.

Ethel.

Just the two of them now. Little baby's grown up and moved to Los Angeles or somewhere.

Norman.

Yes. (They kiss. A long gentle moment passes. They look at one another, and then look away.)

Ethel.

Well, let's go down. (They exit. He follows her across the porch and down the steps.) Hello Golden Pond. We've come to say goodbye.

Picnic

William Inge

❧

This play opened on Broadway in 1952. The action of the play takes place on the porches and in the yards of two modest houses in a small Kansas town in the 1950s. It is Labor Day and a big town picnic is being planned. It is also the last day of summer vacation and Rosemary Sydney, who rents a room in one of the houses and jokingly calls herself an old maid schoolteacher, will go back to work tomorrow. Though she is often raucous, she is desperately lonely. In the following scene she is returning from an evening spent with her boyfriend, Howard, a businessman. Rosemary enters first. "Wearily, a groggy depression having set in, she makes her way to the doorstep and drops there, sitting on porch corner. Howard enters quickly as she sits. He crosses down to down center lawn. She seems preoccupied at first and her responses to Howard are mere grunts."

ROSEMARY, HOWARD

Howard.
Here we are, Honey. Right back where we started from.

Rosemary.

(Her mind elsewhere.) Uhh.

Howard.

(Sits at her left on porch edge.) You were awful nice to me tonight, Rosemary.

Rosemary.

Uhh.

Howard.

Do you think Mrs. Owens suspects anything?

Rosemary.

I don't care if she does.

Howard.

(Rises, crosses l. to c.) A business man's gotta be careful of talk. And after all, you're a schoolteacher. (Fumbling to get away.) Well, I guess I better be gettin' back to Cherryvale. I gotta open up the store in the morning. (Crosses to her.) Good night, Rosemary. Good night. (He kisses her cheek.) Maybe I should say, good morning. (He starts off—crosses to up center lawn.)

Rosemary.

(Just coming to.) Where you goin', Howard?

Howard.

(Crosses down a bit.) Honey, I gotta get home.

Rosemary.

You can't go off and leave me.

Howard.

(Crosses down to down center lawn.) Honey, talk sense.

Rosemary.

You can't go off without me. Not after tonight. THAT'S sense.

Howard.

(A little nervous.) Honey, be reasonable.

Rosemary.

Take me with you.

Howard.

What'd people say?

Rosemary.

(Almost vicious.) To HELL with what people'd say!

Howard.

(Shocked—looks around to see if this is overheard.)
Honey!

Rosemary.

What'd people say if I thumbed my nose at them?
What'd people say if I walked down the street and
showed 'em my pink panties? What do I care what
people say?

Howard.

(Crosses down to right of stump.) Honey, you're not
yourself tonight.

Rosemary.

Yes I am. I'm more myself than I ever was. Take
me with you, Howard. If you don't, I don't know
what I'll do with myself. I mean it.

Howard.

(Crosses to her, leans over her.) Now look, Honey,
you better go upstairs and get some sleep. You gotta
start school in the morning. We'll talk all this over
Saturday.

Rosemary.

(Grabs his arms.) Maybe you won't be back Saturday. Maybe you won't be back ever again.

Howard.

(Pulling away a step.) Rosemary, you know better
than that.

Rosemary.

(Front.) Then what's the next thing in store for me?
To be nice to the next man, then the next . . . till
there's no one left to care whether I'm nice to him
or not. Till I'm ready for the grave and don't have
anyone to take me there.

Howard.

(Crosses l. to c. ridge) Now, Rosemary!

Rosemary.

(Looking him in the eyes.) You can't let that happen to me, Howard.

Howard.

I don't understand. When we first started going together, you were the best sport I ever saw, always good for a laugh.

Rosemary.

I can't laugh any more.

Howard.

(Starts u.s.) We'll talk it over Saturday.

Rosemary.

We'll talk it over NOW.

Howard.

(Stops, crosses down, sits on stump. Squirming.) Well . . . Honey. . . . I . . .

Rosemary.

(Looking at him.) You said you were gonna marry me, Howard. You said when I got back from my vacation, you'd be waitin' with the preacher.

Howard.

Honey, I've had an awful busy summer and . . .

Rosemary.

Where's the preacher, Howard? Where is he?

Howard.

Rosemary, I'm 42 years old. A person forms certain ways of livin', then one day it's too late to change.

Rosemary.

(Rises, crosses to c.) I'm no spring chicken either. Maybe I'm a little older than you think I am. I've formed my ways, too. But they can be changed. (Turns, crosses right to steps.) They GOTTA be changed. It's no good livin' like this, in rented rooms, meetin' a bunch of old maids for supper every night, then comin' back home alone.

Howard.

(Rises, crosses to c.) I know how it is, Rosemary. My life's no bed of roses either.

Rosemary.

(Turning to him.) Then why don't you do something about it?

Howard.

I figure . . . there's some bad things about every life.

Rosemary.

There's too much bad about mine. Each year, I keep tellin' myself, is the last. Something'll happen. Then nothing ever does . . . except I get a little crazier all the time.

Howard.

(Hopelessly.) Well. . . .

Rosemary.

A well's a hole in the ground, Howard.

Howard.

I wasn't tryin' to be funny, Rosemary.

Rosemary.

All this time you just been leadin' me on.

Howard.

(Vehement.) Rosemary, that's not so! I've not been trying to lead you on.

Rosemary.

I'd like to know what else you call it.

Howard.

Well. . . . can't we talk about it Saturday? I'm dead tired and I got a busy week ahead, and. . . .

Rosemary.

(Runs to him, embraces him desperately.) You gotta marry me, Howard.

Howard.

(Tortured.) Well. . . . I can't marry you NOW.

Rosemary.

(Looking at him.) You can be over here in the morning.

Howard.

Sometimes you're unreasonable.

Rosemary.

You gotta marry me.

Howard.

What'll you do about your job?

Rosemary.

(Encouraged.) Alvah Jackson can take my place till they get someone new from the agency.

Howard.

I'll have to pay Fred Jenkins to take care of the store for a few days.

Rosemary.

Then get him.

Howard.

(Turns away down left) Well . . .

Rosemary.

I'll be waitin' for you in the morning, Howard.

Howard.

(After a moment's troubled thought crosses to downstage of steps.) No, I'm not gonna marry anyone that says, "You gotta marry me, Howard." I'm not gonna. (He is silent. Rosemary stares at him. Slowly Howard reconsiders.) If a woman wants me to marry her . . . she could at least say "please."

Rosemary.

(Beaten and humble.) PLEASE marry me, Howard.

Howard.

Well . . . you got to give me time to think it over.

Rosemary.

Oh, God! Please marry me, Howard. Please. . . . (She sinks to her knees.) Please . . . please . . .

Howard.

(Turns.) Rosemary, don't! (He goes to her, lifts her up.) Honey, you go get some sleep. I'll call you in the morning.

Rosemary.

I won't sleep a wink, Howard, till I hear. (He lifts her gently to her feet. She crosses to steps at right. stops on top step.) Good night, Howard.

Howard.

I'll call you first thing. (Crosses to her—squeezes her hand.)

Rosemary.

Good night.

Howard.

'Night, Rosemary. (Crosses up center lawn.)

Rosemary.

(Holding in her tears.) Please call.

Howard.

(Turning back a step.) I'll call. (He starts again.)

Rosemary.

Please call.

Howard.

(Stops.) I will, Rosemary. I will. (Starts.)

Rosemary.

Please call.

Howard.

(Stops.) Honey, don't worry.

Rosemary.

Good night.

Howard.

Good night. (He is gone out alley r.) As we hear Howard's car drive off, Rosemary silently looks up at the sky. Then she turns and goes silently into the house.)

The Potting Shed

Graham Greene

This play, one of the few written by the well-known novelist Graham Greene, takes place in the sitting room of Father Callifer's presbytery in an East Anglian town in England. The play centers around a family and its secret. A well-known scholar has just died and is having his biography written. The scholar's brother is a priest who apparently knows more about his brother than he has revealed. In the following scene, Father Callifer, the brother, is talking to his housekeeper, who has just announced that a visitor is waiting in the hall.

FATHER CALLIFER, MISS CONNOLLY

Miss Connolly.
They'd have written to the Bishop long before this if I'd let them. (A pause.) Don't think they haven't learnt what happened in your last parish and the one before that. If I hadn't begged them time and again to give you a chance, if only for my sake—
Callifer.
(Not turning.) Your sake?

Miss Connolly.

I've been the priest's housekeeper here for twenty years and never had a breath of scandal before. But unless you give me your solemn honest-to-God promise you'll keep off the liquor I'll not be preventing them any longer writing to the Bishop.

Callifer.

Let them write.

Miss Connolly.

If they do it will be the end of you. You won't find another bishop to take you.

Callifer.

(Swinging suddenly around.) Do you think I'd mind that? Let them take away my faculties. Don't threaten a convict with the loss of his chains.

Miss Connolly.

Speak lower if you don't want to advertise your shame to a stranger.

Callifer.

Go and fetch the man, whoever he is.

Miss Connolly.

I'm going to have my say first. Here they want a priest with the faith in him. Don't turn away and pretend you don't understand.

Callifer.

Fetch him in, I say.

Miss Connolly.

You and I have got to have this out once and for all. (With a slight softening.) It's for your sake I'm speaking.

Callifer.

I say the Mass every Sunday at eight-thirty and on week-days at seven for those who care to come. There aren't many of them. What else do you want of me?

Miss Connolly.

Oh, you stand at the altar all right, gabbling your

way through as quickly as possible to get at your breakfast. But you don't believe a word you are saying.

Callifer.

How do you know?

Miss Connolly.

You should have heard poor Father Murphy and the beautiful voice he had. He wouldn't have read other men's sermons because he had no thoughts of his own.

Callifer.

I can tell he never preached to you on charity.

Miss Connolly.

I found your new hiding place this morning. (Callifer turns his back on her and moves away. More gently.) Father, what kind of a priest are you?

Callifer.

A priest who does his job. I say the Mass, I hear confessions, if anyone has a stomach ache in the night, don't I go to him? Who has ever asked for me and I haven't come?

Miss Connolly.

Miss Alexander.

Callifer.

(Slowly, with shame.) Yes, you would remind me of that.

Miss Connolly.

I couldn't wake you. I had to say next day you were sick. Sick!

Callifer.

Miss Connolly, you've looked after a lot of priests. You take it as your right to speak your mind to them. And me—you expect me to serve you, all of you, every day for twenty-four hours. I mustn't be a man. I must be a priest. And in return, after Mass you give me coffee and eggs (in all these years you've never learnt how to make coffee) and you make my bed. You keep my two rooms clean—or nearly. (He runs his finger along the mantelpiece.) I don't ask you for any more than you are paid to do.

Miss Connolly.

The people here have a right to a priest with the faith.

Callifer.

Faith. They want a play-actor. They want snow-white hair, high collars, clean vestments (who pays the cleaner?—not their sixpence) and they want a voice that's never husky with the boredom of saying the same words day after day. All right. Let them write to the Bishop. Do you think I want to get up every morning at six in time to make my meditation before Mass? Meditation on what? The reason why I'm going on with this slave-labour? They give prisoners useless tasks, don't they, digging pits and filling them up again? Like mine.

Miss Connolly.

Speak low. You don't understand what you are saying, Father.

Callifer.

Father! I hate the word. I had a brother who believed in nothing, and for thirty years now I have believed in nothing too. I used to pray, I used to love what you call God, and then my eyes were opened—to nothing. A father belongs to his children until they grow up and he's free of them. But these people will never grow up. They die children and leave children behind them. I'm condemned to being a father for life.

Miss Connolly.

I've never heard such words before out of a priest's mouth.

(A pause.)

Callifer.
You wouldn't have heard them now if the bottle you found hadn't been empty.

Miss Connolly.
They say your breath smells in the confessional.

Callifer.
And so do theirs. Of worse things. I'd rather smell of whisky than bad teeth.

Miss Connolly.
You're full of it now.

Callifer.
Oh no, I'm empty. Quite empty.

Remembrance

Graham Reid

This play was commissioned and produced by the Lyric Theatre in Belfast, Ireland, in 1984 and was performed in New York City in 1990. It takes place in Ireland in the 1980s, a time when the country had seen a great deal of violence caused by the opposing political views and antagonized by religious differences. A man and a woman, both in their sixties, have met at a cemetery where each has buried a son who died violently while fighting for opposing sides. Bert is Protestant and Theresa is Catholic. In their loneliness and grief, they find friendship and are able to share with each other their problems with their re-

maining children. The following scene takes place on a bench in the cemetery. There is a handbag and a box of pastries on the bench. Theresa is pacing up and down. She sits. Pause. She looks around and smiles at someone approaching. Bert arrives a little breathless. There is a reference to Victor who is Bert's very angry son. Deidre and Joan are Theresa's daughters, and Peter is the son who was killed.

BERT, THERESA.

Bert.

Sorry I'm late, love.

Theresa.

I was just beginning to get anxious.

Bert.

I got into an argument with Victor.

Theresa.

You two, what was it this time?

Bert.

I suppose what it really is every time us two just being in the same house together.

Theresa.

It wasn't too nasty, was it?

Bert.

I can cope. I understand Victor, you see. He doesn't think I do, but I do. We talk the same language. I just speak a more standardized version, that's all.

Theresa.

I think my Deirdre and him would have a lot in common.

Bert.

Yes . . . and they'd have a lot not in common.

(They sit for a moment, enjoying the day.)

Theresa.

Isn't it beautiful . . . lovely weather. Listen to the birds. (Pause.) I saw a blackbird this morning . . .

eating a worm. A disgusting, fat slimy thing. (Pulls a face.) I thought, what a horrible thing to have to have for your breakfast . . . so I threw it a bit of currant cake.

Bert.

Did it prefer that?

Theresa.

It flew away . . . and then came back, for the worm.

Bert.

Perhaps it didn't like currants.

(Pause.)

Theresa.

Isn't it a shame you have to be dead to get this sort of peace and quiet?

Bert.

There's not so many use it now. Cremation's the great thing nowadays.

Theresa.

The very thought of it makes me shiver. They'll never get me into one of them furnaces. (Looking around.) This is where I want to be.

Bert.

When you're gone, you're gone, I suppose. You'll be none the wiser.

Theresa.

I've heard it's a take on. They take the bodies out and save the coffins. Earth burial's the Christian way. A nice service and a nice tea afterwards.

Bert.

Talking of tea. (Organizing things.) Have you heard the joke about the Irishman who arrived late for a cremation funeral? He rushed in, just as the coffin was disappearing, smashed two eggs on it, threw a bit of bacon on. He shouted, ''Would you put them through as well, I'd no time for breakfast.'' (He laughs.)

Theresa.
(With a weak smile.) Oh yes, very good.

Bert.
You know, I wonder if I was away tomorrow who'd look after this place? Victor wouldn't, that's for sure.

Theresa.
The young ones . . . neither of those two ladies of mine'll come near the place. It's Joan's nerves, mind. Deirdre could come . . . but she wouldn't.

Bert.
Maybe it's just as well in a way. After all, we mightn't have got together.

Theresa.
The young aren't as thoughtful. (Pause.) You notice, there's never very many young ones about.

Bert.
It's a working day I suppose. Anyway, the young think it's morbid. They don't want to be thinking about it. I suppose you don't when you're young.

Theresa.
My fella didn't get the choice. (Crossing herself.) God rest him.

Bert.
Come on, eat away at them sandwiches.

Theresa.
(Eating.) That's beautiful cooked ham.

Bert.
Didn't I tell you? The best in the city.

Theresa.
Did you forget about the mustard?

Bert.
Aye. I was in a bit of a rush . . . getting it all ready, before that Victor fella came down.

Theresa.
But you didn't . . .
                    (He shakes his head.)

Theresa.

And you forgot the mustard. It's a nice cup of tea, though.

Bert.

It's not too strong?

Theresa.

No, it's grand. I've brought two nice fresh cream doughnuts and some currant cake.

Bert.

The blackbird didn't get it all then?

Theresa.

You know, when I saw the size of that worm, I shuddered. With this being a graveyard and all, you get to wondering why the worms are so fat.

Bert.

You can get fat worms anywhere.

Theresa.

They're all fat here, though. It makes my skin crawl.

Bert.

You don't get that with cremation.

Theresa.

Do you want to be cremated?

Bert.

It's cheaper, so I don't suppose I'll have much choice with that Victor fella.

Theresa.

Surely with all the overtime the polis get, he can afford to give you a decent burial?

Bert.

Anyway, (Looking her her.) maybe it'll not be his responsibility.

Theresa.

(Looks at him shyly.) Do you think him and his wife'll ever get together again?

Bert.

I doubt it. I doubt if Jenny'd be interested. Not in the state he's in at the moment. He's a mess.

Theresa.

It's the strain, I suppose. The fear . . . and the strain.

Bert.

It's the drink.

Theresa.

That's because of the strain and fear. My husband was the same.

(He looks at her.)

Theresa.

He lived in fear of someone offering him a job. (Crosses herself.) God forgive me for speaking ill of the dead, but he was a terrible man and you daren't have looked sideways at him when he'd a drop taken. Many's a clout I got. For a couple of years before he died I barely knew what it was like to see out of both eyes together.

Bert.

It must have had a very bad effect on the children.

Theresa.

It did. Peter always swore he'd never drink when he got married . . . but sure. (Pause.) He was engaged you know. He'd been up seeing her that night . . . must have decided to take a short-cut home. It was a short cut to here.

Bert.

Did they shoot him?

Theresa.

(Emotional.) Eventually they did him that kindness.

Bert.

(Touching her hand and withdrawing.) I remember this used to be the safest city in Europe. You could have walked anywhere.

Theresa.

His wee girl used to visit me, ach for months afterwards.

(Pause.)

Bert.
Isn't it strange. We were here together that morning. A few hundred yards apart. Burying our sons. (Pause. Breaks. Rises.) That sun's strong. (Removes his pullover.) I'm boiled.

Theresa.
Be careful now. Summer chills can be treacherous.

Bert.
I'd hate to be a gravedigger in weather like this. (Looking out.) The ground hard . . . digging, sweating.

Theresa.
(Following his gaze.) I'd hate to be a gravedigger in any weather. Mind you it must be worse for the cremators, weather like this. It's no wonder you never see a fat gravedigger.

Bert.
I suppose now, with all this equality, we'll have women doing it soon.

Theresa.
If I was going to be equal to men, I'd rather be equal to something better than a gravedigger!

Bert.
(Pauses, looks at her. Sits again.) Are we being foolish Theresa, I mean, at our ages?

Theresa.
I suppose to some it'll seem that way. I don't feel foolish. Or if that is what I feel, I like feeling foolish.

Bert.
We can't go on meeting here every day.

Theresa.
Well, either we stop meeting . . . or we meet somewhere else.

Bert.
Your place or mine?

Theresa.

We're old enough to please ourselves.

Bert.

That Victor fella . . . well, he's a bit bigoted I suppose.

Theresa.

He'll make a match for that eldest one of mine then. You'd expect that, In an RUCman. They must live on their nerves. There've been that many of them shot.

Bert.

I'd like to bring you home. If I thought he was out.

Theresa.

Bert, your Victor doesn't frighten me . . . and I think I'm a bit old for hiding around corners.

Bert.

I don't want him offending you. I don't want any sort of unpleasantness.

Theresa.

Is he with you for good?

Bert.

It's beginning to look that way.

Theresa.

We could always go to the pictures.

Bert.

(Enthusiastic.) Would you like to?

Theresa.

Yes . . . but not every night . . . and the days of short walks and long stands up entries are well behind me.

Bert.

We could try it . . . going home, I mean.

Theresa.

You could always come to my place.

Bert.

Well yes, yes . . . but what about your daughters?

Theresa.

What about them?

Bert.

You said the eldest one was . . . bitter.

Theresa.

You're a big lad, Bert. I'm sure you can look after yourself. If I'm not frightened of your monster, there's no reason why you should be frightened of mine.

Bert.

Except you've got two!

Theresa.

Ach, Joan's no problem..I sometimes wish she was.

(Short interlude.)

Bert.

Those doughnuts must be fattening.

Theresa.

(Shocked.) I didn't realize.

Bert.

It's the cream.

Theresa.

I didn't realize your young fella'd been murdered. There's me going on about Peter . . .

Bert.

I'd rather talk about the doughnuts.

Theresa.

No wonder Victor's so bitter.

Bert.

Or the weather. It's bloody hot.

Theresa.

(Looking at him.) You haven't tried the currant cake.

Bert.

I'll have it later.

Theresa.

Later! How long are we staying here?

Bert.

What is there to rush away for?

Theresa.

I'd like to talk about it, Bert. We've really got something in common. Did the ones who did it own up?

Bert.

Yes. They sent a postcard, "Greetings from Hell. Wish you were here." And I was. (Pause. Emotional) . . . Sorry . . .

Theresa.

(Takes his hand.) Oh Bert . . . Bert . . . I know . . . I know. (They look at each other for a moment. Then they kiss . . . for the first time ever. Break apart, embarrassed. Pause. Theresa looks around. Both face front.)

Bert.

I suppose this weather can't really last much longer.

Theresa.

We'll have a water shortage soon. A few days' good weather and we have a water shortage.

Bert.

It's a storage problem.

Theresa.

If you ask me it's an intelligence problem. I think it's all that tea them civil servants drink that causes it.

Bert.

I wouldn't want to stop coming here . . . especially when the weather's fine like this.

Theresa.

They keep this one nice. I like a well-kept cemetery.

Bert.

I don't mind very old ones being overgrown. (Pause. They sit for a moment . . . then look at each other and smile.)

Theresa.

I'm always giving off when I see young ones snogging in the street.

Bert.

It isn't quite the street.

Theresa.

Huh, some people might say it's even worse. I haven't been kissed like that since I was courting my husband.

Bert.

(Pleased with himself.) I was always a good kisser.

Theresa.

(Good-natured.) I meant outside!

Bert.

Elsie was terrible about that, always. Holding hands was as far as she'd go, in public.

Theresa.

I like a kiss or two, the occasional ear-nibble. Mind you I had to be careful. If he'd had a few drinks he'd have bitten the ear off me. He was never really romantic. He was an awkward man. If he was sober, you knew twenty minutes beforehand that he was working up to a kiss. By the time it actually came the notion had gone off me.

Bert.

Even up until near the end Elsie got annoyed..if I kissed her in front of the other patients.

Theresa.

Did she linger long?

Bert.

She was sick for years, a lot of pain. I could never believe it was part of a grand design. Mind you, she had great faith. Until the very end.

Theresa.

He went in the street. His brother had a coal business. He was giving him a hand out, one cold November Wednesday. He had the bag on his back and all. Half-way across the road and down he went, bag and all, dead. Mind you, that Sean one wasn't too far gone with grief that he didn't shovel up every last bit of coal.

(Pause.)

Bert.

You never know how you're going to react. People do strange things. The night Sam was shot on our drive, we ran out, I kicked over the milk bottles and Victor stopped to pick them up! Reflex, I suppose.

Theresa.

He was a stubborn man, Joe, awful stubborn. Wouldn't go near the doctor about the pains in his chest. I think he was just afraid of being told to give up the drink. Still, maybe it's not a bad way to go. (Pause. Looks) There are worse wastes, when you look around you today.

(Pause. They both sit, gloomy.)

Bert.

Would you like to come home with me?

Theresa.

(Nervy.) Today?

Bert.

No . . . Tomorrow. Tomorrow night.

Theresa.

Oh, dear . . . the thought of meeting children's even more frightening than the thought of meeting parents. Will Victor be there?

Bert.

It's my house.

Theresa.

Owning the kennel doesn't stop your dog from biting.

Bert.

(Starts to pack up.) Come on, we'll be a long time in a place like this.

(Gather up all their stuff and go.)

The Road to Mecca

Athol Fugard

The play takes place in 1974 in the home of Miss Helen. She
lives in a small village in the Great Karoo, a semidesert region
in the center of South Africa. The room in which this scene is
set is extraordinary by virtue of someone's attempt to use as
much light and color in the decor as humanly possible. The
walls are all of different colors and liberally decorated with mir-
rors, while the ceiling and floor are covered with multicolored
geometric patterns. The effect is of an extravagant fantasy. The
room is filled with candles of all sizes, shapes, and colors which
apparently caused a small fire at some previous time. There is
also a collection of strange statues. Miss Helen, a frail, bird-like
woman in her late sixties, lives here alone but is being visited
by her devoted friend, a young woman named Elsa Barlow. Elsa
feels that Miss Helen must go into a nursing home. The following scene is between Helen and the local minister, Marius By-
leveld, a man of her own age. A short scene when Elsa enters
with some tea and the application for the old-age home before
returning to the kitchen has been deleted and marked with asterisks.

MARIUS, MISS HELEN

Marius.

. . . . I think Miss Barlow gets a little impatient with our old-fashioned ways and attitudes. But it's too late for us to change now. Right, Helen?

Helen.

Elsa and I have already had those arguments, Marius.

Marius.

I hope you put up a good defense on our behalf.

Helen.

I tried my best.

Marius.

And yet the two of you still remain good friends.

Helen.

Oh yes!

Marius.

And so it should be. A true friendship should be able to accommodate a difference of opinion. You didn't mention anything about her coming up for a visit last time we talked.

Helen.

Because I didn't know. It's an unexpected visit.

Marius.

Will she be staying long?

Helen.

Just tonight. She goes back tomorrow.

Marius.

Good heavens! All this way for only one night. I hope nothing is wrong.

Helen.

No! She just decided on the spur of the moment to visit me. But she's got to go back because they're very busy at school. They're right in the middle of exams.

Marius.

I see. Helen, may I sit down for a moment?

Helen.

Of course, Marius. Forgive me, I'm forgetting my manners.

Marius.

(Hangs up hat and scarf in the hallway and then joins Helen at the table.) I won't stay long. I must jot down a few thoughts for tomorrow's sermon. And thanks to you I know what I want to say.

Helen.

Me?

Marius.

Yes, you. (Teasing her.) You are responsible . . .

Helen.

Oh dear!

Marius.

(A little laugh.) Relax, Helen. I only said thanks to you because it came to me this afternoon while I was digging up your vegetables. I spent a lot of time while I was out in the garden doing that, just leaning on my spade. My back is giving me a bit of trouble again and to tell you the truth, I also felt lazy. I wasn't thinking about anything in particular . . . just looking, you know, the way an old man does, looking around, recognizing once again and saying the names. Spitskop in the distance! Aasvoelkrans down at the other end of the valley. The poplars with their autumn foliage standing around as yellow and bright as that candle flame! And a lot of remembering. As you know, Helen, I had deep and very painful wounds in my soul when I first came here. Wounds I thought would never heal. This was going to be where I finally escaped from life, turned my back on it and justified what was left of my existence by ministering to you people's simple needs. I was very wrong. I didn't escape from life here, I discovered it, what it really means, the fullness and goodness of it. It's a deep and lasting regret that Aletta wasn't alive to share that discovery with me. Anyway, all of this was going on in my head when I realized I was hearing a small little voice, and the small little voice was saying "thank you." With every spade-full of earth that I turned, when I went down on my knees to lift the potatoes out of the soil, there it was: Thank you. It was mine! I was muttering away to myself the way we old folks are inclined to do when nobody is around. It was me saying "thank you." That is what I want to do tomorrow, Helen. Give thanks, but in a way that I've never done before. I know I've stood there in the pulpit many times telling all of you to do exactly that, but oh dear me! the cleverness and conceit in the soul of Marius By-leveld when he was doing that. I had an actor's vanity up there, Helen. I'm not saying I was a total hypocrite, but believe me in those thanksgivings I was listening to my Dominee's voice and its hoped-for eloquence every bit as much as to the true little voice inside my heart . . . the voice I heard so clearly this afternoon. That's the voice that must speak to-morrow! And to do that I must find words as simple as the sky I was standing under or the earth I was turning over with my spade. They have got no van-ities or conceits. They are just "there." And if the Almighty takes pity on us, the one gives us rain so that the other can in turn . . . give us this day our daily potato. (A smile at this gentle little joke.) Am I making any sense, Helen? Answer me truthfully.

Helen.

Yes, you are, Marius. And if all you do tomorrow is say what you have just said to me, it will be very moving and beautiful.

Marius.

(Sincerely.) Truly, Helen? Do you really mean that?

Helen.

Every word of it.

Marius.

Then I will try. (Rests his hand on Helen's. They both withdraw. A pause.) My twentieth anniversary comes up next month. Yes, that is how long I've been here. Twenty—one years ago, May the six-teenth, the Good Lord called my Aletta to his side and just over a year later, June the eleventh, I gave my first sermon in New Bethesda. (A little laugh at the memory.) What an occasion that was! I don't know if I showed it, Helen, but let me confess now that I was more than just a little nervous when I went up into the pulpit and looked down at the stern and formidable array of faces. A very different prop-osition to the town and city congregations I had been preaching to up until then. When Miss de Klerk played the first bars of the hymn at the end of it, I heaved a very deep sigh of relief. None of you had fallen asleep! (Helen is shaking her head.) What's the matter, Helen?

Helen.

Young Miss de Klerk came later. Mrs. Retief was still our organist when you gave your first service.

Marius.

Are you sure?

Helen.

Yes. Mrs. Retief also played at the reception we gave you afterwards in Mr. van Heerden's house. She played the piano and Sterling Retief sang.

Marius.

You know something, I do believe you're right! Good heavens, Helen, your memory is better than mine.

Helen.

And you had no cause to be nervous, Marius. You were very impressive.

Marius.

(A small pause as he remembers something else.) Yes, of course. You were in that congregation. Stefanus was at your side as he was going to be every Sunday after that for . . . how long?

Helen.

Five years.

Marius.

Another five years. That was all a long time ago.

Helen.

More than a long time, Marius. It feels like another life.

******

Marius.

You're quite certain you want to deal with this now, Helen?

Helen.

Yes, Marius.

Marius.

It can wait until tomorrow.

Helen.

No, I'm ready. (Sits at the table.)

Marius.

Right. Just before we start talking, Helen, the good news . . . (Elsa tiptoes back from the kitchen into the bedroom alcove with her tea and begins to work on her papers. Marius hesitates for a moment and then resumes talking.) The good news is that I've spoken to Dominee Gericke in Graaff-Reinet again and the room is definitely yours . . . that is, if you want it, of course. But they obviously can't have it standing empty indefinitely. As it is he's already broken the rules by putting you at the top of the waiting list, but it's a personal favor. He understands the circumstances. So the sooner we decide, one way or the other, the better. But I want you to know that I do realize how big a move this is for you. I want you to be quite certain and happy in your mind that you're doing the right thing. So don't think we've got to rush into it . . . start packing up immediately or anything like that. A decision must be made, one way or the other, but once you've done that you can relax and take all the time you need.

(Spectacles, a little notebook, pen and pencil from a jacket pocket. The way he handles everything . . . care—and precisely . . . reveals a meticulous and orderly mind. He opens the application form. Miss Helen gives Elsa the first of many desperate and appealing looks. Elsa, engrossed in her work, does not apparently notice it.)

Helen.

Marius, I just . . .

Marius.

I know we went over this the last time, Helen, but there still are just a few questions. Yes . . . we put Stefanus' father's name down as Petrus Johannes Martins, but in the Church registry it's down as Petrus Jacobus. (Spectacles off.) Which one is correct, Helen? Can you remember? You were so certain of the Petrus Johannes last time.

Helen.

I still am! But what did you say the other one was?

Marius.

(Holding the notebook up to the candlelight.) Petrus Jacobus.

Helen.

Jacobus . . . Johannes . . . No, maybe I'm not sure.

Marius.

In that case what I think I will do is just enter it as Petrus J. Martins. Just as well I checked. (spectacles on. Back to the form.) And next . . . yes, the date of your confirmation. Have you been able to find the certificate?

Helen.

No, I haven't. I'm sorry, Marius. I have been looking but I'm afraid my papers are all in a mess.

Marius.

(Spectacles off.) I've been through the Church records again but I can't find anything that sheds any light on it. It's not at all that important, of course, but it would have been nice to have had that date as well. (Spectacles on.) Let's see . . . what shall we do? You think you were about twelve at the time?

Helen.

Something like that.

Marius.

What I'll do is just pencil in 1920 and have one more look. I hate giving up on THAT one. But you surprise me, Helen . . . of all dates to have forgotten. That takes care of the form now . . . (His notebook.) . . . Yes. Two little points from Dominee Gericke, after which you can relax and enjoy your supper. He asked me . . . and do believe me, Helen, he was only trying to be practical and helpful, nothing else . . . whether you had taken care of everything by way of a last will and testament, and obviously I said I didn't know.

Helen.

What do you mean, Marius?

Marius.

That in the event of something happening, your house and possessions will be disposed of in the way that you want them to be. Have you done that?

Helen.

(Taking a legal document out of the red box.) I've still got a copy of Stefanus' will. He left everything to me.

Marius.

We're talking about you, Helen. Have you seen a lawyer?

Helen.

No, I . . . I never thought of it.

Marius.

Then it is just as well Dominee Gericke asked. Sit down, Helen. (Helen sits clutching the red box.) Believe me, Helen, in my time as a minister I have seen so many bitterly unhappy situations because somebody had neglected to look after that side of things. Families not talking to each other! Law suits over a few sticks of furniture! I really do think it is something you should see to. We're at an age now when anything can happen. I had mine revised only a few months ago. (His notebook.) And finally, he made the obvious suggestion that we arrange for you to visit the Home as soon as possible. Just to meet the Matron and the other people there and to see your room. He's particularly anxious for you to see it so that you know what you need to bring on your side. He had a dreadful to-do there a few months ago with a lady who tried to move a whole houseful of furniture into her little room. Don't worry, there's plenty of space for personal possessions and a few of your . . . ornaments. That covers everything, I think. All that's left now is for you to sign it. Provided you still want to do that, of course. (Places his fountain pen in readiness on the form.)

Helen.

(Rises, trying to take command.) Marius . . . please . . . please . . . can I talk for a little bit now?

Marius.

But of course, Helen.

Helen.

I've been doing a lot of thinking since we last spoke . . .

Marius.

Good! We both agree that was necessary. This is not a step to be taken lightly.

Helen.

Yes, I've done a lot of thinking and I've worked out a plan.

Marius.

For what, Helen?

Helen.

A plan to take care of everything.

Marius.

Excellent!

Helen.

I'm going in to Graaf-Reinet next week, Marius, to see a doctor. I'm going to make the appointment on Monday and I'll ask Gertruida to drive me in.

Marius.

You make it sound serious, Helen.

Helen.

No, it's just my arthritis. I'm going to get some medicine for it.

Marius.

For a moment, you had me worried. I thought the burns were possibly more serious than we had realized. But why not save yourself a few pennies and see Dr. Lubbe at the Home? He looks after everybody there free-of-charge.

Helen.

(Hanging on.) And spectacles. I'm going to make arrangements to see an optician and get a pair of spectacles.

Marius.

Splendid, Helen! You certainly have been making plans.

Helen.

And finally I've decided to get Katrina to come in two or three times a week to help me with the house.

(Turns and looks at Elsa proudly. She is very pleased with herself.)

Marius.

Katrina?

Helen.

Little Katrina. Koos Magas' wife.

Marius.

I know who you're talking about, Helen, it's just . . . Oh dear! I'm sorry to be the one to tell you this, Helen, but I think you are going to lose your little Katrina.

Helen.

What do you mean, Marius?

Marius.

Koos has asked the Divisional Council for a transfer to their Aberdeen depot and I think he will get it.

Helen.

So. . . .

Marius.

I imagine Katrina and the baby will go with him . .

Helen.

Katrina . .

Marius.

Will be leaving the village.

Helen.

No, it can't be.

Marius.

It's the truth, Helen.

Helen.

But she's said nothing to me about it. She was here just a few days ago and she didn't mention anything about leaving.

Marius.

She most probably didn't think it important.

Helen.

How can you say that, Marius? Of course it is! She knows how much I depend on her. If Katrina goes

I'll be completely alone here except for you and the times when Elsa is visiting. (Miss Helen becomes increasingly distressed.)

Marius.

Come now, Helen! It's not as bad as that. I know Katrina is a sweet little soul and that you are very fond of her, as we all are, but don't exaggerate things. There are plenty of good women in the location who can come in and give you a hand in here and help you pack up . . . if you decide to go. Tell you what I'll do . . . if you're worried about a stranger being in here with all your personal things. I'll lend you my faithful old Nonna. She's been looking after me for ten years now and in that time I haven't missed a thing. You could trust her with your life.

Helen.

I'm not talking about a servant, Marius.

Marius.

I thought we were.

Helen.

Katrina is the only friend I've got left in the village.

Marius.

That's a very hard thing you're saying, Helen. We all still like to think of ourselves as your friends.

Helen.

I wasn't including you, Marius. You're different. But as for the others . . . ? They've all become strangers to me. I might just as well not know their names. And they treat me as if I'm a stranger to them as well.

Marius.

You're being very unfair, Helen. They behave towards you in the way you apparently want them to, which is to be left completely alone. Really, Helen! Strangers? Old Gertruida, Sterling, Jerry, Boet, Mrs.

van Heerden . . ? You grew up in this village with all of them. To be very frank, Helen, it's your manner which now keeps people at a distance. I don't think you realize how much you've changed over the years. You're not easily recognizable to others anymore as the person they knew fifteen years ago. And then your hobby, if I can call it that, hasn't really helped matters. This is not exactly the sort of room the village ladies are used to, or would feel comfortable in having afternoon tea. As for all that out there . . . the less said about it the better.

Helen.

I don't harm or bother anyone, Marius!

Marius.

And does anyone do that to you?

Helen.

Yes! Everybody is trying to force me to leave my home.

Marius.

Nobody is trying to force you, Helen! In Heaven's name where do you get that idea from? If you sign this form it must be of your own free will. You're very agitated tonight, Helen. Has something happened to upset you? You were so reasonable about everything the last time we talked. You seemed to understand that the only motive on our side was to try and do what is best for you. And even then it's only in the way of advice. We can't TELL you what to do. But if you want us to stop caring about what happens to you we can try . . though I don't know how our Christian consciences will allow us to do that.

Helen.

I don't believe the others care about me, Marius. All they want to do is to get rid of me. This village has also changed over the past fifteen years. I don't recognize it anymore as the simple, innocent world I grew up in.

Marius.

If it's as bad as that, Helen, if you are now really that unhappy and lonely here, then I don't think you should have any doubts about leaving.

(Miss Helen's emotional state has deteriorated steadily. Marius' fountain pen has ended up in her hand. She looks down at the application form . . a few seconds' pause and then a desperate cry.)

Helen.

Why don't you stop me, Elsa! I'm going to sign it.

The Subject Was Roses

Frank D. Gilroy

This realistic slice-of-life play, of a type which is sometimes referred to as kitchen drama, takes place in the living room of John and Nettie Cleary's middle-class apartment in the West Bronx in May 1946. This scene opens the play. It takes place the morning after a party for John and Nettie's only son, Timmy, who has just been discharged from the army after serving three years in World War II. The scene opens with John hastily taking off his son's army jacket when he hears his wife entering with a bundle of groceries. Some stage directions in-

*volving Timmy, who overhears the last part of this conversation,
are deleted and marked with asterisks.*

JOHN, NETTIE

Nettie.

It's a lovely day . . . Timmy still asleep?

John.

Haven't heard him . . . Better give me mine.

Nettie.

I thought we'd all have breakfast together.

John.

I have to go downtown.

Nettie.

Today?

John.

Ruskin wants to see me. (She regards him a moment, then begins to set the food before him.) I'm going to stop at St. Francis on the way . . . to offer a prayer of thanks.

Nettie.

Toast?

John.

Yes . . . All those casualties and he never got a scratch. We're very lucky.

Nettie.

What do you want on it?

John.

Marmalade . . . The Freeman boy dead. The Mullin boy crippled for life . . . Makes you wonder . . . Think he enjoyed the party?

Nettie.

He seemed to.

John.

First time I ever saw him take a drink.

Nettie.

He drank too much.

John.

You don't get out of the army every day.

Nettie.

He was sick during the night.

John.

Probably the excitement.

Nettie.

It was the whiskey. You should have stopped him.

John.

For three years he's gotten along fine without anyone telling him what to do.

Nettie.

I had to hold his head.

John.

No one held his head in the army.

Nettie.

That's what HE said.

John.

But that didn't stop you.

Nettie.

He's not in the army any more.

John.

It was a boy that walked out of this house three years ago. It's a man that's come back in.

Nettie.

You sound like a recruiting poster.

John.

YOU sound ready to repeat the old mistakes.

Nettie.

Mistakes?

John.

Pardon me.

Nettie.

You said mistakes.

John.

Slip of the tongue.

Nettie.

I'd like to know what mistakes you're referring to.

John.

The coffee's excellent.

Nettie.

I'd really like to know.

John.

He was eighteen when he went away. Until that time, he showed no special skill at anything, but you treated him like he was a protege.

Nettie.

I think you mean prodigy.

John.

What I really mean is baby.

Nettie.

For a baby he certainly did well in the army.

John.

I didn't say he WAS a baby. I said you treated him like one.

Nettie.

You were surprised he did well. You didn't think he'd last a week.

John.

Bless us and save us, said Mrs. O'Davis.

Nettie.

Do you know why you were surprised?

John.

Joy, joy, said Mrs. Malloy.

Nettie.

Because you never understood him.

John.

Mercy, mercy, said old Mrs. Percy.

Nettie.

I never doubted that he'd do as well as anyone else.

John.

Where he's concerned you never doubted, period. If he came in here right now and said he could fly, you'd help him out the window.

Nettie.

If you're saying I have confidence in him, you're right. And why not? Who knows him better?

John.

Is there more coffee?

Nettie.

He's exceptional.

John.

Here we go again.

Nettie.

Yes—exceptional!

John.

In what way?

Nettie.

I refuse to discuss it.

John.

A person who's going to be famous usually drops a few clues by the time they're twenty-one.

Nettie.

I didn't say famous—I said exceptional.

John.

What's the difference?

Nettie.

You wouldn't understand.

John.

Here's something you better understand—you can't treat him as though he'd never been away. He's not a kid.

Nettie.

If you had stopped him from drinking too much that would have been treating him like a kid?

John.

This is where I came in.

Nettie.

He was trying to keep up with you and you knew it.

John.

You sound like you're jealous.

Nettie.

The two of you so busy drinking you hardly paid attention to anyone else.

John.

You ARE jealous!

Nettie.

Don't be absurd.

John.

He and I got along better yesterday than we ever did before and you're jealous. (She turns away.) Well, well, well. (He finishes the last of his coffee. Rises to leave.)

Nettie.

Can't Ruskin wait till Monday?

John.

No. And don't pretend you're disappointed. What a charming little breakfast you and he will have together.

Nettie.

You're welcome to stay.

John.

My ears are burning already.

Nettie.

I've never said a word against you and you know it.

John.

Don't forget my excursion to Montreal.

Nettie.

It was always your own actions that turned him against you.

John.

And the convention—don't leave that out. (He starts from the room.)

Nettie.

The curtains. (He regards her.) The curtains for Timmy's room. They're coming today.

John.

I don't know anything about curtains.

Nettie.

Yes, you do.

John.

I do not.

Nettie.

They'll be ten dollars.

John.

What's the matter with the old ones?

******

Nettie.

They're all worn out.

John.

They look all right to me.

Nettie.

They aren't all right.

John.

Ten dollars for curtains.

Nettie.

Timmy will want to bring friends home.

John.

The old squeeze play.

******

Nettie.

Are you going to give me the money?

(John extracts a bill from his wallet, slaps it on the table.)

John.

Here!

Nettie.

I need five dollars for the house.

John.

I gave you fifteen yesterday.

Nettie.

That went for the party.

John.

That party cost close to a hundred dollars.

Nettie.

It was worth it.

John.

Did I say it wasn't (He takes another bill from his wallet and puts it down.) There.

The Visit

Friedrich Duerenmatt
Adapted by Maurice Valency

The play was first produced in new York in 1958. It takes place in a shabby and ruined little town somewhere in Central Europe in the mid-1950s. A very wealthy and renowned woman in her fifties, Claire Zachanassian has come back to the town where she was born. The citizens have enthusiastically welcomed her, hoping she can help restore their former prosperity. In the following scene, Claire is in a little wood with Anton Schill, with whom she had an affair when young. He had impregnated her, resulting in her banishment. Since he had been her lover, Anton has been persuaded by the townspeople to use his influence to convince Claire to help them. It is important to realize that Claire has not forgotten the shabby way in which she had been treated by Anton and the town.

CLAIRE, SCHILL

Claire.

(Comes downstage with Schill.) Look, Anton. Our tree. There's the heart you carved in the bark long ago.

Schill.

Yes. It's still there.

Claire.

How it has grown! The trunk is black and wrinkled. Why, its limbs are twice what they were! Some of them have died.

Schill.

It's aged. But it's there.

Claire.

Like everything else. (She crosses, examining other trees.) Oh, how tall they are. How long it is since I walked here, barefoot over the pine needles and the damp leaves! Look, Anton. A fawn.

Schill.

Yes, a fawn. It's the season.

Claire.

(They sit together on bench.) I thought everything would be changed. But it's all just as we left it. This is the seat we sat on years ago. Under these branches you kissed me. And over there under the hawthorn, where the moss is soft and green, we would lie in each other's arms. It is all as it used to be. Only we have changed.

Schill.

Not so much, little witch. I remember the first night we spent together, you ran away and I chased you till I was quite breathless—

Claire.

Yes.

Schill.

Then I was angry and started to go home, when suddenly I heard you call and I looked up, and there you were sitting in a tree laughing down at me.

Claire.

No. It was in the great barn. I was in the hayloft.

Schill.

Were you?

Claire.

Yes. What else do you remember?

Schill.

I remember the morning we went swimming by the waterfall, and afterwards we were lying together on the big rock in the sun when suddenly we heard footsteps and we just had time to snatch up our clothes and run behind the bushes when the old pastor appeared and scolded you for not being in school.

Claire.

No. It was the schoolmaster who found us. It was Sunday and I was supposed to be in church.

Schill.

Really?

Claire.

Yes. Tell me more.

Schill.

(Turns and looks away.) I remember the time your father beat you, and you showed me the cuts on your back, and I swore I'd kill him. And the next day I dropped a tile from a rooftop and split his head open.

Claire.

You missed him.

Schill.

No!

Claire.

You hit old Mr. Reiner.

Schill.

Did I?

Claire.

Yes. I was seventeen. And you were not yet twenty. You were so handsome. You were the best-looking boy in town.

Schill.

And you were the prettiest girl.

Claire.

We were made for each other.

Schill.

So we were.

Claire.

But you married Mathilde Blumhard and her store and I married old Zachanassian and his oil wells. He found me in a whorehouse in Hamburg. It was my hair that entangled him, the old golden beetle.

Schill.

Clara!

Claire.

A cigar.

Schill.

My kitten smokes cigars!

Claire.

Yes. I adore them. Would you care for one?

Schill.

Yes, please. I've never smoked one of those.

Claire.

It's a taste I acquired from old Zachanassian. Among other things. He was a real connoisseur.

Schill.

We used to sit on this bench once, you and I, and smoke cigarettes. Do you remember?

Claire.

Yes. I remember.

Schill.

The cigarettes I bought from Mathilde.

Claire.

No. She gave them to you for nothing.

Schill.

Don't be angry with me for marrying Mathilde.

Claire.

She had money.

Schill.

And what a lucky thing for you that I did!

Claire.

Oh?

Schill.

You were so young, so beautiful. You deserved a better fate than to be stuck in this wretched town without any future.

Claire.

Yes?

Schill.

If you had stayed in Gullen and married me, your life would have been wasted like mine.

Claire.

Oh?

Schill.

My God, Clara, look at me. A broken shopkeeper in a bankrupt town!

Claire.

But you have your family.

Schill.

My family! Never for a moment do they let me forget my failure, my poverty.

Claire.

Mathilde has not made you happy?

Schill.

(Shrugs.) What does it matter?

Claire.

And the children?

Schill.

(Shakes his head.) They're so completely material-
istic. You know, they have no interest whatever in
higher things.

Claire.

How sad for you.

(A moment's pause.)

Schill.

Yes. You know, since you went away my life has
passed by like a stupid dream. I've hardly once been
out of this town. Five days at a lake years ago. It
rained all the time. A trip to Berlin, once. That's all.

Claire.

The world is much the same everywhere.

Schill.

At least you've seen it.

Claire.

Yes, I've seen it.

Schill.

You've lived in it.

Claire.

I've lived in it. The world and I have been on very
intimate terms.

Schill.

Now that you've come back, perhaps things will
change.

Claire.

Naturally. I won't leave my native town in this condition.

Schill.

It will take millions to put us on our feet again.

Claire.

I have millions.

Schill.

One, two, three—

Claire.

Why not?

Schill.

You mean—you will help us?

Claire.

Yes.

Schill.

I knew it—I knew it! I told them you were generous. I told them you were good. Oh, my kitten! (He takes her hand.)

Claire.

(She turns her head away and listens.) Listen! A woodpecker.

Schill.

It's all just the way it was in the days when we were young and full of courage. The sun high above the pines. Great white clouds, piling up on one another. The cry of the cuckoo in the distance. The wind rustling the leaves like the sound of surf on a beach. Just as it was years ago. If only we could roll back time and be together always.

Claire.

Is that your wish?

Schill.

You left me, but you never left my heart. (He raises her hand to his lips.) The same soft little hand.

Claire.

No, not quite the same. It was crushed to a pulp in the plane accident. But they mended it. They mend everything nowadays.

Schill.
Crushed? You wouldn't know it. (Points.) Another
fawn.

Claire.
The old wood is alive with memories—

The Waltz of the Toreadors

Jean Anouilh

*This broad comedy , which opened in New York in 1957, is set
in France in the first decade of the twentieth century. It revolves
around General St. Pe, a man of late middle age, who sees
himself as a debonair man-about-town. He has been having an
affair for seventeen years with a younger woman, Mlle. De Ste
Euverte. Their affair had been limited to an exchange of love
letters but she has just appeared as a visitor, adding to the chaos
of his household, which includes two teenage daughters, his secretary, his servants, and his sick wife. The following scene takes
place in Mme. St. Pe's bedroom. She, an idiosyncratic character,
is propped up in bed. Her husband is standing beside the bed.*

GENERAL, WIFE

General.
We must thrash this matter out, Madam, once and
for all.

Wife.

I tried to kill myself, you monster, isn't that enough for you?

General.

You were stretched out on the tracks—an awkward position but quite safe. The train had already passed.

Wife.

I didn't know! I was waiting for it!

General.

On that branch line you could reckon on a good twenty-four hours of it.

Wife.

Is nothing sacred to you? You brute! I might have died of cold during the night.

General.

We are well into April, and spring is early this year. We are dying of heat.

Wife.

Of sunstroke then—starvation, I don't know . . . Of sorrow—yes, that's it—quite simply of sorrow, in my state of health.

General.

Sorrow you can die of in your bed, Madam, at leisure. It was absurd, like everything else you do.

Wife.

I am seriously ill. How often has the doctor told you that my condition gives cause for the gravest alarm? I did truly mean to kill myself and that alone should make you fall sobbing at my feet, if your heart were not made of granite!

General.

My heart is not made of granite, Madam, but I am thrifty with my tears.

Wife.

I sacrificed my life for you! (Screaming) Murderer!

General.

Be quiet, confound you, or I'll leave the room! Let us talk things over calmly.

Wife.

I'm too unhappy. You aren't unhappy, not you! You have your health and strength, you have. You're up and dressed each morning, you ride your horse, you walk around the garden, you go drinking with your friends! You live! You jeer at me, on your two legs, while I sit glued to my wheel chair. Aren't you ashamed of being well?

General.

You are glued to your wheel chair for no other reason than because you want to be. We know that now.

Wife.

Do you dare to say that I'm not ill?

General.

One has to be an idiot like myself, Madam, to go on believing in your aches and pains by this time. As for your poor ailing legs, thank God we'll hear no more about those for a bit. I strongly suspect you of stretching them in your room every night. They helped you keep your balance mighty well down the wisteria and over to the railway line this morning.

Wife.

It was the last spasm of the stricken beast who longs for death—Call your accomplice Doctor Bonfant, with his rubber mallet; let him test my reflexes!

General.

Death and damnation, Madam, that's too easy!

Wife.

Too easy for you, I daresay. What have you got to complain about? While I lie here, racked with pain, you who can wander fancy free on your great fat legs, where do you go, eh?

General.

From my study to the garden, at your beck and call every ten minutes.

Wife.

And what is there in the garden? Answer me that, you pig, you satyr, you lascivious goat!

General.

Well, I dunno . . . roses . . .

Wife.

(Cackling) Roses! There's Madame Tardieu on the other side of the privet hedge, that frightful woman who exhibits her bodice as she leans over her flower beds. They're a household word hereabouts, Madame Tardieu's breasts! Whalebone, rubber, steel probably—she's propped up like a tumbledown barn.

General.

All right, all right, all right! After all, I haven't been to look.

Wife.

You dream of nothing else. You'll be mighty disillusioned when the great day comes. But on the other side of the fence at the bottom of the garden, walking along the school path at midday and at four, there are younger ones, aren't there? (Turns away.) The little convent girls! You centaur! One of these days the parents will complain.

General.

You're wandering Madam. They say good-morning to me, and I say good-morning back.

Wife.

And what about Prize Giving Day, at which you always manage to officiate, you old faun!—When you kiss them, red as a lobster in your uniform?

General.

It's the custom.

Wife.

What you're thinking isn't the custom and you know it! You tickle their bosoms with your decorations as you lean over them. Don't say you don't. I've seen you.

General.

If nothing worse happens to them as they're growing up we'll make may queens out of them!

Wife.

Queens of the May indeed! You've always been ready to officiate on May Day too. Last year's one, that hussy, as you kissed her, you whispered something in her ear. It was reported to me.

General.

(Chaffingly.) I whispered something? You don't say so?

Wife.

You arranged to meet her, I know. Besides I've seen her since. She's pregnant.

General.

Nonsense, she's putting on weight, that's all.

Wife.

My maids are putting on weight too, one after another.

General.

Let's change the subject, Madam, I have something very serious to say to you. You are untrue to me, Madam, that's the long and short of it. You wrote to Doctor Bonfant that you were in love with him. I have proof of it here in my wallet, down in black and white with two spelling mistakes which identify your hand. Yes. For you, who have always accused me of being a clodhopper, too lumpish to appreciate Baudelaire or Wagner, can't tell a conjunction from a carrot. You never had a day's schooling in your life.

Wife.

How shabby you are! To come on my deathbed and throw my unhappy childhood in my face! For over a year I was a boarder with the daughters of consuls and ambassadors in the most elect ladies' college in Paris.

General.

Where your mother went to do the household mending and where they took you in and fed you out of charity.

Wife.

My poor mother and I suffered a great deal, no doubt. But please to remember that my mother was a woman of infinite distinction, not a little provincial housewife like yours.

General.

One trade is as good as another, but your mother, Madam, was a dresser at the Opera.

Wife.

She accepted the post at the earnest request of the Director, solely for love of music. A woman whose hand M. Gounod kissed at a gala matinee for charity.

General.

Have it your own way. Let us get back to those letters. Did you or did you not write them? Do you or do you not address him as "Armand"? Do you tell him, yes or no, that his hair smells of vanilla when he sounds your chest and that you pretend to have a belly ache so he can come and feel it for you? It's down in black and white with two spelling mistakes in your own handwriting.

Wife.

How could you stoop so low as to come poking about in my correspondence?

General.

I did not poke about in your correspondence, Madam. I obtained possession of those letters. How? That's none of your business.

Wife.

Oh, isn't it? None of my business? Those letters were in the drawer of my bedside table where I keep my curlers and other objects of an intimate nature. You tell me they are in your wallet. And you dare to cross-question ME? It's past belief! But I did think you were still a gentleman.

General.

Dammit, Madam, will you stick to the point?

Wife.

So you ransack a lady's drawers, do you, my lad? You try to dishonor her, you a senior officer? All right, then, I shall tell, I shall tell everybody. I shall get up, I'll recover, for a day, the use of my poor aching legs, and the night of the reception at the annual Tattoo, in front of all the high ranking military personnel, I shall make a sensational entrance and I shall tell all!

General.

I repeat I have not ransacked your drawers.

Wife.

Have you those letters?

General.

I have.

Wife.

Show them to me.

General.

Ha ha! Not on your life.

Wife.

Very well. If you really have those letters in your wallet, there can be nothing more between us but an ocean of contempt. You may go. I am sleepy. I'm asleep. (She lies with her eyes closed.)

General.

No, Madam, you are not asleep. That would be too easy. Open your eyes. Open your eyes, this instant, do you hear, or I'll open them for you! Emily! Do as I say! Open your eyes! (He shakes her, slaps her, forces her eyelids up from their white eyeballs, begins to lose his head.) Come to your senses, damn you! What new game are you playing now?

Wife.

(Weakly.) My heart!

General.

What about your heart!

Wife.

It's shrinking. Good-bye Leon! I never loved anyone else but you.

General.

Oh, no, not your heart attack. We haven't even raised our voices. Your heart attack is for after the big scenes, Madam. You are warm, your pulse is good. I'm not falling for that. (Shaking her.) Wake up, Emily! You can't be as rigid as that. You're doing it on purpose. I'll give you your drops. (He rummages about among the bottles on the side tables.) Holy Moses, what a collection! It would take a qualified druggist to make head or tail of this lot! There's enough here to upset the constitution of a cart horse. Needless to say, no dropper. Where the devil did Eugenie put the thing? Oh well, here goes—one drop more one drop less the way things are now . . . There, Emily, drink this, and if that doesn't do the trick I'll call the doctor. Unclench your teeth, my love—unclench your teeth, damn you, it's dripping all over you! Give me strength— what's the matter with you? Your pulse is all right.

There's no getting away from that. I'll give you your injection.

Wife.

(Feebly) You're still rummaging, Leon. You're suspicious of me even on my deathbed.

General.

I'm NOT rummaging. I'm looking for your capsules.

Wife.

Too late. Call the children.

General.

What are you raving about, my dear, you aren't going to die. You're weak, that's all. I'll get the doctor. (Starts—She pulls him back—he lands sprawling on stool.)

Wife.

Too late. I implore you, don't move, Leon. Stay with me. Hold my hand as you did the old days long ago, when I was ill. You took care of me then, you were patient with me. You used to bathe my temples with eau de cologne and murmur sweet nothings in my ears . . .

General.

(Looking for the bottle and mumbling.) I can still dab you with a bit of cologne . . . (Pours on handkerchief.)

Wife.

But without the sweet nothings! It's that that's killing me—you murderer!

General.

(Not seeing—puts in her mouth then quickly to her head.) There. That will revive you.

Wife.

(Leaves hankie on head.) It frightens you, eh, to hear me say it? I'm dying for want of your love, Leon!

General.

(On knees.) No, no, no, don't be silly now. To begin with you are not dying at all, and you know perfectly well, my love, that I am always full of attention for you..(Tucks blanket.)

Wife.

(Throws hankie to wall.) Attentions! What do I want with your attentions (Grabs his arms.) I want you to love me, Leon, as you used to long ago, when you took me in your arms and called me your little girl, when you bit me all over . . . Aren't I your little girl any more, to be carried naked to my bath? (Tips his face up—looks into it.)

General.

(Uncomfortably.) Emily, we all have to grow up sometime. (Struggling to get away.)

Wife.

(Plaintively.) Why don't you bite me all over like a young terrier any more?

General.

(More and more embarrassed.) Dammit, Madam, young terriers grow into old ones—(Rises and turns left.) after twenty years. Besides I've lost my teeth. (Sinks into left chair.)

Wife.

(Sitting up with astonishing vigour considering her heart attack.) You've teeth enough for others, you mealy-mouthed old fraud! You can talk about those letters which were never even sent. I have evidence of another sort, in a trinket box underneath my mattress, letters both sent and received, where there's no question of your having lost your teeth. Letters in which you play the young man for another's benefit—and there you flatter yourself incidentally, my poor Leon—for apart from your summary prowess with the maids, you needn't think you're capable of much in that line either—

General.

(Rises, crosses left to window.) Be quiet, Madam! What do you know about it?

Wife.

I know as much as all women left unsatisfied. Learn first to satisfy one woman, to be a man in her bed, before you go scampering into the beds of others.

General.

(Turns right to her.) So I have never been a man in your bed, Madam, is that it?

Wife.

Soon weary, my friend, soon asleep, and when for a wonder you had a little energy, soon replete. We would both close our eyes in the bed, but while you performed your little task picturing the Lord knows whom, you don't imagine, do you, that it was you I thought about?

General.

(Turns away left.) How vulgar you are, Madam— vulgar and shameless. However, if that was so, why the reproaches and the scenes, why so many tears for so long?

Wife.

Because you belong to me, Leon! You are mine like my house, mine like my jewels, mine like my furniture, mine like your name. (Starts kneeling.)

General.

And is that what you understand by love?

Wife.

(In a great and frightful cry, standing on her bed in her nightshirt, a nightmarish figure.) Yes!

General.

(Crosses to foot of bed.) Death and damnation, Madam, I do not belong to you!

Wife.

To whom then?

General.

(Crosses to below right end of bed.) To no one. To myself perhaps.

Wife.

No! Not any longer. I am your wife. Your wife before God and before the law.

General.

Hell's bells, Madam, I'll escape you!

Wife.

Never!

General.

I'll pretend not to know you.

Wife.

I'll scream, I'll cause a riot! I'll break things. I'll run up debts to ruin you—

General.

(Crosses to below center, right of bed.) I tell you I'll take a train and disappear into thin air. You won't know where I am.

Wife.

You'd never dare, and if you did, I'd follow you to the far ends of the earth!

General.

(Turns to her, left corner of bed.) And when I die, hell's teeth! Will you make that journey too?

Wife.

When you die, I shall cry out loud—"I was his wife!" I shall put on widow's weeds, I, and I alone, will have the right and I shall visit your grave on All Soul's Day. I'll have my name engraved on your tombstone and when my turn comes to die I shall come and lie beside you for eternity. Unknown people as they pass will still read that I was your wife, on the stone!

General.

(Crosses to down left corner of bed.) By God, I hate you, Madam.

Wife.

(Leans forward.) What difference does that make? I am your wife.

General.

(Crosses to left of her.) I hate the sight and sound of you! And I'll tell you something else that's stronger even than my hatred and disgust. I am dying of boredom, Madam, by your side.

Wife.

You bore me too, but I am your wife just the same and about that you can do nothing.

General.

(Crosses down left.) But devil take it, you hate me just as much!

Wife.

Yes, I hate you. You ruined my career. I had a superb voice, a dazzling future—you insisted that I give up the stage. All that was brilliant in me you crushed underfoot. Other men worshipped me; you frightened them away with your great sword. You created a desert around me with your stupid jealousy, you made me unlearn how to be beautiful—unlearn how to love and be loved. Expected me to keep house for you like a servant, to feed your sickly children, I, whose breasts were famous throughout Paris!

General.

(Down left.) Your breasts famous? Don't make me laugh. Where did you exhibit them anyway? In Lohengrin?

Wife.

At festivals of Art. Before people whose refinement and luxurious living your petty tradesman's world can't even guess at. (Gets back down in bed—leans

back on head board.) Have you ever thought, you
desperado, of all I sacrificed for you?

General.

Death and damnation. (Paces to right and then left.)
Madam, that is ancient history! I am resolved to sue
for a divorce. (Left at foot of bed.)

Wife.

A divorce! You could never live alone, you're far
too frightened. And who do you think would have
you, you poor devil?

General.

I've found someone who will have me.

Wife.

She must be very old and pretty ugly—or pretty
poor to be reduced to that.

General.

It's a lie. She is young and beautiful. She's true to
me. She is waiting for me.

Wife.

Since when?

General.

Since—since seventeen years.

Wife.

You must be joking, my dear. Seventeen years! And
you think she loves you? And you think you love
her? And they've been waiting seventeen years,
poor lambs!

General.

(Sits left chair.) Yes Madam, and because of you.

Wife.

Oh Leon, if I weren't so ill, I'd laugh! I'd laugh like
a mad thing! It's too silly—really too silly! Seventeen years! But if you really loved her, you poor
imbecile, you would have left me long ago!

General.

I stayed out of respect for your grief and pity for your
illness, which I long took to be genuine, Madam.

Wife.

What a fool you are! Do you think I couldn't dance
if I wanted to? (She gets out of bed—right side.)
Look! You see how well I can stand! Come and
dance with me. Come! (Crosses down and left to
him. She sings and dances a few steps.)

General.

Let me go! You're mad! Go back to bed.

Wife.

(Tries to pull him right.) No. You are my true love
and I want to dance with you. Like at the Ball at
the Military College in Saumur, the one of '93 seventeen years ago funnily enough. (Stops dancing—
below bed.) Do you remember?

General.

Confound you, why?

Wife.

Because you were so handsome and scintillating and
sure of yourself with the women at that Ball. "Major
St. Pe!" How smartly you clicked your heels,
German fashion, when you introduced yourself! How
fetchingly you smoothed your whiskers, how prettily
you kissed their hands! (Sits foot of bed.) I shall
never forget that ball. I was still in love with you
then, and I had stayed faithful, idiot that I was, in
spite of your lady friends whom you forced me to invite to dinner. But at that ball I suddenly had enough,
all at once, in the space of a second. You were dancing a waltz with a ninny of a girl—I saw you whisper
in her ear and she made eyes at you and simpered.
The Waltz of the Toreadors—I even remember the
tune. (She sings.) I was too wretched. I had to get
away, out of the ballroom. I went out into the hall to
order my carriage. There was a man there, younger
and handsomer than you, and he helped me. And

when he found our carriage he said I couldn't possibly go home alone and he climbed in to escort me.

General.

Well?

Wife.

Well, you were still waltzing, my poor dear, with your superb half turns and your airs and graces. What do you suppose women are made of? He became my lover.

General.

What? You have had a lover, Madam, and it was at that Saumur Ball that you made his acquaintance? A man who had merely helped you find our carriage, a complete stranger?—I won't even ask you his rank. How horrible! But I'd like to believe that you had a few doubts, dear God!—a few misgivings, before taking such a step. I fondly hope you did at least wait a little?

Wife.

Of course, my dear. I was a respectable woman. I waited.

General.

How long?

Wife.

Three days.

General.

(Exploding.) Holy suffering rattlesnakes! (Rises, crosses down left to window.) I waited seventeen years, Madam, and I'm waiting still!

Wife.

(Rises, crosses to right of bed—leans over.) And when that one was posted, I forget where, to the devil—to the Far East, I took another just as handsome, and another, and again another, and so on before I grew too old and there would only be you left who would have me.

General.

(Turns to her.) But dammit, if you were untrue to me why the tears and the reproaches—why the immense heartaches and the torment—why this illness?

Wife.

To keep you, Leon. To keep you for always because I am your wife. For I do love you, Leon, on top of everything. I hate you for all the harm you did to me, but I love you—not tenderly, you fool, not with seventeen years of waiting and letter-writing. (Climbs on bed and stands.) Not for the bliss of being in your arms at night—we have never made love together, you poor wretch, and you know it— not for your conversation—you bore me—not for your rank either, nor your money—I've been of-fered more—I love you because you are mine, my object, my thing, my hold-all, my garbage bin—

General.

No! (Turns down left.)

Wife.

Yes, and you know it! And whatever you may promise others you know you will never be anything but that.

General.

(Wildly.) No!

Wife.

Yes! You will never be able to bring yourself to hurt me, you're too cowardly. You know it, and you know I know it too.

General.

No! (Crosses left to down left corner.)

Wife.

(Gets off left side.) Yes! Come now, darling, dance with me. The Waltz of the Toreadors, the last waltz, with me this time. (Crosses to him, arms out.)

General.
No! (Pushes her right away.)
Wife.
(Backs off right—below bed.) Yes! I want you to.
And you want whatever I want. Come, dance with
your chronic invalid, your old bag of bones. Come
dance with your remorse! Come dance with your
love!
General.
(Backs up left.) Don't touch me, for pity's sake,
don't touch me! (She pursues him. He cringes in a
corner. All of a sudden he stretches out his arms,
grips her throat and yells—forces her back on bed,
her head flopping over foot—body upstage.) Phan-
tasmagoria!! (The General's wife struggles in her
voluminous nightgown, trying to tear his hands
away from her throat.)

The Young Man from Atlanta

Horton Foote

❧

*This is the last scene of the play. Will and Lily Dale have had
their share of troubles. Not only have they suffered the recent
death of a son, Bill, under questionable circumstances, and the
loss of Will's job, but Will has just had a heart attack. Added
to this, a young friend of Bill's has been secretly visiting Lily*

*Dale and telling her many things about her son that give her a
sense of comfort. He has also "borrowed" a great deal of money,
unbeknownst to Will. A distant relative has visited who knew
both Bill and his friend in Atlanta and has presented a very
different version of Bill's behavior prior to his death. It is
strongly advised that the reader refer to the other scene from
this play (see pages 530–542) for a better understanding of these
two characters.*

WILL, LILY DALE

Will.

Why did you give that boy money, Lily Dale? Behind my back after I had asked you not to see him
again or go near him? Didn't I ask you that?

Lily Dale.

Yes, you did.

Will.

Then why, Lily Dale? Why?

Lily Dale.

I don't know. I felt sorry for him. He had a sick
mother, he lost his job, his sister was deserted with
three small children.

Will.

All lies, as we know now. But even if they were
true, after I had asked you—

Lily Dale.

I know. I know. I have never deceived you before,
Daddy, except for one time. It was when you went
to Chicago for a business trip and my cousin Mary
Cunningham came to stay with me and she talked
me into letting two men come over to the house.
And you came back from Chicago unexpectedly and
they ran out of the back door. (A pause.) That was
twenty years ago I don't know why I had to tell you
that. It has bothered me all these years—not that I

would have done anything wrong . . . (A pause.) I get lonely, Will. You've always had your work, gone away so much of the time, and then Bill went off to school, and then of course I had my music, but when Bill died I couldn't go near the piano anymore and I decided I should dedicate myself to God, and then this young friend of Bill's comes and he was sweet to me, and I missed Bill so, and I would always talk to him about Bill. And I never told you this, but just before Alice Temple committed suicide I went to see her and she told me that Bill had committed suicide, that everyone said that, and it upset me so, and I didn't want to tell you because I was afraid it would upset you, so I called his sweet friend in Atlanta and he told me he did not because he had talked to him the night before and all he talked about was God.

Will.
That boy is a liar, Lily Dale.

Lily Dale.
He may be, Will, but it did comfort me to hear him say it, and I needed comforting, Will. I've spent my days here crying since Bill died, and I wouldn't have done anything in the world to hurt you, Will, because you know how much I love you and how grateful I am for all you've given me, and I do believe in prayer, Will, and I'm going to pray that you get well and strong and you'll find a way to start your business.

Will.
Bill did kill himself, Lily Dale.

Lily Dale.
Don't say that, Will.

Will.
I'm sorry, but I think he did.

Lily Dale.

You think? But you don't know. What a terrible thing to say about your son!

Will.

Why did he come swimming in the middle of the afternoon in the lake in Florida and walk and continue to walk until he got water over his head? Why? Lily Dale, why? (A pause.) Lily, Lily Dale, why? I failed him, Lily Dale. Some way I failed him. I tried to be a good father, but I just think now I only wanted him to be like me, I never tried to understand what he was like. I never tried to find out what he would want to do, what he would want to talk about. Life goes so fast, Lily Dale. My God. It goes so fast. It seems like yestereday he was a baby, and I was holding him in my arms, and before I turned around good he was off to school and I thought, when he comes back he'll come into the business and I'll be close to him. (A pause.) I was never close to him, Lily Dale. How was your day? Fine, son, how was yours? And then he was gone. (A pause.) I want my son back, Lily Dale. I want him back. (A pause.)

Lily Dale.

I know. I know. So do I. (A pause.) I have to tell you this one last thing, Will. I saw Bill's friend today. He stood in the driveway as I was backing the car out and if I hadn't stopped I would have run over him, and he came to the car and I told him what Carson said and he said Carson was the liar—that—(Will has closed his eyes.) He said that Carson was jealous of his friendship with Bill and. . . . (A pause.) Will, I haven't told you the whole truth about those two men that came to the house with me and Mary Cunningham. They didn't come to our house because Mary invited them. We were riding down Main Street in

Mary's car and these two men passed us slowly in their car and looked back at us, and Mary said, they want to flirt, let's flirt back. Well, Mary, I said, I'm a married woman, Will wouldn't like that. What Will doesn't know won't hurt him, she said—besides, flirting is harmless, so she stepped on the gas and passed those men and looked back in this bold kind of way and as she did so, they stepped on the gas and drove right up beside us and introduced themselves, and Mary, before I could stop her, told them her name and my name and they told us theirs and they asked us to go to their apartment and Mary said we weren't that kind of girl and they said they meant no harm by it, as they just wanted to go someplace where we could talk and get to know each other, and then without asking my permission she said we could all go to my house and gave them the address. (A pause.) And do you know why I've stopped seeing Mary Cunningham? She said that one time when she was visiting Mama and Pete in Houston, Pete tried to put his arm around her and kiss her when Mama went out of the room. I said, I do not believe a word of that, and she said the same thing happened to our cousin Mable Thornton when she was visiting them, and their mama wouldn't allow them to stay at Mama's any longer after that. Do you believe that?.

Will.

I don't know. Who knows about anything, Lily Dale? I'm just very tired, that's all I know. Just very tired. Very, very tired.

Lily Dale.

Who are we to believe, Daddy? Pete's great-nephew Carson, or Bill's friend? Bill's friend asked if you would please see him and let him tell you what he told me. He says he is not a liar, that every word he has said to us is the truth. That Bill was very religious and he did pray loud and clear so that everybody in the boardinghouse could hear him, he said, and he cried as he was telling me. (A pause.) I feel so sorry for him, Daddy. He's not able to find work and he is alone here in Houston . . . (A pause.)

Will.

I ran into Ted Jr. at the bank, Lily Dale. He said they would like to find something for me to do at the company again, and I wanted to say, Go stuff it, but I didn't. I thanked him, and I have to tell you I may have to swallow my pride and go back there and see what they'll dole out to me.

Lily Dale.

Whatever you think best, Will. And you know what I've been thinking—maybe I could start teaching music and that would help us out, too.

Will.

If you like. It might give you something to think about. (A pause.)

Lily Dale.

Will?

Will.

Yes? (He takes her hand.) We're going to make it, Lily Dale. We always have.

Lily Dale.

I know. (A pause.) Will?

Will.

Yes.

Lily Dale.

Would you do me one last favor?

Will.

What is it?

Lily Dale.

Would you speak to Bill's friend? Let him tell you his side of the story. That is all he asks. Then he says he'll go away and leave us alone forever if you want him to. Would you see him, Will? He's outside in my car.

Will.

No.

Lily Dale.

Will.

Will.

No.

Lily Dale.

Why, Will? Why can't you just talk to him?

Will.

Because I don't want to, Lily Dale. Because there are things I'd have to ask him and I don't want to know the answers.

Lily Dale.

Like what?

Will.

You know the money I gave Bill at Christmas?

Lily Dale.

Yes. And that he spent.

Will.

And I told you I didn't know how he spent it. Well, I didn't tell you the truth. In his safety box there were some canceled checks totaling a hundred thousand dollars and they were all made out to his friend.

Lily Dale.

Will, maybe there was a reason.

Will.

Maybe so. But I don't want to know what it is. Ever. So tell him that for me. That I know my son gave him a hundred thousand dollars and maybe it was for his sick mother, too, or his sister, but I don't believe it. And I don't believe—anyway, whatever the reason, I don't want to know. There was a Bill

I knew and a Bill you knew and that's the only Bill
I care to know about.

Lily Dale.

What will I tell him?

Will.

Just tell him to please go away and leave us alone.

Lily Dale.

All right, Will. (She goes. Will goes to the phone.
He dials.)

Will.

Tom? . . . How about my coming in tomorrow? . . .
Early afternoon—all right. I'll be there. Thank you.
(He hangs up the phone. Lily Dale comes in.)

Lily Dale.

I told him, Will. He cried, Will, when I told him. He
said Bill insisted on giving him the money, for buying nice things. He said he was like a father to him
and he'd never known his father, and that—and he'd
go back to Atlanta now and not bother us anymore
and he was sorry if he had upset us in any way. He is
a sweet boy, Will, I don't care what anybody says. (A
pause.) He said, too, that he wished he could have
gone down in the water that day with Bill. That's how
much he loved him and missed him. (She's crying.)
Oh my God, Will, oh my God.

Will.

Don't cry, Lily Dale. Everything is going to be all
right. If I go back to work and you start teaching,
everything will be all right. (He holds her as the
lights fade.)

Scenes for Groups
of Three or More

The Chalk Garden

Enid Bagnold

❧

The Chalk Garden *opened in New York in 1955. This scene from the play takes place in a well-appointed room in a manor house in Sussex, England. Miss Madrigal has come to interview for a governess position with the old, overpowering Mrs. St. Maugham, whose granddaughter, aged sixteen, has frightened off many other governesses. There is something odd and secretive about Miss Madrigal and by the end of the play we find that she has just been released from prison after being granted a reprieve from her sentence for the murder of a stepsister, though there was some doubt about who actually committed the crime. The man in the scene is Maitland, a servant who has been with the St. Maugham family for years. In the following scene at the beginning of the play, Miss Madrigal is waiting for Mrs. St. Maugham who finally appears. A very short interlude with a nurse is deleted and marked with asterisks.*

MRS. ST. MAUGHAM, MISS MADRIGAL,
MAITLAND

Mrs. St. Maugham.
(Right of Maitland. Takes gloves off) I've tried all
the dentists! You can't fit false teeth to a woman of
character. (Gloves on up stage table. Hat off) As one
gets older and older, the appearance becomes such
a bore. (She sees Madrigal) Good morning. (Dis-
pleased—to Maitland) But I expected four appli-
cants!

Maitland.
Four came. Three have gone.

Mrs. St. Maugham.
And one wrote me such a good letter! Gone?

Maitland.
But I've kept this one.

Mrs. St. Maugham.
(to Madrigal) Shall we sit? (Gives Maitland her hat)
You can go, Maitland.
(Madrigal crosses down stage to sofa and sits. Maitland exits to pantry.)
(With a sudden and alarming charm) Now what
questions do total strangers put to one another? (Sits
armchair.)

Madrigal.
(Colourlessly) The name is Madrigal.
(Mrs. St. Maugham takes spectacles from apron
pocket and selects the ''Madrigal'' letter from the
table.)
I am the daughter of the late Ronald Bentham Madrigal, Rajputuna Hussars, Indian Army. He was the
son of General Bentham Madrigal—the Honourable
East India Company.

Mrs. St. Maugham.

No, no! That you can't be! The Honourable East India Company was dissolved in 1860! I'm an expert! My great-grandfather was Tarra Bethune, Governor of Madras, tried for corruption in 1859 and found guilty!

Madrigal.

(Calmly) My grandfather had my father at the age of seventy-five.

Mrs. St. Maugham.

(Admitting the point) That might make it possible. What experience have you?

Madrigal.

I have all private means. I have not taken such a post before.

Mrs. St. Maugham.

Why do you apply to me?

Madrigal.

The advertisement tempted me. I have been—somewhat alone.

Mrs. St. Maugham.

You will be able, I suppose to give me references?

Madrigal.

(Coldly) That will be difficult.

Mrs. St. Maugham.

What?

Madrigal.

In fact impossible.

******

Mrs. St. Maugham.

Ask ME questions, Miss Madrigal.

Madrigal.

Does one have a room to oneself?

(Maitland enters. Takes tray from up stage table.)

Mrs. St. Maugham.

Life without a room to oneself is a barbarity. Lunch-

eon is here with me and my granddaughter. Your
evening meal served in your room on a tray—

Maitland.

(Stopping on way out) That can't be done!

Mrs. St. Maugham.

(Automatically) Ma'am.

Maitland.

(As automatically) Ma'am.

Mrs. St. Maugham.

And why can't it?

(Telephone rings off left.)

Maitland.

(Left of her) Because I shall be busy serving at
Madam's table.

Mrs. St. Maugham.

I hear the telephone. (Maitland exits.) Now—now—
Miss Madrigal! We are so continuously interrupted—
Are you Church of England?

Madrigal.

(Whose mind is only on the telephone) My religion
is private. I should tell you—in case you should ask
me to—I don't answer the telephone.

Mrs. St. Maugham.

(Immediately interested) For what reason?

Madrigal.

I prefer not to. (As though realizing by Mrs. St.
Mauagham's attitude that more explanation is
needed) It disturbs me to join two worlds.

Mrs. St. Maugham.

Which—?

Madrigal.

The outside . . . and the inside one.

Maitland.

(Returning) They want you to open the village Summer Festival.

Mrs. St. Maugham.

Are they holding on?

Maitland.

They are.

Mrs. St. Maugham.

Ask them what attendance they can insure? Last time I opened something there was nobody there.

Maitland.

Madam is so unpopular.

Mrs. St. Maugham.

How do you know?

Maitland.

I heard it on all sides.

Mrs. St. Maugham.

They tell me that when I send you down to the post. Give me my engagement book. (Spectacles out.)

Maitland.

That's last year's.

Mrs. St. Maugham.

Give it me all the same. The dates are not so different. Have you lived in a village, Miss Madrigal? (Maitland, now Right of her, hands her the book.)

Madrigal.

(Mumbling) No, Mrs. St. Maugham—

Mrs. St. Maugham.

(Vaguely leafs through book) All the graces of life here go unvalued. In a village one is down to the bones of things. When I was at my height—though I lived here—I never knew them! They were waiting for my old age like wolves it seems! Tell them I won't open it. (Hands book back) (Maitland returns it to desk and exits to pantry.) Ah—where were we? My advertisement asks for handicraft. What handicraft do you suggest?

Madrigal.

I have ornamented a chapel.

Mrs. St. Maugham.

With your needle?

Madrigal.

With my brush. I have painted a twining plant on
the altar candles.

Mrs. St. Maugham.

(Immediately interested) But—as the candles burnt
down the painting must have melted away!

Madrigal.

THAT was the beauty of it! Is this a quiet house?

Mrs. St. Maugham.

Absolutely.

(Wild screams are heard off stage up the garden.
Maitland bursts in, rushes through to the garden.)

Maitland.

That child again—(Disappears up Right.)

Mrs. St. Maugham.

(Calm) My daughter's child. My granddaughter.
She's so fond of screaming.

Madrigal.

While I was waiting a young girl passed through the
room.

Mrs. St. Maugham.

That was she! She lives with me. Did she say anything?

Madrigal.

(Colourless) Nothing of consequence.

Mrs. St. Maugham.

Not the suicide of her father!

Madrigal.

I think she mentioned it!

Mrs. St. Maugham.

(Delighted) Oh Laurel—to make a drama—! He
died—poor man—of his liver!

Madrigal.

(As though it were a foible) She does not care for
the truth?

Mrs. St. Maugham.

No. But I encourage her. She loves a small lime-

light! One must be tender with her. Alas, he died
when she was three. Rich and a fine estate. Four
Van Dykes and unique Sheraton furniture. (Bitterly)
Her mother's one success—(Rises, to Left of table.)
But why speak of it! She married again.

Madrigal.

And where IS her mother?

Mrs. St. Maugham.

She follows the drum—as they say—in Arabia. Sta-
tioned abroad is the term, but I dislike military language. She is coming by ship—I am expecting her.

Madrigal.

(Rising) Would you sooner postpone—

Mrs. St. Maugham.

(To her) But she does not come here!—I should be
your employer.

Madrigal.

(Cautiously) She IS coming?

Mrs. St. Maugham.

In front of the child—we don't mention it. She is
coming.

(Madrigal sits again.)

One does not know why, though I shrewdly suspect
it. (Pauses, looks at miniature on the table) I have
an unworldy daughter. She was always crying out
after being simple. That's hard to understand. It
seems such a waste, with all the chances of life, to
want to be simple. Privilege and power make selfish people—but gay ones—(Breaks off) Forgive
me, Miss Madrigal, for being personal. (Miniature
back) But irritation is like a rash on the heart! (Sits
again.)

Madrigal.

(To change the subject) The child—is she fond of
her stepfather?

Mrs. St. Maugham.

(Indifferent) I never asked. His rank is Colonel. My grand-daughter has developed an interesting mother-hatred, which is clearly explained in Freud. You have had experience? You feel competent to deal with such things?

Madrigal.

(Dreamily) For the worse—or the better—

Mrs. St. Maugham.

You seem absent in mind!

Madrigal.

(Pulling herself together again) Not in mind—but in manner. (Pursily) The child is naturally alienated—that a sexlife has broken out again in her mother.

Mrs. St. Maugham.

You put it well. Exactly. The child was frenzied. (The house phone rings.) When nothing would stop the wedding—she ran from the hotel into the dark—

(Second ring.)

Madrigal.

There seems to be bell ringing.

(Phone stops.)

Mrs. St. Maugham.

(Getting up and talking as she crosses Right to house telephone)—and by some extra-ordinary carelessness she was violated in Hyde Park at the age of twelve. It has upset her nerves. We are waiting as it were for calmer weather. (Picking up house telephone) You want me, Pinkerbell? One moment—(Hand over phone) Of course we put it less strongly to her mother. Apart from certain fixations connected with fire, she is a charming intelligent girl. I should value your impressions. (Into phone) What's that! (Listens.) I did. I ordered it. The Extract of Humus—for the seed boxes. (Listening) It should have come. I'll ring. I'll ring and ask him. (Is about to put the receiver from her but is recalled by the voice) I know! I know! But one can't get perfection, Pinkbell! (Replaces receiver on hook. To herself) Oh. . . . isn't jealousy terrible! (Moving above chair.)

Madrigal.

(With surprising force) Yes.

Mrs. St. Maugham.

You made me jump. He's my butler. Forty years my butler. Now he's had a stroke but he keeps his finger on things. (Rings handbell. Keeps bell.)

Madrigal.

He carries on at death's door.

Mrs. St. Maugham.

His standards rule this house.

Madrigal.

(Absently) You must be fond of him.

Mrs. St. Maugham.

Alas no. (Below chair) He trains Maitland—but now Maitland won't go near him. But I shall overcome it. (Sits.) He's so good with the garden. (Rings bell again, over back of chair.)

Madrigal.

Maitland?

Mrs. St. Maugham.

Pinkbell. He directs mine from his window. All butlers dream of gardening. (Puts bell on table) We spoke of references. Who will speak for you?

Madrigal.

(In her sing-song voice.) No one will speak for me— Extract of Humus is too rich for summer biennials.

(Maitland enters up Centre from garden. To Left of Mrs. St. Maugham.)

Mrs. St. Maugham.

Has a bag of humus been delivered at the back door?

Maitland.

There's a sack there.

Mrs. St. Maugham.

When did it come?

Maitland.

Days ago.

Mrs. St. Maugham.

And you walk by it and ignore it! How do you know someone hasn't sent me a brace of pheasants! Mr. Pinkbell says you must report and at once everything that comes to the back door.

Maitland.

(Suddenly reaching his limit) I WON'T TAKE ORDERS FROM THE OLD BASTARD!

Mrs. St. Maugham.

Am I to have trouble with you, Maitland?

Maitland.

(Breaking) Oh, if I could please and be sure of myself!

Mrs. St. Maugham.

(Quiet, menacing) Maitland—

Maitland.

Oh, if things would go smoothly!

Mrs. St. Maugham.

MAITLAND! (With deliberation and distinctness) Bring me the Creme de Menthe and two glasses. (Maitland's chest fills with emotion. He seems about to burst. He obeys and rushes out through his door. Fanning her face with handkerchief) Touch and go! How frail is authority. What were you saying?

Madrigal.

When?

Mrs. St. Maugham.

About humus and summer biennials.

Madrigal.

(Tonelessly, sleepwalking) Don't pep up the soil before birth. It leads them on to expect—what life won't give them.

Mrs. St. Maugham.

(Suddenly reminded) What was that plant you painted on the candles?

Madrigal.

(With inner pleasure, as though she were eating a sweet) Lapagaria. Sub-tropical. With waxy umbels.

Mrs. St. Maugham.

Lady Dorchester had it in her wedding bouquet after the battle of the Marne! I had forgotten it! Could I grow it in my greenhouse?

Madrigal.

(By rote.) It needs the early actinic rays. Exclude the sun again at midday. Counteract the high lime-content in your soil with potash.

Mrs. St. Maugham.

Where did you learn about such things?

Madrigal.

I was put in charge of—

Mrs. St. Maugham.

What?

Madrigal.

A garden.

Maitland.

(Enters, carrying everything most correctly—liqueur bottle, two small glasses, silver tray, and even a clean napkin over his arm. Sets down tray. Then, straightening himself) I wish to give my notice.

Mrs. St. Maugham.

(Eyes like steel) If I take it you will not get it back again.

Maitland.

I am prepared for that.

Mrs. St. Maugham.

(Terrible) Are you?

Maitland.

(Immediately broken) You know I can't stand criticism! Every time a word's said against me a month's work is undone!

Mrs. St. Maugham.

We all make mistakes.

Maitland.

(Passionately) But nothing should be said about them! Praise is the only thing that brings to life again a man that's been destroyed! But oh if I leave—what will you do without me! (Another scream is heard from the garden.)—and what will the child do! (Runs off into the garden up Right.)

Mrs. St. Maugham.

(Smiling in triumph) Do you know the secret of authority, Miss Madrigal? Changes of mood. The inexplicable. The thunder, the lightning, and the sudden sun. He won't leave me! Will you have a Creme de Menthe?

Madrigal.

(Stiffly) I never touch alcohol.

Mrs. St. Maugham.

(Filling glass) Certainly he makes scenes. But I like them. He has been a prisoner.

Madrigal.

(Pause) A prisoner!

Mrs. St. Maugham.

Five years. Now that there are no subject races, one must be served by the mad, the sick, and those who can't take their place in the outside world—and served I must be. (Drinks.)

Morning's at Seven

Paul Osborn

❧

This play takes place in a small town in the Midwest in the 1930s. Four sisters, all in their sixties, live in this same town. Two of them, Cora and Ida, live next door to each other, and their back porches and backyards provide the setting of the play. The third sister, Arry, who is unmarried, lives with Cora and Cora's husband, Thor. Though Ida and another sister, Esther, have suspected an ongoing relationshiop between Arry and Thor, we discover that there has been just one indiscretion between them forty years ago. No other intimacies have occurred in the intervening years, but they have obviously continued to be fond of each other and enjoy each other's companionship. At the end of the play, Arry elects to leave Cora and Thor alone in a new house.

ARRY, ESTHER, IDA, THOR, CORA

(The door of the house at right opens and Esther comes out. She has hold of Arry's hand and is pulling her. Arry is drawing back.)

Arry.

What do you want to talk to me about?

Esther.

Oh, come on, Arry. We're not going to hurt you.

Arry.

(Drawing back.) I don't trust you, Esty. When you start talking—. (She suddenly comes out with a rush. Ida, who has given her a push, appears in the door behind her—steps to the right of her.) Hey! Quit that! What'd you push me for?

Ida.

I didn't push you.

Arry.

You did too.

Ida.

I just wanted to come out and you were blocking the way.

Arry.

What's going on here anyway? (They are at each side of her—she looks from one to the other.) I'm going back in. (She starts to duck into the house. Ida grabs one arm—Esther the other.)

Esther.

Oh, no, you're not.

Ida.

You're coming right along with us.

Arry.

(Struggling.) You let go of me. Let go of me!

Esther.

Oh, be quiet, Arry.

Arry.

Let go of me! (Screaming.) Let go of me!

Esther.

Oh, my goodness. Let go of her, Ida.

                    (They let go of Arry.)

Arry.

Thank you. Thank you so much. (She starts up steps.)

Esther.

Go on back in. If you don't want to hear what we have to say, you don't need to.

Arry.

(Stops—turns slowly.) I didn't say I wouldn't like to hear what you had to say, Esty, but when one person wishes to talk to another, there are certain rules of nice behavior they try to observe.

Esther.

(Trying not to giggle.) I'm sorry, Arry.

Arry.

I doubt very much whether in the best society you would find one person approaching the back of another person and pushing them from behind.

Ida.

I'm sorry, Arry. We just wanted to have a little talk with you. Of course, if you don't care to—

Arry.

I'd be very glad to. (She walks over to the stump, sits. Faces Esther and Ida.) Well, Esther!

Esther.

Well, Arry, I'll tell you. It's about Thor and Cora moving up to Homer's house—.

(Arry jumps up and starts to run in.)

Arry.

Oh, no, you don't! I know you, Esty!

Esther.

(As she and Ida stop Arry.) Now wait a minute, Arry.

Arry.

(Between them.) I don't want to talk about it.

Ida.

You GOT to talk about it.

Arry.

I knew I shouldn't have trusted you—.

Esther.

Why? What do you think we're going to say?

Arry.

You're going to say Thor and Cora ought to move up there.

Esther.

Well, don't you think they should?

Arry.

No, I don't.

Ida.

Why not?

Arry.

Just because I don't, that's all.

Esther.

But if Cora wants to—and Thor wants to—.

Arry.

Thor doesn't want to.

Ida.

How do you know?

Arry.

(Hesitating.) Well, I—I don't think he does—

Esther.

Why, have you talked to him?

Arry.

Well, I—Not much.

Esther.

Then you're not sure, are you?

Arry.

No, I'm not sure—.

Ida.

Then if he does want to and Cora wants to—why, it would be pretty nice for them, don't you think? (Arry, trapped, moves back to the stump. They watch her.)

Arry.

(Sullenly—sits.) I don't know what business it is of yours anyway.

Esther.

Strictly speaking, I don't suppose it is. But after all, we're sisters. And it means so much to Cora . . . I'm just thinking of her happiness.

Arry.

And what about MY happiness?

Esther.

Well, in this case, certainly Cora's happiness is the one to consider.

Arry.

I don't see why.

Esther.

Don't you? Cora wants to live alone with Thor, Arry.

Arry.

(Suddenly vicious.) Well, she's not going to!

Ida.

Oh, isn't she?

Arry.

Over my dead body she is. If they try anything there's a few things I can tell—.

Ida.

You've made that threat a lot of times, Arry—.

Arry.

I mean it.

Esther.

What could you tell, Arry?

Arry.

Plenty.

Esther.

What could you tell that all of us don't already know? That we haven't all known for years? (Sudden pause. Arry looks up at Esther, startled.)

Arry.

(Softly.) What do you mean, Esty? (She looks at Ida, frightened, and back at Esther. In a whisper.) What do you mean?

Ida.

Do you think we're all blind, Arry?

Esther.

Don't you think all of us know by this time about you and Thor?

(Pause.)

Arry.

(Frightened.) No—no—Esty—.

Ida.

We've all known for years. All of us.

Arry.

No—no—.

Esther.

But we've all kept our mouths shut for Cora's sake. If you want to make a nasty business out of it go on and do it. But it won't get you anywhere, Arry. And you won't look so nice, carrying on for years with the husband of your own sister right under her very nose—.

Arry.

(Shocked—rises.) Esty! Esty, what do you mean? You don't think—Ida, you don't think—that Thor and me—all this time—Oh, my God!

(She buries her face in her hands. Ida and Esther watch uneasily.)

Ida.

What do you mean, Arry?

Arry.

(Moaning—sits stump.) Oh, my God! Oh, my God!

Esther.

(Uneasily.) But you've always hinted in front of everyone, Arry—.

Arry.

You've all thought that Thor and me—all these years—Does Cora think that?

Esther.

I don't know, Arry. Nobody's ever said anything to Cora. I guess Cora doesn't think anything.

Arry.

(Suddenly she turns toward the house. Rises, and yells with a sudden frenzied frightenedness.) Thor! Thor! Thor!

Esther.

(She and Ida move down right.) Arry—. Wait—.

Arry.

Thor! Thor!

Thor.

(Hurries out of the house right.) What's the matter? What's the matter, Arry?

Arry.

They say that—. They think that—.

(Cora has entered between the houses. She stops, frozen, watching the scene.)

Cora.

Why, Arry, what's the matter?

(Arry hesitates a minute—looks at Cora—then suddenly runs into the house, weeping.)

Thor.

What's the matter with her?

Esther.

(Starting into house.) I don't quite know. I'll find out.

Thor.

What did you say to her, Esty?

Cora.

(Hard.) Yes. What did you say to her?

Esther.

(Looking at Cora.) We just had a little fuss, Cora.

Cora.
About what?

> (Pause. Esty looks at Cora.)

Esther.
I'll tell you later. (She exits.)

Cora.
Thor! (He turns and sees her watching him.) I wonder what she could have said to Arry?

Thor.
I don't know, Cora. Maybe she said something Arry
didn't like so much.

Cora.
Yes, she must have. I wonder what it could have been?

Thor.
I don't know, Cora.

> (Pause. Cora turns to Ida brightly.)

Cora.
Ida, has Carl still got those packing cases he used
to have in his garage?

Ida.
(Mystified.) Why—I don't know, Cora—.

Cora.
Harold Blake hasn't got any. He says he can move
Thor and me up day after tomorrow, but he just
hasn't got any packing cases.
(Thor looks at her startled.)

Thor.
(Hesitantly.) Day after tomorrow?

Cora.
Uh-huh! (To Ida.) Can we go over and see if they're
still there? (She has started off left.)

Ida.
(Following) Yes—of course—.

Thor.
But Cora—but Cora—. (They go off left—Thor
watches them. He sits on ledge—depressed.) The
day after tomorrow! Good God!

The Octette Bridge Club

P. J. Barry

❧

This play takes place in a Rhode Island town in 1944. Eight sisters have been meeting to play bridge for many years. Betsy, the youngest, who is forty-seven, had been hospitalized at Quidnekka Hall, a mental hospital, and has just rejoined the group. In the following scene, the last in the play, they are in the living room of one of the sisters where they are celebrating Halloween by being in costume.

ANN, ALICE, LIL, MARY, CONNIE, MARTHA, BETSY, NORA

Ann.
  (Returning.) Here we are, Lil.
Alice.
  Open it.
Lil.
  Of course I'll open it. If I didn't you'd all kill me. Oh, what pretty wrapping, Ann.
Mary.
  Isn't it?

419

Connie.

Let's hear it for the pretty wrapping!

All.

Rah! Rah! Rah!

Martha.

I wonder what it is.

Lil.

(Getting it open.) Oh. It's . . . it's . . . what is it, Ann? Oh, it's . . . ?

Ann.

Bubble bath. Evergreen bubble bath balls. Just what you needed, Lil.

Lil.

Oh. I see.

Connie.

Certainly Little Red Riding Hood needs a good evergreen bubble bath.

Ann.

It's supposed to be very soothing. Evergreen.

Betsy.

It is. They have wonderful evergreens at Quidnekka Hall. I took long walks most—

Ann.

That time is over with! Stop bringing it up . . . it's unpleasant and it's over. Don't dwell on it.

Betsy.

You're beginning to sound like Martha.

Ann.

(Warmer.) It's in the past. You're well now. You're recovered. You're back with us . . . and that makes all of us happy. For five months there was no Octette Bridge Club.

Lil.

If you keep talking about it again and again you have no choice but to remember sad things because it was a sad time for you. So let's be happy.

Mary.

    Yes.   **Alice.** Please.

Betsy.

But I want to be aware of what I went through. It was painful, but it was good. Quidnekka Hall helped me. Dr. Chisholm—

Ann.

Betsy, you must remember . . . like I do . . . that it does no good to think about oneself too much. The best thing to do is—

Betsy.

There's nothing wrong with thinking about yourself.

Ann.

There are better things to do . . . such as utilizing that spare time, filling up that time with prayers for Danny off fighting for his country. I know that helps me.

Betsy.

And do you fill up that spare time praying for your husband? Do you pray that he'll stop drinking?

Ann.

(Taken aback.) Yes, I pray that his drinking will . . . lessen. Would anyone like any more tea or coffee or ginger ale? Cookies?

Betsy.

I'm not even sure if I believe in God anymore.

Alice.

Of course you believe in God. We all do.

Betsy.

In Quidnekka Hall—

Martha.

That is enough. Stop talking about—

Betsy.

(Determined.) In Quidnekka Hall, IN THAT HOS-PITAL, I thought a lot about us. And when things were dark and bad, I'd be glad that the Octette

Bridge Club would go on and on . . . come rain or come shine . . .

Lil.

Sleet or snow!

Alice.

War or peace!

Betsy.

But us . . . we eight sisters . . . (Rising.) . . . I realized that we never talk to one another about anything serious.

Lil.

We all talk too much . . . if you ask me.

Betsy.

Sisters . . . but not close.

Lil.

Let's have some songs.

Alice.

Oh, yes.

Lil.

How about SHINE ON HARVEST MOON? (Begins to play.)

Betsy.

Can't I finish talking?

Lil.

I'm trying to cheer you up.

Betsy.

(Crossing to Lil.) You're trying to shut me up. (Lil stops playing.) I was so depressed . . . so unhappy . . . and I tried to—

Alice.

Betsy, don't.   **Martha.** NO.

Betsy.

I tried to commit suicide.

Alice.

This is our Thirteenth Anniversary. Don't spoil it.

Betsy.

(Her courage growing.) I remember our third anni-

versary . . . ten years ago . . . here. That was the
night the trouble started for me. Connie gave me a
ride home, and I went inside, paid Mary Lou for
babysitting, got my scissors from my sewing basket
and I cut up the kitchen curtains I'd just made. And
for . . . well, the next ten years . . Doctor Carroll
would call my . . . misbehaviors the flu, . . . or
nerves . . . and I'd be in bed for a week or two. Once
I remember smashing all my Norataki China . . .
Ann came over and helped me clean it up, and the
next day I went to that psychiatrist who had such
bad teeth and he gave me those pills that made me
so groggy all the time. But every other Friday . . .
the Octette Bridge Club was always something I
looked forward to . . . safe. Oh, all of you seemed to
think I was stupid, but—

Nora.

No.

Betsy.

I had the chance here to prove that I wasn't! I could
win! I became something, a good bridge player . . .
my claim to fame and fortune. (Pause.) I don't know
why I did what I did. (Pause.) It was a beautiful
day; and I was cleaning our room. When I finished
I took Dan's pants and jackets and went out in the
backyard and had a bonfire, and when everything
was burned I went back inside and went into the
bathroom and slashed my wrists.

Ann.

Don't.

Martha.

You weren't yourself.

Betsy.

Dan had to commit me . . . he didn't have much
choice. But I wanted to go, I think I wanted to go
years before. I needed help. (Pause; attempting to
override her tears.) Why didn't you come to see me?

Oh, you sent gifts and cards and flowers . . . but not one of you came to see me. My sisters. (Pause.) That hurt so much.

Nora.

(Long pause.) The doctor said..Dan said . . . it was best that we didn't visit.

Betsy.

That was only in the beginning, Nora, for the first month.

Lil.

We didn't know what to do.

Alice.

We wanted to visit.

Ann.

We thought it was best. All of us agreed, it was a mutual agreement. We went to mass together for you, we prayed for your quick recovery. Our prayers were answered.

Connie.

Baloney! We didn't want anybody gossiping about the wonderful saintly Donavan girls . . . the scandal! or anybody seeing us going in and out of Quidnekka Hall as if anybody would in Woonsocket. But when Martha had her operation we were there in full force. And when Mary had her stroke . . . we were there. But going inside THAT place? Quidnekka Hall? (Pause) I guess we were all frightened. More baloney! No excuses . . . Pretty disgraceful conduct . . . all of us.

Ann.

We agreed—

Connie.

I know we agreed.

Martha.

(Restrained.) It was a majority rule.

Connie.

And it was wrong. (To Betsy.) I should've gone to visit you. We all should've. I'm ashamed.

Nora.

So am I.

Mary.

So am I.

Lil.

Me, too. (Ann, Alice and Martha nod reluctantly.)

Connie.

Can you forgive us?

Betsy.

(Pause.) In time.

Connie.

Alice has a new Bulova. Give her thirty seconds, Alice.

Betsy.

More time than that.

Connie.

Okay. We're patient.

Betsy.

What I wanted to say earlier, I couldn't say it, I wanted to dance first, surprise you all.

Martha.

You did.

Betsy.

What I wanted to say was that this is my last game with the Octette Bridge Club.

Lil.

What do you mean?

Betsy.

Tonight is my last game.

Nora.

No.

Mary.

Betsy.   **Martha.** What?

Ann.

Is this some kind of revenge because we didn't come to visit you?

Betsy.

No, it's more than that. I get lost with all of you. I want to do my own walking.

Connie.

You've always been a walker.

Betsy.

You know what I'm saying.

Alice.

Betsy, please change your mind.

Lil.

Please, Betsy.

Nora.

You're part of us.

Mary.

Please.

Martha.

Don't beg. Baby brat.

Betsy.

Damn it, I'm trying to grow up.

Martha.

Stop that swearing!

Betsy.

I'll speak as I please.

Martha.

(A volcano slowly erupts; rising.) Oh, aren't you brave, you're so brave! Well, go, desert us! Good riddance to bad rubbish, I say.

Connie.

That's a rotten thing to—

Martha.

You think you're the only one who's ever suffered? Well, I know heartbreak, too, I know adultery! Michael was deserting us, leaving his family, moving out to live with a waitress, a tramp with dyed red hair. She even had the nerve to show up at his wake!

Nora.

None of us knew that.

Martha.

Do I broadcast my pain? Did I ever? No, not like some! No one knew, no one! Michael said he couldn't stand being around such a self righteous..prude anymore. Broke my heart . . . I know heartbreak! (Uncontrollable sobbing takes over; pause.) Don't anyone touch me, don't! (Pause.) I begged him to reconsider . . . got down on my knees and begged him. He agreed to stay the week. In the morning on his way to work just as he started across Main Street that drunken driver hit him. (Gaining control of herself; pause.) I don't know why I told you all that. Unless there's a lesson to be learned. Yes, yes, there is, Betsy. You see what happens to deserters? God is watching. Do you see?

Betsy.

(Laughs.) I don't think I will get hit by a car tonight on my way home. If there is a God, I think he's merciful.

Martha.

IF? You should have your face slapped.

Betsy.

You'd be happy to do that . . . the way you did when I was a child.

Martha.

You were only slapped if you misbehaved.

Betsy.

I always misbehaved according to your—

Martha.

You deserved it!

Betsy.

You go to hell!

Mary.

(Near tears.) Betsy—Martha, STOP! (Pause.) Listen, Betsy, please. We are close. Eight of us born from the same woman, STRONG when we're together. And for me . . . it's been the joy of my life. I am so grateful for the gift of my sisters. I love you all so much. (Pause.) I won't be here much longer. There. I've said it out loud. (Pause.) Don't cry, Alice. I'm not afraid. (Pause.) Betsy, I'm not very demonstrative . . . maybe that's what you mean about us . . . come to me now. (Mary offers her arms. Betsy doesn't move.) Come . . . and embrace me. (Betsy moves to her, kneels down and they embrace.) Hug your sister, each of you. (All hesitate, looking to one another. Then they all begin. It is slow and awkward, but an attempt. It takes time. Long pause.)

Connie.

(After awkwardly hugging Ann.) You have bad breath.

Ann.

I do not.

(Lil sings a brief excerpt from a popular toothpaste jingle of the period.)

Connie.

We were never great huggers, any of us.

Betsy.

Except me.

Connie.

You're the exception to a lot. (And Connie hugs Betsy.)

Mary.

Nice if we could live forever.

Lil.

How about an old favorite? (And she's off to the piano.)

Nora.

Good idea, Lil.

Betsy.

I meant what I said.

Connie.

I know you did. But tonight's tonight. And it's our Thirteenth Anniversary!

Alice.

Thirteen is an unlucky number.

Nora.

Always was.

Ann.

Always will be.

Martha.

We're Catholics. We're not superstitious. (They all laugh.)

Connie.

(Moving Mary to the piano.) Mary, before you run off into the woods with John Alden, let's sing.

(Lil begins to play and sing an old favorite and they begin to move toward the piano, joining in the song. Nora approaches Betsy and kisses her on the cheek. Then Nora joins the singers and then Betsy does the same. But in a moment she turns around, aware of Martha a distance from her. She moves a step or two toward her. The two now stand on a parallel line, space between them as the singing continues and Betsy glances at Martha as the lights fade.)

THE END

The Oldest Profession

Paula Vogel

❦

This play has a long production history, first being staged as a reading in 1981 and then produced in Canada in 1988, at Brown University in 1990, and in Hartford, Connecticut, in 1991. As the title would indicate, all five characters of the play are prostitutes. Paula Vogel, a quality playwright whose work is becoming well-known, deals with these elderly characters in a touching, humorous, and slightly tongue-in-cheek fashion. Mae, eighty-three and the madam, is concerned for her "girls." The others accept her leadership role and their different personalities are revealed as the scene unfolds. They are Vera, the youngest at seventy-two; Edna, seventy-four, next in line and a good-time girl; Lillian, seventy-five, a woman of style and audacity; and Ursula, seventy-nine, bossy, set, and determined. The setting is a park bench on 72nd Street and Broadway in New York City on a sunny day in 1980. Mae has insulted and chased off a young prostitute.

VERA, EDNA, LILLIAN, URSULA, MAE

Mae.

When a woman can't defend her territory or her girls, it's time to get out of the Life. I tell you, it makes me sad. When I see the new generation of prostitutes working right on the street—gypsies, all of them—on their own with no group, no house to call their own, no amenities for customers, no tradition or . . . or finesse . . . where's the pride in the name of prostitute? It's all gone downhill since the government poked their nose in our business and booted decent self-respecting businesswomen out of Storeyville. Remember the House where we all first met? A spick-and-span establishment. The music from Professor Joe in the parlor; the men folk bathed, their hair combed back and dressed in their Sunday best, waiting downstairs happy and shy. We knew them all: knew their wives and kids, too. It was always Mr. Buddy or Mr. Luigi; never this anonymous "john" for any stranger with a Jackson in his billfold.

Ursula.

And we were called Miss Ursula and Miss Lillian too . . . Men who treated their wives and mothers right treated their mistresses right, too.

Mae.

There was honor in the trade . . . My father went to Storeyville often when I was a girl. Mother used to nod to Miss Sophie right in the street before Mass in the Quarter. Miss Sophie saved our lives, she did. The depression of '97—Papa lost work and there were seven of us to feed. So every morning before folks were up and about, Miss Sophie came and put groceries on the back step—Papa was a regular customer, she couldn't let us starve. And none of the neighbors knew a thing. Finally Papa got work again; the money came in for food on the table and Saturday nights at Miss Sophie's. And then my mother got pregnant again—I guess there was plenty of my father to go around. Mother had a boy. So Miss Sophie said she'd be real pleased if they named that boy after her gentleman protector. So they named my brother—

Lillian and Vera.

(In unison) Radcliffe.

Vera.

I love that story. It's such a nice name, too. So re-fined.

Ursula.

(Irritated) We've heard that old story before, Mae. The best thing that ever happened was the day the Navy closed Storeyville down because too many boys were jumping ship.

Edna.

You always say that, Ursula. I liked Storeyville when it was legal.

Ursula.

Oh, sure. The working girls loved Storeyville.

Mae.

We would have been Number One in the District if those military police hadn't of busted us. Hauled us to jail and slammed the door shut. And then the bulldozers came in overnight.

Ursula.

(Frustrated) I just can't get you to understand the Law of Supply and Demand. Anything Black Mar-ket fetches a higher price. Prohibition was the best thing for the liquor market—

Lillian.

Uh-oh!! Ursula's off again about Prohibition! Check the bathtubs!

Ursula.

That's not funny! I was making a pretty penny in 1927 until someone—one of you! snitched on me. Butted their nose in my business. I'm still gonna find out who it was—

(Ursula glares at Lillian; Lillian, Vera and Edna look blank.)

Mae.

Hold the line right here! Lillian, Ursula's arrest record is not a subject for levity. You hear me?

Lillian.

(Mild.) I can still hear you.

Mae.

Second thing, for the record, I'm glad someone put a stop to your bathtub gin, Ursula. We were new here, and the last thing we could afford was to bring the law down on us. We're in the Life, not the distillery business.

Ursula.

Well, we're not going to stay in the Life, Mae, unless you stop living in the past! It's a New Age: We've got to get off our fannies and sell!

Mae.

Oh? Exactly what are you trying to tell me, Ursula?

Ursula.

Smell the coffee! "Fair words butter no parsnips!" It takes different strategies to stay afloat in today's competitive market; that little chippy will be back.

Mae.

If that little clapbox shows again, I'll—

Ursula.

What? Beat her with your purse? Call her names? Have a stroke in the process?

Mae.

Well, have you got any better ideas?

Ursula.

I won't mince words, Mae. We've been working

together too long for that. What's needed around here are new management ideas at the helm; someone who can make this business cost-effective.

Vera.

Cost-effective?

Mae.

And I suppose that person is you, Ursula.

Ursula.

That's right. "He that is wise is he that is rich."

Mae.

And what exactly would you do differently from me?

Ursula.

Advertise.

Lillian.

Advertise! Just lift your skirts, Ursula.

Ursula.

Advertising's the soul of the modern marketplace. First thing to do is to place pithy personals in the VILLAGE VOICE.

Mae.

VILLAGE VOICE? Who reads the VILLAGE VOICE?

Ursula.

A younger clientele. We've got to face the facts: Our gentlemen callers are a dying breed. Or they're in the hospital; or when you do get them in bed at home they can't get it up anymore.

Mae.

Still, they do the honorable thing by us. They pay.

Lillian.

You mean we'd have younger customers? We'd end up paying them.

Ursula.

No, I don't think so. New York's a city of diversified tastes. I think we could specialize. You know, we could seek out a HAROLD AND MAUDE situation. (Grandly.) We could cater to the complexes of a small circle.

Vera.

Edna, what is she talking about? Who the hell is Harold?

Mae.

(To Ursula.) I don't think we want to know any more ideas that are cost-effective. You're upsetting the girls.

Lillian.

Not me. She's entertaining me.

Ursula.

Wait. Let me have my say. We should up our fees. Change to a price list. Instead of seven dollars an hour, we could start with a seven-dollar minimum, and charge for the extras. We have to increase the rate of turnover, and make the girls more time-efficient. Lillian here stays in bed with Mr. Loman much too long . . .

Lillian.

Well, I just can't jump into bed and jump out anymore, Ursula. It's not my fault, it's the arthritis—

Ursula.

"It's a poor workman that blames his tools . . ."

Mae.

Are you through?

Ursula.

Then there's Entertainment Surcharge, Linen Tax, Mastercharge, Visa and—

Edna.

She's been reading the WALL STREET JOURNAL again.

Lillian.

No, Dale Carnegie's HOW TO WIN FRIENDS AND INFLUENCE PEOPLE. She's halfway through the course; she can influence people.

Ursula.

Well, I'll keep my advice to myself in the future. "A bumblebee in a cow turd thinks himself a king."

Mae.

I've listened to you, and now you're going to listen to me, Ursula Thaller. I've kept you girls together for over forty-five years. When we were closed down in Storeyville, I paid your bail: all of you got your train tickets North and a place to live. All of our gentlemen here are nice, and good to us, with a codicil in the will now and then. There's always been money for the doctor when any of you girls are sick, and food on the table. And you know I've never held back on anyone. If any of you girls want to leave this stable for greener pastures, you can go. No hard feelings. Well?

Lillian.

I stick with Mae.

Vera.

Oh, dear. I hate to see fighting on such a beautiful day. Let's forget the whole thing.

Edna.

Well, I think . . . I think . . it's not time for a change. Not now.

Mae.

Well. That's settled, then. You should be proud, Ursula, that you're apprentice to a Madam.

Ursula.

I say whoopee-ding. For the past fifteen years—you call that merit promotion?

Mae.

When I go, you'll get your chance. You're Second-in-Command. I think we're all agreed upon that. When you carry me out feet first, Ursula's in charge and you're all going to listen to her as if to me. It's important to me that we keep together. When I pass away, I'd like to think of you all carrying on.

Lillian.

Nonsense, Mae. You're as strong as a horse.

Vera.

(Trembling.) Oh, Mae . . .

Mae.

(Looking at Ursula.) I don't intend to go anywhere, yet.

Ursula.

I'm only trying to point out the facts of life. "Old Vessels Leak." You forgot to collect the money from this morning, Mae. You're losing your touch.

Mae.

(Sniffs.) I did NOT forget. I was . . . (Clears her throat.) . . . I was just about to get around to that. You know, Ursula, you're a whore with the soul of a businesswoman. And I'm a businesswoman with the soul of a whore. And THAT is the difference between us. (Briskly.) Ladies, please get out your purses and have your money ready.

(The women rustle through their handbags.)

Mae.

All right, then: Vera, what do you have to report?

(Vera stands and walks toward Mae; she hands over her money.)

Vera.

I have seven dollars plus a one-dollar tip.

Mae.

Seven dollars plus a one-dollar tip. That's eight.

Edna.

(As Vera walks back.) Well? Did he come today?

(The other women laugh.)

Vera.

I don't think it's nice of you to make fun of Mr. Francis behind his back . . . he tries so hard.

Lillian.

That answers your question, Edna.

Ursula.

I don't understand why the fool tips if he doesn't get anything out of the deal . . .

Vera.

(Tenderly) It's not just for the sex, Ursula. I . . . I hold him when he cries . . . He's a very nice man.

Edna.

Mr. Francis's idea of a lay is lying down.

Mae.

He's a good and regular customer. Always pays up. Edna? What do you have?

(Edna struts over with pride to Mae and hands her the money.)

Edna.

Fourteen AND two dollars and fifty cents in tips.

Lillian.

Good show.

Mae.

Yes, that's good. Fourteen plus $2.50. That makes $16.50.

(Edna walks back.)

Edna.

And I had to work my ass for every penny. Mr. Andrew was a lamb, as always, but Mr. Benjamin! All around the room he was! I told him, "Mr. Benjamin, you'd make an eighteen year old scream!!" God, he's one cocky man . . .

Ursula.

(Dour) It must be the medication he's on.

Vera.

Whatever it is, I wish he could lend Mr. Francis some . . .

Mae.

Mr. Benjamin's very fond of you, Edna. He's told me. So then, we're up to Lillian. Lillian? (Lillian does not rise.) Well, Lillian, what about this morning?

Lillian.

(hesitating.) I hope you won't be mad at me, Mae. But I didn't know what to do . . . I

Ursula.

Do about what?

Mae.

Didn't you go up to Mr. Loman's room at 11:30?

Lillian.

Yes, I went. But . . .

Mae.

(Warning.) Ursula. . . .

Lillian.

I went at the appointed time; I kept my side of the bargain . . . but he's not very well.

Mae.

Did he cancel?

Lillian.

No, not exactly . . . he's all right in that department. I gave him the usual, but when it came time for payment . . .

Mae.

Ah, I see. Short of cash, long on horn?

Lillian.

No, he paid. He paid with these. (Draws out of her purse long silk stockings circa 1945, with the seam running down the middle.) He insisted that I take these for payment. Said he's paid a lot of money for them while on the road in Boston; he . . . he said they were hard to get, what with the war going on and all. Mr. Loman thinks that stockings and chocolate are a better bet than our currency as long as . . . as long as the "Japanese are beating the pants off our boys in the Pacific Theatre." Those were his exact words.

Mae.

Ah, I see.

(There is a respectful silence as the women realize that Mr. Loman has lost his marbles.)

Mae.

Well, I think you did the right thing, Lillian.

Ursula.

The right thing! Look at them! No one's wearing stockings with garter belts anymore! What good are they?

Lillian.

I've been wearing a garter belt on Saturday morning for Mr. Loman; he's partial to 'em.

Edna.

I agree with Mr. Loman. They make women look sexy; it's definitely a "turn-on" . . .

Ursula.

That's besides the point! This is worse than passing a bad check . . .

Lillian.

Mae, what are we going to do? About Mr. Loman I mean?

Mae.

(Slowly.) I don't know. He's been left alone for too long.

Lillian.

He looks forward to my visit once a week so much . . .

Ursula.

Well, we can't have charity cases hanging on— we're not Meals on Wheels! (To herself.) Chocolates and stockings! What good are they? They're not even staples . . .

Edna.

Maybe we should say something to someone in charge at Jefferson Square . . .

Mae.

That's the least we can do. Thing is, though, Jefferson Square's just apartments; the front desk doesn't look out for the tenants. They think they've done their responsibility just because they've installed handle bars by the toilet and the tub. If we tell them that Mr. Loman's deteriorating, they'll say he should go to a home.

(Pause.)

Lillian.

He was doing just fine . . . until this morning. Maybe it's temporary.

Mae.

It's not a good sign. Maybe he should go to a home. Jefferson Square's designed for folks with all their fixtures in working condition. Does he have any relations, Lillian?

Lillian.

Two good-for-nothing sons who are only God-knows-where.

Mae.

(Wearily.) Well, I'll drop by there tonight and have a chat with him.

(Pause, as if a requiem for Mr. Loman. Then Mae, shaking her head, gets back to business.)

Mae.

All right now. We're up to you, Ursula. How did you make out?

Ursula.

(Stiffly hands over the money.) Seven dollars.

Mae.

(Frowning.) No tip?

Ursula.

No tip.

Lillian.

Mr. Ezra, last of the big time spenders!

Ursula.

Well, he pays. I don't mind. At least he's not a gabber; he doesn't bend my ears with ramblings and soft words . . .

Lillian.

I bet he doesn't.

Ursula.

That suits me just fine. I like 'em silent. I come into his room and he's in bed, ready and undressed. No small talk. A man of business. I say, "Good morning, Mr. Ezra." He says, "Good morning." And then he gets right to the point—

Lillian.

Premature ejaculation?

(Mae check over the money and counts it again; she makes out a Citibank deposit slip.)

Ursula.

I get the same rate for five minutes that you all get for twenty. "The more fool he."

Vera.

I like to cuddle with some of the gentlemen. Like Mr. Francis. He's got the softest gray hair on his chest. I could lie there for hours ..

Ursula.

That's what I mean by faster turnover. If they want to cuddle, give 'em their hot water bottle.

Mae.

Well, we're a little short, today.

Ursula.

It came to $31.50.

Mae.

Thank you, Ursula, we can all count.

Ursula.

That doesn't even pay the rent.

Lillian.

Thank God Mr. Zabar's rooms are rent controlled. We're safe.

Mae.

Edna, can you approach Mr. Benjamin on Thursday and ask him to consider three times a week? He can afford it.

Ursula.

If spermatozoons were nickels, that man would be a millionaire by now.

Edna.

I don't know if I can take him three times a week. But I'm willing to die trying.

Mae.

Good girl. Well, ladies, if you'll give me your undivided attention for a few minutes. Here's how matters stand: Earned income for each of us is forty-seven dollars and sixty cents per week. I pay each of you sixty dollars a week. Which means we are depleting our savings account to the tune of fifty dollars per month.

Vera.

Oh, dear.

Mae.

Some measures need to be taken, Lillian . . .

Lillian.

Yes.

Mae.

Next Tuesday you start with Mr. Sidney. As he's a new customer, we'll up the fee to ten dollars. We keep the fee the same for our regulars. Only new customers will be increased.

Lillian.

Right.

Mae.

Secondly . . . there will be no increase in your weekly allowance. It's adequate . . .

Lillian.

Barely.

Mae.

Well, we have no expenses right now. No carfare. We can walk down the seven blocks it takes . . . Remember, President Reagan has called on all

Americans to reduce the deficit, and to balance the budget. We can start here. We can tighten our belts. No more two-hour lunches.

(There is a united groan from the women.)

Vera.

I get gas when I don't digest properly, Mae. And there's nothing more embarrassing . . .

Mae.

Well, then, moan or something. Cover it over, Mr. Francis doesn't hear too well, anyway. To continue. All of our customers should be encouraged to increase the number of our visits. Mr. Benjamin. Mr. Franklin. Mr. Samuel. If it's not hazardous to their health. And Ursula . . . I want you to give a little extra to Mr. Ezra. If you give extra, he'll give extra. No more flat fees.

Ursula.

It's squeezing water from a stone.

Mae.

Then SQUEEZE . . . All of you are hard workers; there's not a shirker in the bunch. We can't rely on legacies from our gentlemen. We have to pull our own weight. All of our gentlemen are very pleased; and I'm very proud when I stroll in the evening and meet our friends down the block—they all have lovely things to say. I'm very proud. But I'd appreciate it if you would all try especially hard in the next few weeks. Say nice things about how they look, and don't talk politics or money or about anything in the newspaper—it puts them off their feed. And it raises their blood pressure, too. Make them feel romantic and strong, and those tips will keep rolling in. Any questions, Edna?

Edna.

No.

Mae.

Vera?

Vera.

No, Mae.

Mae.

We need to straighten up and fly right. We've got to be prepared.

Ursula.

Just what are we preparing for?

Mae.

Change. I think now would be a good time to tell them, Vera.

Vera.

Oh, Mae, I don't know.

(The women look at Vera with expectation.)

Mae.

I think we'd all like to share in your good news.

Vera.

Well . . . Mr. Simon has asked for my hand in marriage.

(There is a considerable stir on the bench.)

Edna.

Mr. Simon!

(Ursula begins to laugh. She laughs for a long time, which makes Edna and Vera laugh. Ursula tries to stop, but can't—the effort makes her cry. Pause.)

Ursula.

I don't know when I've had such a laugh.

Lillian.

I don't know that it's that funny.

Vera.

I don't mind, Lillian. It is funny, come to think of it.

Ursula.

It's just that . . . Mr. Simon's going to make an honest woman of her. (Starts laughing again.)

Edna.

Isn't he Mr. Jonathan's former golf partner?

Vera.

Yes. The three of us used to . . . have a good time together.

Edna.

Are you going to accept?

Vera.

I haven't made up my mind yet. I don't know.

Ursula.

If he's fool enough to ask, you should be fool enough to accept.

Lillian.

I don't know, Vera.

Mae.

And why not, Lillian?

Lillian.

Hasn't he already had three wives?

Mae.

Yes. So?

Lillian.

Well, doesn't it make you wonder? Why they all died before him?

Vera.

They didn't all die. Two of them left him first. Then they died.

Edna.

But we do know why they left. Boredom.

Mae.

Mr. Simon has a pension. And money in the bank. It's security.

Vera.

I don't know that I will.

Mae.

Be sensible, Vera. He's much older than you are. He's eighty-six.

Ursula.

(Bristling.) That's not so old.

Lillian.

I think he's a dull, stodgy old fart. Don't do it, Vera.

Vera.

I haven't made up my mind yet.

Ursula.

Well, Vera, I don't suppose you'll marry in white. (Laughs.)

Mae.

Look, Ursula, this kind of thing happens all the time. Remember Jeannette? Pretty little girl. Left the Life, got married to an accountant.

Ursula.

Of course he was an accountant. Knew a bargain when he saw one. Used goods go cheap.

Mae.

Well, as far as we know, she made a good match.

Ursula.

That was different.

Edna.

Why?

Ursula.

Jeannette was all of eighteen. Vera's not just a Woman with a Past; she's a Woman with an Epic.

Edna.

Does Mr. Simon love you?

Vera.

Well, I make him feel clever. He talks and I listen.

Lillian.

Well, I wouldn't care if he was the King of Siam. I wouldn't do it.

Mae.

There won't be many more offers down the pike. And when Mr. Simon's time is up, all of his benefits will go to Vera.

Ursula.

Mr. Simon's better off marrying Vera than one of those grandmother floozies in Jefferson Square.

Edna.

Have you told Mr. Francis yet?

Vera.

(Desperate.) I haven't made up my mind yet!

Edna.

He's going to be very upset.

Vera.

Edna, if I do decide to marry Mr. Simon, you'd look after Mr. Francis, wouldn't you?

Edna.

Of course I would.

Vera.

So I wouldn't have to worry.

Edna.

But even if you did marry Mr. Simon, couldn't you visit Mr. Francis now and then?

Mae.

Vera will do nothing of the kind. Once a girl leaves the Life, she has to go straight all the way.

Ursula.

That's right, Vera. It's "Till Death do you part."

Edna.

I don't know. I think Mr. Simon would look cute with horns.

Lillian.

Oh, God. Marital sex is so dull.

Ursula.

Wait a moment. What about Vera's customers?

Vera.

Yes, that's right. I can't do this to you. I'll just thank Mr. Simon for the honor but—

Mae.

We can figure it out. Make up new schedules.

Ursula.

That's a lot of lost income, Mae, to just let whistle down the drain—

Mae.

Vera should do what makes her happy.

Ursula.

Of course, there will be less expenses this way, too.

Vera.

Stop it! All of you! I'm not ready for this! I need to make up my own mind.

Ursula.

If we're going to be so hard-pressed, Mae, why don't you take on some trade as well?

Mae.

I'll pretend I didn't hear that suggestion, Ursula.

Lillian.

What's wrong with you today, Ursula? You've been riding Mae all day. . . . It's because of Mae in the first place that you even have one five-minute fuck—

Ursula.

You're talking mighty big for someone who swaps for stockings . . .

Lillian.

Listen, sister, I've just about had it with—

Ursula.

You were just a scrawny virgin with big eyes in Storeyville while I was satisfying the troops—

Lillian.

Seniority be damned . . . who cares if you were fucking at Gettysburg!

Ursula.

Gettysburg!

Mae.

(Overlapping.) Girls, girls! Enough! Now stop it— right on the street. I'm going to have to separate you just like you were in grammar school again. Edna, sit in between Lillian and Ursula. Lillian, move down next to Vera.

(Edna gets up, sits in between, and smiles pacifically at Ursula.)

Lillian.

Suits me fine. Hi, Vera.

Mae.

Edna—it's 4:30 now. Are you aware of the time?

Edna.

Yes.

Mae.

Be especially nice to Mr. Lawrence today.

Edna.

I'll give him a good time.

Vera.

4:30 already, is it? That's why my stomach is growling . . . it's almost time for dinner. I have the strangest hankering for dinner tonight . . . I feel like going to the produce market up the street—the one on 76th street is the best—and buying two pints of the first raspberries of the season. Did you notice that raspberries are back again? God only knows, I love those things . . . but they're so expensive. They're a very delicate fruit. What I'd like most is just a bowl of raspberries, washed ever so carefully, with cream on top. No sugar. Nothing else. My mother used to make babies in a blanket: raspberries wrapped in pastry and then sprinkled with confectionery sugar. I'd make myself ill eating those. But raspberries plain are the best.

BLACKOUT

Pygmalion

George Bernard Shaw

❧

This play by the renowned Irish critic and playwright is familiar to many because of My Fair Lady, *the musical comedy and film based on* Pygmalion. *Eliza Doolittle, a flower girl on the streets of London, has appeared at the home of Henry Higgins, a professor of phonetics. Higgins has befriended her and taken her into his home out of curiosity about her Cockney dialect and the challenge of correcting it. In the following scene, Mrs. Pearce, Higgins's housekeeper, announces the arrival of Eliza's father to Professor Higgins and his friend, Colonel Pickering.*

HIGGINS, PICKERING, DOOLITTLE, MRS. PEARCE

Pickering.
Excuse the straight question, Higgins. Are you a man of good character where women are concerned?

Higgins.
(Moodily.) Have you ever met a man of good character where women are concerned?

451

Pickering.

Yes: very frequently.

Higgins.

(Dogmatically, lifting himself on his hands to the level of the piano, and sitting on it with a bounce.) Well, I haven't. I find that the moment I let a woman make friends with me, she becomes jealous, exacting, suspicious, and a damned nuisance. I find that the moment I let myself make friends with a woman, I become selfish and tyrannical. Women upset everything. When you let them into your life, you find that the woman is driving at one thing and you're driving at another.

Pickering.

At what, for example?

Higgins.

(Coming off the piano restlessly.) Oh, Lord knows! I suppose the woman wants to live her own life; and the man wants to live his; and each tries to drag the other on to the wrong track. One wants to go north and the other south; and the result is that both have to go east, though they both hate the east wind. (He sits down on the bench at the keyboard.) So here I am, a confirmed old bachelor, and likely to remain so. ·

Pickering.

(Rising and standing over him gravely.) Come, Higgins! You know what I mean. If I'm to be in this business I shall feel responsible for that girl. I hope it's understood that no advantage is to be taken of her position.

Higgins.

What! That thing! Sacred, I assure you. (Rising to explain.) You see, she'll be a pupil' and teaching would be impossible unless pupils were sacred. I've taught scores of American millionairesses how to

speak English: the best looking women in the world.
I'm seasoned. They might as well be blocks of
wood. I might as well be a block of wood. It's—
(Mrs. Pearce opens the door. She has Eliza's hat in
her hand. Pickering retires to the easy-chair at the
hearth and sits down.)

Higgins.

(Eagerly.) Well, Mrs. Pearce: is it all right?

Mrs. Pearce.

(At the door.) I just wish to trouble you with a word,
if I may, Mr. Higgins.

Higgins.

Yes, certainly. Come in. (She comes forward.)
Don't burn that, Mrs. Pearce. I'll keep it as a curiosity. (He takes the hat.)

Mrs. Pearce.

Handle it carefully, sir, please. I had to promise her
not to burn it; but I had better put it in the oven for
a while.

Higgins.

(Putting it down hastily on the piano.) Oh! thank
you. Well, what have you to say to me?

Pickering.

Am I in the way?

Mrs. Pearce.

Not at all, sir. Mr. Higgins: will you please be very
particular what you say before the girl?

Higgins.

(Sternly.) Of course. I'm always particular about
what I say. Why do you say this to me?

Mrs. Pearce.

(Unmoved.) No, sir: you're not at all particular
when you've mislaid anything or when you get a
little impatient. Now it doesn't matter before me:
I'm used to it. But you really must not swear before
that girl.

Higgins.

(Indignantly.) I swear! (Most emphatically.) I never swear. I detest the habit. What the devil do you mean?

Mrs. Pearce.

(Stolidly.) That's what I mean, sir. You swear a great deal too much. I don't mind your damning and blasting, and what the devil and where the devil and who the devil—

Higgins.

Mrs. Pearce, this language from your lips! Really!

Mrs. Pearce.

(Not to be put off.)—but there is a certain word I must ask you not to use. The girl has just used it herself because the bath was too hot. It begins with the same letter as bath. She knows no better: she learnt it at her mother's knee. But she must not hear it from your lips.

Higgins.

(Loftily.) I cannot charge myself with having ever uttered it, Mrs. Pearce. (She looks at him steadfastly. He adds, hiding an uneasy conscience with a judicial air.) Except perhaps in a moment of extreme and justifiable excitement.

Mrs. Pearce.

Only this morning, sir, you applied it to your boots, to the butter, and to the brown bread.

Higgins.

Oh, that! Mere alliteration, Mrs. Pearce, natural to a poet.

Mrs. Pearce.

Well, sir, whatever you choose to call it, I beg you not to let the girl hear you repeat it.

Higgins.

Oh, very well, very well. Is that all?

Mrs. Pearce.

No, sir. We shall have to be very particular with this girl as to personal cleanliness.

Higgins.

Certainly. Quite right. Most important.

Mrs. Pearce.

I mean not be slovenly about her dress or untidy in leaving things about.

Higgins.

(Going to her solemnly.) Just so. I intended to call your attention to that. (He passes on to Pickering, who is enjoying the conversation immensely.) It is these little things that matter, Pickering. Take care of the pence and the pounds will take care of themselves is as true of personal habits as of money. (He comes to anchor on the hearthrug, with the air of a man in an unassailable position.)

Mrs. Pearce.

Yes, sir. Then might I ask you not to come down to breakfast in your dressing-gown, or at any rate not to use it as a napkin to the extent you do, sir. And if you would be so good as not to eat everything off the same plate, and to remember not to put the porridge saucepan out of your hand on the clean tablecloth, it would be a better example for the girl. You know you nearly choked yourself with a fishbone in the jam only last week.

Higgins.

(Routed from the hearthrug and drifting back to the piano.) I may do these things sometimes in absence of mind; but surely I don't do them habitually. (Angrily.) By the way: my dressing-gown smells most damnably of benzine.

Mrs. Pearce.

No doubt it does, Mr. Higgins. But if you will wipe your fingers—

Higgins.

(Yelling.) Oh very well, very well: I'll wipe them in my hair in future.

Mrs. Pearce.

I hope you're not offended, Mr. Higgins.

Higgins.

(Shocked at finding himself thought capable of an unamiable sentiment.) Not at all, not at all. You're quite right, Mrs. Pearce: I shall be particularly careful before the girl. Is that all?

Mrs. Pearce.

No, sir. Might she use some of those Japanese dresses you brought from abroad? I really can't put her back into her old things.

Higgins.

Certainly. Anything you like. Is that all?

Mrs. Pearce.

Thank you, sir. That's all. (She goes out.)

Higgins.

You know, Pickering, that woman has the most extraordinary ideas about me. Here I am, a shy, diffident sort of man. I've never been able to feel really grown-up and tremendous, like other chaps. And yet she's firmly persuaded that I'm an arbitrary overbearing bossing kind of person. I can't account for it.

(Mrs. Pearce returns.)

Mrs. Pearce.

If you please, sir, the trouble's beginning already. There's a dustman downstairs, Alfred Doolittle, wants to see you. He says you have his daughter here.

Pickering.

(Rising.) Phew! I say! (He retreats to the hearthrug.)

Higgins.

(Promptly.) Send the blackguard up.

Mrs. Pearce.

Oh, very well, sir. (She goes out.)

Pickering.

He may not be a blackguard, Higgins.

Higgins.

Nonsense. Of course he's a blackguard.

Pickering.

Whether he is or not, I'm afraid we shall have some trouble with him.

Higgins.

(Confidently.) Oh no: I think not. If there's any trouble he shall have it with me, not I with him. And we are sure to get something interesting out of him.

Pickering.

About the girl?

Higgins.

No. I mean his dialect.

Pickering.

Oh!

Mrs. Pearce.

(At the door.) Doolittle, sir. (She admits Doolittle and retires.)

(Alfred Doolittle is an elderly but vigorous dustman, clad in the costume of his profession, including a hat with a back brim covering his neck and shoulders. He has well marked and rather interesting features, and seems equally free from fear and conscience. He has a remarkably expressive voice, the result of a habit of giving vent to his feelings without reserve. His present pose is that of wounded honor and stern resolution.)

Doolittle.

(At the door, uncertain which of the two gentlemen is his man.) Professor Higgins?

Higgins.

Here. Good morning. Sit down.

Doolittle.

Morning, Governor. (He sits down magisterially.) I come about a very serious matter, Governor.

Higgins.

(To Pickering.) Brought up in Hounslow, Mother Welsh, I should think. (Doolittle opens his mouth, amazed. Higgins continues.) What do you want, Doolittle?

Doolittle.

(Menacingly.) I want my daughter: that's what I want. See?

Higgins.

Of course you do. You're her father, aren't you? You don't suppose anyone else wants her, do you? I'm glad to see you have some spark of family feeling left. She's upstairs. Take her away at once.

Doolittle.

(Rising, fearfully taken aback.) What!

Higgins.

Take her away. Do you suppose I'm going to keep your daughter for you?

Doolittle.

(Remonstrating.) Now, now, look here, Governor. Is this reasonable? Is it fairity to take advantage of a man like this? The girl belongs to me. You got her. Where do I come in? (He sits down again.)

Higgins.

Your daughter had the audacity to come to my house and ask me to teach her how to speak properly so that she could get a place in a flower-shop. This gentleman and my housekeeper have been here all the time. (Bullying him.) How dare you come here and attempt to blackmail me? You sent her here on purpose.

Doolittle.

(Protesting.) No, Governor.

Higgins.

You must have. How else could you possibly know that she is here?

Doolittle.

Don't take a man up like that, Governor.

Higgins.

The police shall take you up. This is a plant—a plot to extort money by threats. I shall telephone for the police. (He goes resolutely to the telephone and opens the directory.)

Doolittle.

Have I asked you for a brass farthing? I leave it to the gentleman here: have I said a word about money?

Higgins.

(Throwing the book aside and marching down on Doolittle with a poser.) What else did you come for?

Doolittle.

(Sweetly.) Well, what would a man come for? Be human, Governor.

Higgins.

(Disarmed.) Alfred, did you put her up to it?

Doolittle.

So help me, Governor, I never did. I take my Bible oath I ain't seen the girl these two months past.

Higgins.

Then how did you know she was here?

Doolittle.

("most musical, most melancholy") I'll tell you, Governor, if you'll only let me get a word in. I'm willing to tell you. I'm wanting to tell you. I'm waiting to tell you.

Higgins.

Pickering, this chap has a certain natural gift of rhetoric. Observe the rhythm of his native woodnotes wild. "I'm willing to tell you: I'm wanting to tell you: I'm waiting to tell you.'' Sentimental rhetoric! that's the Welsh strain in him. It also accounts for his mendacity and dishonesty.

Pickering.

Oh, please, Higgins: I'm west country myself. (To Doolittle.) How did you know the girl was here if you didn't send her?

Doolittle.

It was like this, Governor. The girl took a boy in the taxi to give him a jaunt. Son of her landlady, he is. He hung about on the chance of her giving him another ride home. Well, she sent him back for her luggage when she heard you was willing for her to stop here. I met the boy at the corner of LongAcre and Endell Street.

Higgins.

Public house. Yes?

Doolittle.

The poor man's club. Governor: why shouldn't I?

Pickering.

Do let him tell his story, Higgins.

Doolittle.

He told me what was up. And I ask you, what was my feelings and my duty as a father? I says to the boy, ''You bring me the luggage.'' I says—

Pickering.

Why didn't you go for it yourself?

Doolittle.

Landlady wouldn't have trusted me with it, Governor. She's that kind of woman: you know. I had to give the boy a penny afore he trusted me with it, the little swine. I brought it to her just to oblige you like, and make myself agreeable. That's all.

Higgins.

How much luggage?

Doolittle.

Musical instrument, Governor. A few pictures, a trifle of jewelry, and a bird-cage. She said she didn't want no clothes. What was I to think from that, Governor? I ask you as a parent what was I to think?

Higgins.

So you came to rescue her from worse than death, eh?

Doolittle.

(Appreciatively: relieved at being so well understood.) Just so, Governor. That's right.

Pickering.

But why did you bring her luggage if you intended to take her away?

Doolittle.

Have I said a word about taking her away? Have I now?

Higgins.

(Determinedly.) You're going to take her away, double quick. (He crosses to the hearth and rings the bell.)

Doolittle.

(Rising.) No, Governor. Don't say that. I'm not the man to stand in my girl's light. Here's a career opening for her, as you might say; and—

(Mrs. Pearce opens the door and awaits orders.)

Higgins.

Mrs. Pearce; this is Eliza's father. He has come to take her away. Give her to him. (He goes. back to the piano, with an air of washing his hands of the whole affair.)

Doolittle.

No. This is a misunderstanding. Listen here—

Mrs. Pearce.

He can't take her away, Mr. Higgins: how can he? You told me to burn her clothes.

Doolittle.

That's right. I can't carry the girl through the streets like a blooming monkey, can I? I put that to you.

Higgins.

You have put it to me that you want your daughter. Take your daughter. If she has no clothes go out and buy her some.

Doolittle.

(Desperate.) Where's the clothes she come in? Did I burn them or did your missus here?

Mrs. Pearce.

I am the housekeeper, if you please. I have sent for some clothes for your girl. When they come you can take her away. You can wait in the kitchen. This way, please.

(Doolittle, much troubled, accompanies her to the door: then hesitates; finally turns confidentially to Higgins.)

Doolittle.

Listen here, Governor. You and me is men of the world, ain't we?

Higgins.

Oh! Men of the world, are we? You'd better go, Mrs. Pearce.

Mrs. Pearce.

I think so, indeed, sir. (She goes, with dignity.)

Pickering.

The floor is yours, Mr. Doolittle.

Doolittle.

(To Pickering.) I thank you, Governor. (To Higgins, who takes refuge on the piano bench, a little over-whelmed by the proximity of his visitor: for Doo-little has a professional flavor of dust about him.) Well, the truth is, I've taken a sort of fancy to you, Governor: and if you want the girl, I'm not so set on having her back home again but what I might be open to an arrangement. Regarded in the light of a young woman, she's a fine handsome girl. As a daughter she's not worth her keep: and so I tell you straight. All I ask is my rights as a father; and you're the last man alive to expect me to let her go for nothing; for I can see you're one of the straight sort, Governor. Well, what's a five-pound note to you? And what's Eliza to me? (He returns to his chair and sits down judicially.)

Pickering.

I think you ought to know, Doolittle, that Mr. Higgins's intentions are entirely honorable.

Doolittle.

'Course they are, Governor. If I thought they wasn't I'd ask fifty.

Higgins.

(Revolted.) Do you mean to say, you callous rascal, that you would sell your daughter for 50 pounds?

Doolittle.

Not in a general way I wouldn't; but to oblige a gentleman like you I'd do a good deal, I do assure you.

Pickering.

Have you no morals, man?

Doolittle.

(Unabashed.) Can't afford them, Governor. Neither could you if you was as poor as me. Not that I mean any harm, you know. But if Liza is going to have a bit out of this, why not me too?

Higgins.

(Troubled.) I don't know what to do, Pickering. There can be no question that as a matter of morals it's a positive crime to give this chap a farthing. And yet I feel a sort of rough justice in his claim.

Doolittle.

That's it, Governor. That's all I say. A father's heart, as it were.

Pickering.

Well, I know the feeling; but really it seems hardly right—

Doolittle.

Don't say that, Governor. Don't look at it that way. What am I, Governors both? I ask you, what am I? I'm one of the undeserving poor: that's what I am. Think of what that means to a man. It means that he's up agen middle class morality all the time. If there's anything going, and I put in for a bit of it, it's always the same story: ''You're undeserving; so you can't have it.'' But my needs is as great as the most deserving widow's that ever got money out of six different charities in one week for the death of the same husband. I don't need less than a deserving man: I need more. I don't eat less hearty than him; and I drink a lot more. I want a bit of amusement, 'cause I'm a thinking man. I want cheerfulness and a song and a band when I feel low. Well, they charge me just the same for everything as they charge the deserving. What is middle class morality? Just an excuse for never giving me anything. Therefore, I ask you as two gentlemen, not to play that game on me. I'm playing straight with you. I ain't pretending to be deserving. I'm undeserving; and I mean to go on being undeserving. I like it; and that's the truth. Will you take advantage of a man's nature to do him out of the price of his own daughter what he's brought up and fed and clothed by the sweat of his brow until she's growed big enough to be interesting to you two gentlemen? Is five pounds unreasonable? I put it to you, and I leave it to you.

Higgins.

(Rising and going over to Pickering.) Pickering: if we were to take this man in hand for three months, he could choose between a seat in the Cabinet and a popular pulpit in Wales.

Pickering.

What do you say to that, Doolittle?

Doolittle.

Not me, Governor, thank you kindly, I've heard all the preachers and all the prime minsters—for I'm a thinking man and game for politics or religion or social reform same as all the other amusements—and I tell you it's a dog's life any way you look at it. Undeserving poverty is my line. Taking one station in society with another, it's—it's—well, it's the only one that has any ginger in it, to my taste.

Higgins.

I suppose we must give him a fiver.

Pickering.

He'll make a bad use of it, I'm afraid.

Doolittle.

Not me, Governor, so help me I won't. Don't you be afraid that I'll save it and spare it and live idle on it. there won't be a penny of it left by Monday. I'll have to go to work same as if I'd never had it. It won't pauperize me, you bet. Just one good spree for myself and the missus, giving pleasure to ourselves and employment to others, and satisfaction to you to think it's not been throwed away. You couldn't spend it better.

Higgins.

(Taking out his pocket book and coming between Doolittle and the piano.) This is irresistible. Let's give him ten. (He offers two notes to the dustman.)

Doolittle.

No, Governor. She wouldn't have the heart to spend ten; and perhaps I shouldn't neither. Ten pounds is a lot of money: it makes a man feel prudent like; and then goodbye to happiness. You give me what

I ask you, Governor: not a penny more, and not a penny less.

Pickering.

Why don't you marry that missus of yours? I rather draw the line at encouraging that sort of immorality.

Doolittle.

Tell her so, Governor: tell her so. I'm willing. It's me that suffers by it. I've no hold on her. I got to be agreeable to her. I got to give her presents. I got to buy her clothes something sinful. I'm a slave to that woman, Governor, just because I'm not her lawful husband. And she knows it too. Catch her marrying me! Take my advice, Governor: marry Eliza while she's young and don't know no better. If you don't you'll be sorry for it after. if you do, she'll be sorry for it after; but better you than her, because you're a man, and she's only a woman and don't know how to be happy anyhow.

Higgins.

Pickering: if we listen to this man another minute, we shall have no convictions left. (To Doolittle.) Five pounds I think you said.

Doolittle.

Thank you kindly, Governor.

Higgins.

You're sure you won't take ten?

Doolittle.

Not now. Another time, Governor.

Higgins.

(Handing him a five-pound note.) Here you are.

Doolittle.

Thank you, Governor. Good morning. (He hurries to the door, anxious to get away with his booty.)

Social Security

Andrew Bergman

❧

This humorous urban play opened on Broadway in 1986 and
has been proven popular with readers, actors, and audiences. It
is set in an elegant Manhattan apartment in 1986. Sophie
Greengrass, a feisty woman in her eighties, is staying with her
middle-aged daughter, Barbara, and Barbara's husband David.
They are entertaining a guest, Maurice Koenig, a man in his
nineties who is a well-known artist and quite natty. Barbara
and Sophie have had one of their usual altercations, this time
about Sophie dressing for dinner, and Barbara has found it
necessary to lock Sophie in the guest room. This scene opens
immediately after Barbara unlocks the door and Sophie enters,
all dressed up.

SOPHIE, MAURICE, BARBARA, DAVID

(Sophie enters the room—without her walker. She has
transformed herself: black dress and a gardenia in her
hair.)
Barbara.
  Mother!

David.

Billie Holiday. We didn't expect you.

Sophie.

Fresh boy. (Maurice begins to stand, slowly.) Please don't. You'll be up all night.

Maurice.

It is my pleasure. (Sophie steadily makes her way toward the sofa.)

Barbara.

You're really okay without your walker?

Sophie.

What walker? (Singing.) "Ha-lo everybody, Ha-lo . . ." Remember that commercial, David?

Sophie.

(To Maurice) It was a shampoo commercial. I used to sing it around the house day and night, right, Bobbsy?

Barbara.

That's right.

Sophie.

That you remember.

Barbara.

I certainly do. Mother, I'd like you to meet Maurice Koenig. Maurice, my mother, Sophie Greengrass.

Maurice.

(Kissing her hand.) I am very, very happy to meet you.

David.

Sophie, you look ravishing.

Sophie.

(To Maurice.) I heard all about you from my daughter. She was so nervous about tonight. I said, for what? Dinner is dinner.

Maurice.

Exactly.

Barbara.

Mother . . .

David.

The point is, here you are.

Sophie.

Here I am. So let me just sit. . . . (David helps Maurice to sit. Barbara helps Sophie.) Thank you darling. Who locked that door? Not me.

Barbara.

I might have locked it without thinking.

David.

We're too crime-conscious.

Sophie.

(To Maurice.) Locked in my room. Like a meshugena.

Barbara.

Not at all.

Maurice.

Oh, no.

Sophie.

Maybe if I was locked in, it was for my own good, right, Maurice?

Maurice.

Barbara and David are so fond of you, they overprotect you.

David.

There's been a wave of mother-snatching.

Sophie.

Sure. (To Barbara.) Is he a doll.

Barbara.

I told you.

David.

Sophie, how about some wine?

Sophie.

What a face.

David.

Sophie, wine?

Sophie.

Why not, David. How often do I go to dinner parties?

Maurice.

Live it up.

Sophie.

Live it up.

David.

White or red, Sophie?

Sophie.

What?

Barbara.

WHITE WINE OR RED WINE?

Sophie.

Maurice, what are you having?

Maurice.

Excuse?

Sophie.

What kind of wine are you having? (To Barbara.) His hearing isn't so good.

David.

Amazing.

Maurice.

I am having white wine, and it is marvelous.

Sophie.

Then that's what I'll have: white wine.

David.

(Going to the bar.) Done.

Sophie.

(Moving closer to Maurice.) A little birdy told me you're pushing a hundred.

Maurice.

That is an unchangeable fact.

Sophie.

I would have said ninety, tops. You look fantastic.

Maurice.

I have had a very good life.

Sophie.

That's the secret. "It's the circumstances, not the years." I read that in MODERN MATURITY..

Maurice.

MODERN . . . ?

Barbara.

It's for senior citizens.

Sophie.

An *alte kocker* magazine. But very interesting. Even Barbara looks at it.

Barbara.

What do you mean, "even Barbara"?

David.

Honey . . .

Maurice.

I am so busy. No time for magazines.

Sophie.

You're still working?

Maurice.

Oh, yes.

David.

(Returning with Sophie's wine.) Maurice is a painter, Sophie.

Sophie.

I know what he is. (To Maurice.) My son-in-law is some character, isn't he?

Maurice.

He is a very brilliant dealer of art. As is your daughter.

Barbara.

Thank you.

Sophie.

I'm sure he is.

Barbara.

(To Sophie.) "As is your daughter."

David.

Give up.

Sophie.

My daughter lives like a queen here. He must be good.

Barbara.

We live well. A "queen . . ."

Sophie.

That ability David has, that's something you're born with, am I right?

Maurice.

Good taste. Vision.

Sophie.

Sure. (To Barbara.) You thought I couldn't make conversation?

Barbara.

I never said you couldn't make conversation, Mother.

David.

Heavens, no. We were counting on your conversational powers.

Sophie.

(To Maurice.) My daughter and I had a little discussion before you arrived.

Barbara.

Mother.

Maurice.

Yes. A heart to heart?

Sophie.

Exactly.

David.

Might I propose a toast?

Barbara.

Yes.

Sophie.

(Ignoring them, to Maurice.) You have a wonderful face.

Barbara.

This isn't happening!

David.

Might I propose a toast?

Maurice.

David?

David.

A toast. To this evening. To the four of us.

Sophie.

Very nice.

David.

To our continued good health and creativity.

Maurice.

And to this wonderful idea, to have us all together with your wonderful mother, Barbara.

Barbara.

Thank you. (To no one in particular.) I can hear my heart beating.

Sophie.

You remind me so much of Sid, my late husband.

Maurice.

Yes?

Barbara.

He doesn't really look like Dad.

Sophie.

He was a painter, too. A housepainter. (A look to Barbara.) I know that's not the same.

Maurice.

But it's an art.

Sophie.

But it's an art. Bobbsy, remember what they used to call Daddy?

Barbara.
The Rembrandt of Dinettes.
Sophie.
The Rembrandt of Dinettes—my Sid!
Maurice.
Yes? (To David.) This is true?
David.
I believe he even signed some of his dinettes.
Sophie.
When Sid worked, apartments weren't like they are today. They had foyers, nooks, moldings. Sid was too dedicated, he'd stay up all night worrying. "That two-bedroom in Woodside," he'd say, "I don't know whether to go with a gloss or a semi-gloss."
Maurice.
He cared.
Barbara.
He really did.
Sophie.
You know how much he cared, Maurice? And not just about painting. During the war—something about Hitler being a housepainter . . .
Maurice.
Yes? Upset him?
Sophie.
Very much.
Barbara.
He had sort of a breakdown.
David.
Took to his bed.
Sophie.
He just stopped painting. For years, wouldn't take a job.
Maurice.
Because of Hitler.

Sophie.
He worked for a friend, Nat Meltzer, repairing radios. Then the Rosenberg case came along, and it turned out Rosenberg was a radio repairman. Poor Sid didn't know what to do.

David.
Sid took these things to heart He was a sweet soul, really.

Sophie.
He finally decided it wasn't his responsibility any more. So he went back to housepainting. That was really his first love.

Barbara.
He did love it. Went on and on about all the colors. He had this book, remember, Mother, with all the colors? (To David, holding up her glass.) Another.

Sophie.
The big book. Do I remember?

Maurice.
You remember well.

Sophie.
Like it was yesterday.

Barbara.
I guess nobody's hungry.

Sophie.
He had such pride in his work.

Maurice.
And you felt the pride also.

Sophie.
Of course. So, I can imagine what your late wife felt when you showed her one of your beautiful pictures.

David.
How does she know Maurice's wife died?

Barbara.
I have no idea. This is so incredible.

Sophie.
  She must have burst with pride.
Maurice.
  She was very proud. Very supportive.
Sophie.
  Sure she was. That's what a wife is for..
Maurice.
  That's what a wife is for, Sophie. Sophie. (Maurice takes Sophie's hand.)
David.
  (To Barbara.) Why do I find myself trembling un-controllably?
Barbara.
  (Pointing to Sophie and Maurice.) David! Look at this.
Sophie.
  He's holding my hand, Bobbsy. What should I do?
CURTAIN

A Thousand Clowns

Herb Gardner

❧

The scene from this play, which opened on Broadway in 1962, takes place in an office in Manhattan in the early 1960s. Murray Burns, a bright, middle-aged man, has recently left a script-writing job for a kiddy show, a job which he could no longer endure. He is a single parent and has a hearing coming up which he hopes will grant him custody of his son Nick. The scene opens with Murray entering his older brother's office in a theatrical agency.

ARNOLD, MURRAY, LEO (Offstage)

(Murray enters wearing new suit and carrying a pine-apple.)

Murray.

Good afternoon, Mr. Burns.

Arnold.

(Coming around the desk to meet him.) Good afternoon, Mr. Burns. Hey, you really did get a new suit, didn't you? How'd the appointment go with—?

Murray.

(Crossing to window, putting pineapple on desk.) Arnold, every time I see you, the agency's put you on a higher floor. I swear, next time I come you'll be up in a balloon.

Arnold.

Murray, the appointment—

Murray.

I can't get over this office, Arnie. (He is at window and he pulls the drape back a bit and sits on the sill.) Twenty-second floor. You can see everything. (Shocked by something he sees out the window.) My God, I don't believe it: it's King Kong. He's sitting on top of the Time-Life Building. He—he seems to be crying. Poor gorilla bastard, they shoulda told him they don't make those buildings the way they used to—

Arnold.

(Raising his hand in the air.) HELLO, Murray, hello there, here we are in my office. Welcome to Tues-

day. Now, come ON, how'd it go with Jimmy
Sloan?

Murray.

He took me to lunch at Steffano's East 53rd. Christ,
it's been a couple years since I hustled around
Lunchland. There is this crazy hum that I haven't
heard for so long, Arnie; eight square yards of idea
men busily having ideas, eating away at their Chef's
Salad like it's crackerjacks and there's a prize at the
bottom.

Arnold.

And Sloan—?

Murray.

(Sitting on the sofa.) Sloan lunches beautifully, can
out-lunch anybody. A killer, this one, Arnie, notches
on his attache-case. Told me this idea he had where
I'd be a lovable eccentric on his panel-show. This
somehow led him very logically to his conception
of God, Who he says is "probably a really Fun
guy."

Arnold.

What'd you tell him about the offer?

Murray.

I told him good-bye. I don't think he noticed when
I left; he focuses slightly to the right of you when
he talks, just over your shoulder, so if you stay out
of range he can't tell that you're gone. Probably
thinks I'm still there.

Arnold.

Murray, you told me this morning to get any job I
could; Sloan's offer wasn't so bad—

Murray.

Sloan is an idiot.

Arnold.

(Sitting next to him on sofa; angrily, firmly.) Listen,
Cookie, I got NEWS for you, right now you NEED

idiots. You got a bad reputation for quitting jobs, I even had trouble grabbing Sloan for you. Why did you have to go and build your own personal blacklist; why couldn't you just be blacklisted as a Communist like everybody else?

Murray.

Don't worry, Arnie; I figured I'd go back with Chuckles. He's ready to take me back, isn't he?

Arnold.

Yeah, he's ready. I just spoke to him. (Solemnly.) Hey, Murray, Leo says he came up to your place last January, a week after you quit him, to talk you into coming back with the show. And right in the middle you went into the kitchen and started singing "Yessir, That's My Baby." Just left him standing there. Your way of saying "good-bye."

Murray.

Well, that was four months ago, Arnie—

Arnold.

(Attempts to conceal his amusement, then turns to Murray, smiling.) So, what'd you do with him, you just left him standing there? (He laughs.) Like to have been there, seen that, must have been great.

Murray.

Arnie, it was beautiful.

Arnold.

(Chuckling.) It's about time somebody left Leo Herman standing around talking to himself. (Rubbing his head.) I wish to God I didn't enjoy you so much. Crap, I don't do you any good at all. (Then solemnly again.) Murray, no fun and games with Leo today, understand? He is absolutely ALL we got left before the hearing Thursday.

Murray.

Yes, I understand.

Arnold.

(Rising, goes to pick up phone on desk.) I wish we coulda got something better for you, kid, but there just wasn't any time.

Murray.

Well, Chuckles won't be so bad for a while—

Arnold.

No, Murray. (Puts phone down firmly.) Not just for a while. You'll really have to stick with Chuckles. I had our Agency lawyer check the facts for me. Most the Board'll give you is a probationary year with Nick; a trial period. The Board's investigators will be checking on you every week—

Murray.

That's charming.

Arnold.

Checking to see if you've still got the job, checking with Leo on your stability, checking up on the change in your home environment.

Murray.

Sounds like a parole board.

Arnold.

(Into intercom phone.) Margo; get me Leo Herman on the speaker-phone here, his home number. Thanks. (To Murray.) He's waiting for our call. Look, Murray, maybe he's not the greatest guy in the world; but y'know, he really LIKES you, Murray, he—

Murray.

Yeah. I have a way with animals.

Arnold.

(Pointing at Murray.) That was your last joke for today. (A click is heard from the speaker-phone; Arnold turns it on.) You there, Leo?

Leo's Voice.
Right, Arn. I'm down here in the basement, in my gymnasium; lot of echoing. Am I coming through, am I coming through O.K.?

Arnold.
Clearly, Leo. Murray's here.

Leo's Voice.
Murray! Murray the wonderful wild man; fellah, how-are-ya?

Murray.
(Taking his hat off, waving "hello" to speaker-phone.) O.K., Leo, how're YOU doing?

Leo's Voice.
Oh, you crazy bastard, it's damn good to hear that voice again. You're an old monkey, aren't ya?

Murray.
You sound about the same too, Leo.

Leo's Voice.
Not the same. I'm MORE IMPOSSIBLE than I used to be. Can you imagine that?

Murray.
Not easily, Leo, no.

Leo's Voice.
Murray, I need you, fellah; I need you back with the show. Murr' we'll talk a while now, and then I'll come over to your place tonight. go over some ideas for next week's shows. It'll be great, sweetie— Oh, there's that word again: "Sweetie." I said that word again. Oh, am I getting SICK of myself. Big phoney. The truth, fellah, I'm the biggest phoney you ever met, right?

Murray.
Probably, Leo.

Leo's Voice.
(After a pause; coldly.) "Probably," he says. There he goes, there goes Murray the old joker, right?

You're a jester, right? Some fooler. You can't fool with a scheduled show, Murray; a scheduled show with a tight budget. (Softly, whispering.) Murray, come closer, tell you a secret—(Murray comes closer to the box.) You're gonna hate me, Murray; I gotta tell you something and I know you're gonna hate me for it, but we can't have the same Murray we used to have on the show. Who appreciates a good joke more than anybody? ME! But who jokes too much? (Suddenly louder.) YOU!

Murray.

Leo, couldn't we talk about this tonight when we get together?

Leo's Voice.

(Softly again.) It hurt me, Murr' it hurt me what you used to do. When all those thousands of kids wrote in asking for the definition of a Chipmonk and you sent back that form letter sayin' a Chipmonk was a—was a what?

Murray.

A cute rat.

Leo's Voice.

(Still soft.) A cute rat; yeah, I remember my skin broke out somethin' terrible. Some jester you are, foolin' around at the script conferences, foolin' around at the studio. Now, we're not gonna have any more of that, are we?

Murray.

(Subservient, apologetic.) No we won't, I'm sorry, Leo.

Leo's Voice.

Because we can't fool with the innocence of children, can we? My God, they believe in the little Chipmonk, don't ask me why; I'm nothing, God, I know that. I've been damned lucky. A person like me should get a grand and a half a week for doin' nothin'. I mean, I'm one of the big NO-TALENTS of all time, right?

Murray.

Right—I mean, no, Leo, no.

Leo's Voice.

Oh, I know it's the truth and I don't kid myself about it. But there'll be no more jokin'; right, Murr? Because I'll tell you the truth, I can't stand it.

Murray.

Right, Leo.

Leo's Voice.

(Softly.) Good. Glad we cleared that up. Because my skin breaks out somethin' terrible. (Up again.) You're the best, Murray, such talent, you know I love ya, don't ya? You old monkey.

Murray.

(To Arnold.) Please, tell him we'll talk further tonight, too much of him all at once—

Arnold.

Say, Leo, suppose we—

Leo's Voice.

Murray, I want you to put some fifteen-minute fairy tales into the show. You've got your Hans Christian Andersens there, your Grimm Brothers, your Goldilocks, your Sleepin' Beauties, your Gingerbread Men, your Foxy-Loxies, your legends, your folk tales—do I reach ya, Murr?

Murray.

(Quietly.) Yeah, Leo—

Leo's Voice.

Now, what I want in those scripts is this, Murray, I want you to give 'em five minutes a action, five minutes a poignancy, and then five minutes of the *MORAL MESSAGE*; race-relations-thing, world-peace-thing, understanding-brings-love-thing. I don't know. Shake-em up a little. Controversy, An-

gry letters from parents. Kid's show with something
to say, get some excitement in the industry, wild . . .

Murray.

(Leans over, very close to speaker-phone, whispers
into it.) Hey, Leo, I might show up one day with
eleven minutes of poignancy, no action, and a
twelve-second moral message—

Arnold.

Murray. Stop it—

Murray.

(Suddenly shouting into speaker-phone.) AND
THEN WHERE WOULD WE BE? (There is a
pause; no sound comes from the speaker-phone,
then:)

Leo's Voice.

See how he mocks me. Well, I guess there's plenty
there to mock. Plenty mocking. Sometimes I try to
take a cold look at what I am . . . (Very soft.)
Sweaty Leo jumping around in a funny costume trying to make a buck out of being a Chipmonk. The
Abominable Snowman in a cute suit. But I'll tell
you something, Murray—sit down for a minute.
(Murray is standing; Leo's voice is still fairly pleasant.) Are ya sitting down, Murray? (Murray remains
standing; Leo's voice is suddenly loud, sharp, com-
manding.) MURRAY, SIT DOWN! Good. Now I'm
gonna tell you a story—

Murray.

(Softly, painfully.) Arnold, he's gonna do it again—
the story—

Leo's Voice.

Murray—

Murray.

(Softly, miserable.) The story I got tattooed to my
skull—

Leo's Voice.

On June the third—

Murray.

(Hunching over in his chair, looking down at the floor.) Story number twelve—the ''Laughter of Children'' story—again—

Leo's Voice.

I will be forty-two years old—

Murray.

(To Arnold; painfully, pleading.) Arnie—

Leo's Voice.

And maybe it's the silliest, phoniest, cop-out thing—

Leo's Voice and Murray.

(In unison.)—you ever heard, but the Chipmonk, Chuckles, the little guy I pretend to be, is real to me—

Leo's Voice.

—as real to me as—as this phone in my hand; those children, don't ask me why, God I don't know, but they believe in that little fellah—(Murray looks up from the floor now and over at the speaker-phone which is on the other side of the room; his eyes are fixed on it.) Look, Murr', I do what I can for the cash-monies; but also, and I say it without embarrassment, I just love kids, the laughter of children, and we can't have you foolin' with that, Murr', can't have you jokin'—(Murray stands up, still looking at the speaker-phone.) because it's this whole, bright, wild sorta child kinda thing—(Murray is walking slowly toward the speaker-phone now. Arnold, watching Murray, starts to rise from his chair.) It's this very up feeling, it's all young, and you can't joke with it; the laughter of children; those warm waves, that fresh, open, spontaneous laughter—you can feel it on your face—

Murray.

(Picking up the speaker-phone up off the desk.) Like a sunburn—

Leo's Voice.

Like a sunburn—

Arnold.

(Coming towards Murray as if to stop him.) Murray—wait—

Leo's Voice.

And it's a pride thing—(Murray turns with the speaker-phone held in his hands and drops it into the wastepaper basket next to the desk. He does this calmly. Arnold, too late to stop him, stands watching dumbly paralyzed. Leo, unaware, goes right on talking, his voice somewhat garbled and echoing from the bottom of the wastepaper basket.) So then how lovely, how enchanting it is, that I should be paid so well for something I love so much—(Pause.) Say, there's this noise—there's this—I'm getting this crackling noise on my end here—what's happened to the phone?

Arnold.

(Sadly, solemnly; looking down into the basket.) Leo, you're in a wastepaper basket.

Leo's Voice.

That you, Murray?—there's this crackling noise—I can't hear you—hello?—what's going on?—

Arnold.

Leo, hold it just a minute, I'll get you.

Leo's Voice.

There's this funny noise—where'd everybody go? Where is everybody?—Hello, Murray—hello—come back—come back—

Arnold.

(Fishing amongst papers in basket for speaker—phone.) I'll find you, Leo, I'll find you. (Finally lifts speaker out of basket, holds it gently, tenderly in his hands like a child, speaks soothingly to it.) Look Leo—Leo, we had a little—some trouble with the phone, we—(Realizes that he is getting no reaction from the box.) Leo—Leo?—(As though the box were a friend who he thinks might have died, shaking the box tenderly to revive it.) Leo—Leo, are you there?—Are you there?—It's dead. (Turning to look at Murray, as though announcing the demise of a dear one.) He's gone.

Murray.

Well, don't look at me like that, Arnie; I didn't KILL him. He doesn't LIVE in that box—or maybe he does.

Arnold.

A man has a job for you so you drop him in a basket.

Murray.

Arnie, I quit that nonsense five months ago—

Arnold.

Murray, you're a NUT, a man has a job for you, there's a hearing on Thursday—

Murray.

A fool in a box telling me what's funny, a Welfare Board checking my underwear every week because I don't look good in their files—and I'M the nut, right? I'M the crazy one—

Arnold.

Murray, you float like a balloon and everybody's waitin' for ya with a pin. I'm trying to put you in TOUCH, Murray—with REAL THINGS; with—

Murray.

(Angrily, taking in the office with a sweep of his hand.) You mean like this office, REAL things, like this office? The world could come to an end and you'd find out about it on the phone—(Pointing at two framed photographs on Arnold's desk.) Pictures of your wife six years ago when she was still a piece and your kids at their cutest four years ago when they looked best for the office—Oh, you're in TOUCH all right, Arnie—

Arnold.

(Softly, soothing.) Murray, you're just a little excited, that's all, just relax, everything's gonna be fine—

Murray.

(Shouting.) Damn it—get angry; I just insulted you, personally, about your wife, your kids; I just said lousy things to you. Raise your voice, at least your eyebrows—(Pleading, painfully.) Please, have an argument with me—

Arnold.

(Coaxing.) We'll call Leo back, we'll apologize to him—(Murray goes to the end table, picks up an apple from the bowl of fruit.) Everything's gonna be just fine, Murray, you'll see—just fine—

Murray.

Arnie?

Arnold.

Huh?

Murray.

Catch.

(Murray tosses the apple underhand across the room. Arnold catches it. Murray exits.)

Arnold.

(His hand out from catching the apple.) Aw, Murray—(Lowers his hand to his side; speaks quietly, alone now in the office.) Murray, I swear to you, King Kong is NOT on top of the Time-Life Building . . . (Arnold discovers the apple in his hand; bites into it.

(The lights fade quickly.)

Tone Clusters

Joyce Carol Oates

This play was first performed in 1990 at a festival for outstanding new plays. It is clear that the author of this piece deserves her status as a very accomplished writer, though she usually writes prose. For this play, she suggests the use of a light and sound design with changing rhythms and intensities, writes fractured dialogue, and employs many other unusual effects. All these attempts to be unrealistic seem to make this unusual play more powerful and moving. Oates describes her play as "about the absolute mystery—the NOT-KNOWING—at the core of our human experience. That the mystery is being exploited by a television documentary underscores its tragi-comic nature." There is a huge screen on stage and Frank Gulick, fifty-three, and his wife, Emily, fifty-one, are being questioned by a Voice about a murder. The interview is being filmed and taped. The characters are, in the author's words again, "never wholly accustomed . . . always slightly disoriented, awkward, confused, inclined to speak slowly and methodically or too quickly." This description of the characters' words plus the author's desire to create a mood of fragmentation and confusion are underscored by the nonstandard spacing she has used in the dialogue.

FRANK GULICK, EMILY GULICK, VOICE

Voice.

In a case of murder (taking murder as an abstraction) there is always a sense of the inevitable once the identity of the murderer is established. Beforehand there is a sense of disharmony.

And humankind fears and loathes disharmony, Mr. and Mrs. Gulick of Lakepointe, New Jersey would you comment?

Frank.

. . . Yes I would say, I think that

Emily.

What is that again, exactly? I . . .

Frank.

My wife and I, we . . .

Emily.

Disharmony . . . ?

Frank.

I don't like disharmony. I mean, all the family, we are a law-abiding family.

Voice.

A religious family   I believe?

Frank.

Oh yes. Yes,

We go to Church every

Emily.

We almost never miss a. a Sunday

For awhile,   I helped with Sunday School classes

The children,   the children don't always go but they believe,   our daughter Judith for instance she..and Carl

Frank.

Oh yes yessir.

Emily.

and Dennis,   they do believe they were raised to believe in God and, and Jesus Christ

Frank.

We raised them that way because   we were raised that way.

Emily.

there IS a God whether you agree with Him or not.

Voice.

"Religion" may be defined as   a sort of adhesive matter invisibly holding together nation-states,   nationalities,   tribes,   families   for   the   good   of those so   held together,   would you comment?

Frank.

Oh,   oh yes.

Emily.

For the good of . . .

Frank.

Yes I would say so.   I think so.

Emily.

My husband and I, we were married in church, in

Frank.

In the Lutheran Church.

Emily.

In Penn's Neck.

Frank.

In New Jersey.

Emily.

All our children,

Both.

they believe.

Emily.

God sees into the human heart.

Voice.

Mr. and Mrs. Gulick   from your experience would you theorize for our audience: is the Universe "predestined" in every particular   or   is man capable of   acts of   "freedom"?

Both.

. . .

Emily.

. . . I would say,   that is hard to say.

Frank.

Yes. I believe that man is free.

Emily.

If you mean, like, I guess   choosing good and evil?
Yes

Frank.

I would have to say   yes. You would have to say
mankind is free.

Frank.

Like moving my hand.   (Moves hand.)

Emily.

If nobody is free   it wouldn't be right would it
to punish anybody?

Frank.

There is always   Hell.
I believe in Hell.

Emily.

Anybody at all

Frank.

Though I am not free to, to   fly up in the air am
I? (laughs.) because   Well I'm not built right for
that am I? (laughs.)

Voice.

Man is free.   Thus man is   responsible for his acts.

Emily.

Except, oh   sometime if,   maybe for instance if
    A baby born without

Frank.

Oh one of those ''AID'' babies

Emily.

Poor thing

Frank.

"crack" babies

Or if you were captured by some enemy,
y'know and tortured

Some people never have a chance,

Emily.

But God sees into the human heart,

God knows who to forgive   and who not.

Scene 2.

(Screen shows a suburban street of lower-income
homes . . . : the Gulicks stare at the screen and their
answers are initially distracted.)

Voice.

Here we have Cedar Street   in Lakepointe, New
Jersey . . . neatly kept homes (as you can see) American suburb   low crime rate, single-family homes
suburb of Newark, New Jersey   population 12,000
and neighborhood of Mr. and Mrs. Frank Gulick the
parents of   Cal Gulick. Will you introduce yourselves to our audience please?

(Houselights come up.)

Frank.

. . . Go on, you first

Emily.

I, I don't know what to say.

Frank.

My name is   Frank Gulick, I   I am fifty- three
years old   that's our house there   2368 Cedar
Street

Emily.

My name is Emily Gulick, fifty-one years old.

Voice.

How employed,   would you care to say? Mr. Gulick?

Frank.

I work for the post office.   I'm a supervisor for

Emily.

He has worked for the post office for twenty-five years.

Frank.

. . . The Terhune Avenue Branch.

Voice.

And how long have you resided   in your attractive home   on Cedar Street''

(Houselights begin to fade down.)

Frank.

. . . Oh I guess how long   if this is   this is 1990?

Emily.

(Oh just think: 1990!)

Frank.

we moved there in, uh,   Judith wasn't born yet so

Emily.

Oh there was our thirtieth anniversary a year ago.

Frank.

wedding

no that was two years ago

Emily.

was it?

Frank.

or three. I   twenty-seven years, this is 1990

Emily.

Yes: Judith is twenty-six   now I'm a grandmother

Frank.

Carl is twenty-two

Emily.

Denny is seventeen, he's a senior in high school

No none of them are living at home now

Frank.

not now

Emily.

Right now poor Denny is staying with my sister in

Voice.
Frank and Emily Gulick you have been happy
here   in Lakepointe raising your family like any
American couple   with your hopes and aspirations
until recently?

Frank.
. . . Yes, oh yes.

Emily.
Oh for a long time we WERE

Frank.
Oh yes

Emily.
It's so strange to,   to think of
The years go by so

Voice.
You have a   happy family life like so many millions
of Americans

Emily.
Until this, this terrible thing

Frank.
INNOCENT   UNTIL   PROVEN   GUILTY—
THAT'S A LAUGH!

Emily.
Oh it's a, a terrible thing

Frank.
Never any hint beforehand of meanness of people's
hearts.
I mean the neighbors.

Emily.
Oh now don't start that, this isn't the

Frank.
Oh God you just try to comprehend

Emily.
this isn't the place, I

Frank.

Like last night: this carload of kids drunk, beer-
drinking foul language in the night

Emily.

oh don't, my hands are

Frank.

Yes but you know it's the parents set them going
And telephone calls   our number is changed now,
but

Emily.

my hands are shaking so
we are both on medication   the doctor says,

Frank.

oh you would not believe, you would not believe
the hatred like Nazi Germany

Emily.

Denny had to drop out of school,   he loved school
he is an honor student

Frank.

everybody turned against us

Emily.

My sister in Yonkers, he's staying with

Frank.

Oh he'll never be the same   boy again,
none of us will.

Voice.

In the development of   human identity there's the
element of chance,   and there is genetic determin-
ism.
Would you comment please?

Frank.

The thing is,   you try your best.

Emily.

oh dear God yes.

Frank.
 Your best.
Emily.
 You give all that's in your heart
Frank.
 you
    can't do more than that can you?
Emily.
 Yes but there is certain to be   justice.
    There IS a, a sense of things.
Frank.
 Sometimes there is a chance, the way they turn out
    but also   what they ARE,
Emily.
 Your own babies.
Voice.
 Frank Gulick and Mary   what is your assessment
 of
    American civilization   today?
Emily.
 It's Emily.
Frank.
 My wife's name is,
Emily.
 It's
    Emily.
Voice.
 Frank and EMILY Gulick
Frank.
 . . . The state of the   civilization?
Emily.
 It's so big.
Frank.
 We are here to tell our side of,

Emily.
    . . . I don't know: it's a   a Democracy
Frank.
    the truth is,   do you want the truth?
        the truth is where we live
        Lakepoint it's changing too
Emily.
    it has changed
Frank.
        Yes but it's all over, it's
        terrible, just terrible
Emily.
    Now we are grandparents we fear for
Frank.
    Yes what you read and see on t.v.
Emily.
    You don't know what to think,
Frank.
    Look: in this country   half the crimes are com-
    mitted by the,   by half the population against the
    other half.
    (laughs.)
    You have your law-abiding citizens,
Emily.
    taxpayers
Frank.
    and you have the rest of them.
        Say you went downtown into a city like   New-
    ark, some night
Emily.
    You'd be crazy if you got out of your car
Frank.
    you'd be dead.   That's what.
Voice.
    Is it possible,   probable   or in your assessment
    IMprobable that the slaying of   fourteen-year-old

Edith Kaminsky   on February 12, 1990 is related to
   the social malaise   of which you speak?
Frank.
   . . . "ma-lezz"?
Emily.
   oh it's hard to,   I would say yes
Frank.
   . . . whoever did it, he
Emily.
   Oh it's terrible the things that keep happening
Frank.
   If only the police would arrest the right person,
Voice.
   Frank and Emily Gulick   you remain adamant in
   your belief   in your faith in your twenty-two-year-
   old son   Carl
      that he is innocent   in the death   fourteen-year-
   old
      Edith Kaminsky?
      on February 12, 1990?
Emily.
   Oh yes
Frank.
   on yes that is the single thing we are convinced of.
Emily.
   On this earth.
Both.
   With God as our witness,
Frank.
   yes
Emily.
   Yes.
Frank.
   The single thing.
                              (Lights down.)

Waiting in the Wings

Noël Coward

❦

The action of the play takes place in the 1950s in the Wings, a charity home for leading or featured actresses who, for various reasons, are living in retirement. Their moods vary like those of anyone, but having spent their lifetimes as actresses, they may, at times, be especially dramatic. The scene opens just after lunch on a sunny Sunday afternoon in June. Bonita Belgrave and Cora Clarke, both in their sixties and still attractive and well-groomed, are playing cards. Maudie Melrose, a diminutive soubrette of seventy, is curled up in an armchair reading. May Davenport, aged about seventy-five, is seated bolt upright by the fire working slowly and majestically on an embroidery frame. Outside on the terrace Almina Clare and Estelle Craven, both in their eighties, are muffled up against the June weather and sitting on deck chairs. Appearing a little later is Deirdre O'Malley, a spry, white-haired woman who speaks in a strong brogue.

BONITA, CORA, MAUDIE, MAY, ALMINA,
ESTELLE, DEIRDRE

Bonita.
(To Cora.) Well, that's that. You owe me two and
six.
Cora.
You owe me a shilling from last Sunday.
Bonita.
In that case you only owe me one and six.
Cora.
We'd better hold it over until next time we play.
Bonita.
(Sharply.) Why—may I ask?
Cora.
(Sweetly.) Because you always do, dear.
Maudie.
(Looking up from the ''Sunday Times.'') I see
they're hoping to get Buck Randy for the Midnight
Matinee this year.
May.
Who in heaven's name is Buck Randy?
Maudie.
Really, May—you MUST have heard of Buck
Randy. He's the rage of America.
May.
I haven't been to America since 1913. What does
he do?
Maudie.
He sings, stripped to the waist, to a zither.
May.
Why should he be stripped to the waist?
Bonita.
Because he's supposed to have the most beautiful
male body in the world, dear. He was Mr. America
of 1955 and 1956.

May.

Why a zither?

Maudie.

He accompanies himself on it. Last year one of his records sold over two million. He has to have police protection wherever he goes.

May.

I'm not surprised.

Maudie.

(Back at the "Sunday Times.") They say that Carolita Pagadicci is going to appear too. She's flying over from Rome especially.

May.

Is that the one with the vast bust who came last year and just stood about?

Cora.

I'm sure it's very kind of all of them to take so much trouble for a bunch of old has-beens like us.

Bonita.

Speak for yourself, dear.

Cora.

I know they get a lot of publicity out of it but even so I shouldn't think from their point of view it was worth all the effort.

May.

It is always possible, my dear Cora, that just one or two of them might do it from sheer kindness of heart.

Cora.

I said it was kind of them to take the trouble and Bonita flew at me.

Bonita.

I didn't fly at you for that. It was because you said we were a bunch of old has-beens.

Cora.

We wouldn't be here if we weren't.

May.

In essence you are quite right, my dear Cora, and I am sure that there are many who would salute your rather devastating honesty. On the other hand there is a wide gulf between honesty and crudeness. Please remember before you say things like that again that it is painful to some of us to be so vulgarly reminded that we are dependent on the charity of our younger colleagues.

Cora.

Oh dear! I'm sure I'm sorry I spoke.

May.

So are we all, Cora. So are we all.

(At this moment Deirdre O'Malley stamps in from the television room.)

Deirdre.

I'm telling you all here and now that I would like to take the windpipe of the man who invented television in me ould rheumatic hands and strangle the bloody life out of him.

Bonita.

Has it gone wrong again?

Deirdre.

It has indeed and for no reason in the world other than pure devilment. I was sitting there quiet as the grave listening to Father Dugan giving his Sunday afternoon talk when suddenly the damned contraption gets up to its blasphemous tricks and before me very eyes I see the blessed Father begin to wobble about like a dancing dervish with one side of his saintly face pulled out of shape as though it was made of india-rubber.

Bonita.

(Getting up.) Miss Archie will fix it, dear. I'll go and ask her.

Deirdre.

I'm grateful for the thought but spare yourself the

trouble. By the time Miss Archie's fiddled with the damn thing the blessed Father will have finished his talk and be having his tea. I'm going up to have me forty winks. (She starts to go upstairs.) It's a dark world we're living in when a bit of soulless machinery can suddenly turn a holy man into a figure of fun. (She disappears into the upper regions.)

Bonita.

(Laughing and sitting on the sofa near to May.) That old girl's wonderful, she really is. You must have seen her in the old days, May; was she really good?

May.

(After a moment's thought.) Good, but unreliable. She's never played a scene the same way twice.

(At this moment Almina and Estelle come in from the terrace. Almina waddles over to the sofa and subsides on it with a sigh. Estelle goes across to the fire place and warms her hands.)

Estelle.

I'm perished to the bone and it's no good pretending I'm not.

Almina.

(Quaveringly.) Do you think we shall ever get it?

Bonita.

Get what, dear?

Almina.

The solarium lounge.

Maudie.

The letter went off to the committee over two weeks ago.

Bonita.

It probably came up at Friday's meeting.

Almina.

Even if they say yes I shall be dead and gone before they get round to building it. My heart's been pounding again, I hardly slept a wink last night.

May.

You know perfectly well, Almina, that that's only indigestion. Doctor Jevons told you so. You eat far too much far too quickly.

Estelle.

That east wind comes straight across the valley and cuts you in two.

Cora.

The committee could well afford it if they chose. Perry told me so himself.

May.

As official secretary to the Fund he had no right to. That young man talks far too much.

Bonita.

Now then, May, you know perfectly well you dote on him, we all do. You gossip away with him for hours whenever you get the chance.

May.

What nonsense you talk, my dear Bonita.

Maudie.

I suppose he'll be down as usual this afternoon.

Cora.

Of course he will, it's Sunday. Also he'll be sure to come today in order to welcome—

Bonita.

(Warningly.) Cora!

Cora.

(With a hurried glance at May.) Well, you know what I mean.

May.

(After a slightly awkward silence.) In order to welcome who?

Maudie.

(Embarrassed.) We've got a new addition to our cosy little family arriving this afternoon.

May.

Why wasn't I told? Who is it?

Bonita.

Oh dear, the cat's out of the bag now with a vengeance. I suppose we'd better say.

May.

What are you all talking about? Why all this mystery?

Bonita.

It's Lotta Bainbridge.

May.

(Stiffening.) Lotta Bainbridge.

Bonita.

Yes.

May.

(Ominously.) Lotta Bainbridge—coming here?

Bonita.

(Hurriedly.) We all thought—knowing that you and she are not exactly the best of friends—that it would be better not to say anything about it.

May.

How long have you known?

Maudie.

Perry told us last Sunday.

May.

(Accusingly.) You mean you were all prepared to let me meet her face to face without even warning me.

Bonita.

Old Dora, her dresser, who's been with her for years, is leaving her to get married, and the maisonette she had just off the Fulham Road is being pulled down to make way for office buildings—

May.

(Rising.) I am not in the least interested in where she lives and what is being pulled down. I only know that I find your combined conspiracy of silence difficult to forgive. (She moves towards the stairs.)

Maudie.

(Jumping up from her chair and putting her hand on her arm.) It was only that we didn't want to upset you.

May.

Do you seriously imagine that it would have upset me less to find her here in this house without being prepared?

Bonita.

Don't be angry with us, May. After all, it was a long, long time ago, wasn't it? The quarrel, I mean—

May.

(Beginning to go upstairs.) There was no quarrel, my dear Bonita. You have been misinformed.

Bonita.

(Weakly.) Well, whatever it was then—

May.

I have not spoken to Lotta Bainbridge for thirty years and I have no intention of doing so now.

Maudie.

Oh May, dear—don't be like that—it's all over and done with.

May.

(Grandly.) One of you had better explain the situation to her when she arrives. Don't be afraid she won't understand. She'll understand perfectly.

(May goes off to her room. There is an embarrassed silence for a moment or two.)

Bonita.

Well, that's that, isn't it?

Maudie.

I suppose we ought to have told her, really.

Bonita.

They'll probably settle down together in time; they can't go on not speaking forever, but the next few weeks are going to be hell.

Maudie.

Who was it that said that there was something beautiful about growing old?

Bonita.

Whoever it was, I have news for him.

Estelle.

Since I've been here I somehow can't remember not being old.

Bonita.

Perhaps that's something to do with having played character parts for so long.

Estelle.

I was an ingenue for years. I was very very pretty and my eyes were enormous. They're quite small now.

Maudie.

What started it—the feud between her and May?

Bonita.

Come off it, Maudie. You weren't toddling home from school with your pencil box in 1918.

Maudie.

(Equably.) As a matter of fact that's exactly what I was doing, eight times a week. I was in MISS MOUSE at the Adelphi and I had a number in the last act called "Don't play the fool with a schoolgirl!" It used to stop the show.

Cora.

As far as I can remember it was the notices that stopped the show.

(At this moment there is the noise of a motorbicycle coming to a noisy halt.)

Cora.

Here's Perry. He's earlier than usual.

Bonita.

(Immediately opening her bag and touching up her face.) Bless his heart.

Maudie.

Don't trouble to do that, dear—it's locking the stable door.

Bonita.

All right, all right, I know—it's just habit.

Almina.

He's tell us whether we're going to get the solarium or not.

Cora.

Oh no, he won't. He'll just say that the committee has it under consideration.

Bonita.

In any case we shall know by his tone whether there's any hope.

Cora.

I don't know why you're all working yourselves up about that damned solarium. It'll be waste of money even if we do get it. Just so much more glass for the rain to beat against.

Bonita.

That's right, dear. Keep us all in hysterics.

(Perry enters.)

The Whales of August

David Berry

❧

Two elderly sisters, Sarah and Libby, are spending the summer at their cottage on an island off the Maine coast. In the following scene, they have a visitor, another elderly woman, Tisha, who is much more flamboyant than they are. For more background on this play, see the introduction to a prior scene from this play which appears on page 98.

SARAH, LIBBY, TISHA

Sarah.
It's whale time, Tisha. The herring are running.
Tisha.
Ayuh. I've seen the fishermen's spotter planes out over the bay.
Sarah.
Remember how many there used to be?
Tisha.
Gorry. I remember when there weren't ANY. So do you.
Sarah.
I mean whales, Tisha, not planes.

510

Tisha.

Oh.

Sarah.

The very first summer we met, we watched the whales together. You kept grabbing the glasses from me.

Tisha.

Well, you were piggy with 'em. Still are. (Joins Sarah.) Ayuh, whales and Northern Lights. I saw the Lights last week. The Maine coast is tellin' us summer's a goner.

Sarah.

Yes. . . . but not 'til the whales come. How nice we still watch them together every year.

Tisha.

Ayuh.

Sarah.

I wish there were as many as before the war.

Tisha.

Which war, dear?

Sarah.

The last one.

Tisha.

I expect all those German submarines scared 'em away.

Sarah.

Oh, you and your German submarines. I never did put much stock in 'em.

Tisha.

No, you didn't, but I saw 'em several times— 'specially in Forty-two.

Sarah.

They were never verified.

Tisha.

Well, those Coastal Watchers—or whatever they were called—NEVER followed up on my sightin's.

Sarah.

Perhaps because you saw too many, dear?

Tisha.

Good Heavens, Sarah! In war time, you can't be too careful.

Sarah.

You know, I haven't see any porpoises.

Tisha.

Ayuh, and nary a seal.

Sarah.

They say the water temperature has something to do with it.

Tisha.

If y'ask me, it's the Russians. They've got the bomb. There's no tellin' what else they're up to.

Sarah.

(Pause.) Do you suppose we still might find some ambergris?

Tisha.

My land! I haven't thought about our ambergris hunts for years!

Sarah.

We were going to make our fortunes.

Tisha.

Ayuh . . . the new perfume queens. Ten dollars an OUNCE that stuff was! Weren't we the pair?

Sarah.

Yes . . . poking around Whaleback Cove all those afternoons—

Tisha.

Oh, yes—

Sarah.

Keeping just ahead of the tide, loaded down with our rocks—

Tisha.

'Cause we knew for a fact that every sperm whale in the ocean had come into the bay to vomit—just for us!

Sarah.

Yes . . . and there was that time we ran into all those proper ladies from the Knickerbocker Hotel—

Tisha.

They were goin' to the Inn for tea—

Sarah.

And Mrs. Miltimore was right in the middle of them—

Tisha.

That old snoot!

Sarah.

And when you said hello, you dropped your whole load of rocks smack on her foot!

Tisha.

And the only thing she said was, "My dear Miss Benson, will you kindly tell us what you girls are doing?" Girls?! We were thirty if we were a day!

Sarah.

I couldn't look at you!

Tisha.

"THIS IS AMBERGRIS, MRS. MILTIMORE, ENOUGH TO MAKE US MILLIONAIRES."

Sarah.

"My de-ah young lady, look again. Your treasure is merely pumice stone."

Tisha.

An old snoot with eyes like a sparrow hawk—

Sarah.

I NEVER forgave her for ruining our dreams.

Tisha.

Well, at least I got seaweed on her lily-white shoes!!

(Tisha bursts into laughter and Sarah joins her.)

Libby.

(Re-awakened by the laughter within.) Sarah? Sarah!

Sarah.

I nearly forgot . . . (Crosses to porch door.) Tisha's here. Will you come in and join us?

Libby.

I expect I've had enough sun. (Rises and goes toward door.)

Sarah.

(Holding door open for Libby.) Will you have some tea?

Libby.

No, Sarah. (Enters living room, crosses toward platform rocker.)

Tisha.

Libby Strong, you're lookin' younger ever day.

Libby.

Hmmph.

Tisha.

Yes indeedy, like a stout oak, dear.

Libby.

You two were certainly carrying on. (Sits in platform rocker.)

Sarah.

We were laughing about our old ambergris hunts.

Tisha.

(Getting berry pail and crossing to Libby.) I brought you some blackberries, Libby. (Extends pail for Libby to taste one.) Gorry, what a walk to find so few berries! I swear there aren't as many as there used to be.

Libby.

It's those nuns.

Tisha.

Nuns, Libby?

Libby.

That's what I said. They flock around our blueberries like a bunch of penguins.

Tisha.

Well, nuns are entitled to pick berries, too.

Libby.

Not in our woods.

Sarah.

Oh, for pity's sake, Libby.

Tisha.

(Taking a seat.) Girls, I do have some news. (Expectant pause.) Helen Parsons told me that Hilda Partridge passed away yesterday at the Medical Center.

Sarah.

Oh, no. . . .

Tisha.

Ayuh. They took her off-island on the fireboat just the day before.

Libby.

We hadn't even heard she was ill.

Tisha.

Very sudden it was . . . and mercifully quick for her.

Sarah.

Hilda was so young . . .

Libby.

I know for a fact she was eighty-three.

Tisha.

I had no idea. (Slight pause.) Y'know, Mr. Maranov's been stayin' at Hilda's this summer.

Sarah.

What will he do now?

Libby.

Yes, whom will he grace?

Sarah.

Libby . . .

Tisha.

Helen said he was still there as of today, but she wasn't sure about his plans.

Sarah.

(A small sigh.) When is the funeral?

Tisha.

Monday comin' in Portland.

Sarah.

Which home?

Tisha.

Nulty and Sons.

Libby.

That's a Catholic home!

Tisha.

Hilda's daughter married one, and I guess he's makin' the arrangement.

Libby.

When my time comes, Sarah, don't you dare—

Sarah.

I know, dear, I know.

Tisha.

I'm sure gonna miss Hilda. She was a crackerjack bridge partner. (Pause.) Oh, you'll never guess who finally bought a hearin' aid!

Sarah.

Who, dear?

Tisha.

Alice Trueworthy. Ayuh, and now she's become our duplicate champion. (Pause.) I bet she never heard the biddin' before. (They all share the laugh.)

Sarah.

We received a lovely note from Lydia Frothinham.

Tisha.

Is the hip mendin'?

Sarah.

Not well at all.

Libby.

You know how it is with hips. She'll be meeting him soon.

Tisha.

Meetin' who, dear?

Libby.

The escort.

Sarah.

(Quickly turning the conversation.) Have you seen anything of Charlie Mayhew lately?

Tisha.

You haven't heard?

Sarah.

What?

Tisha.

He got up and married that young waitress from the Abenaki House.

Sarah.

You don't say!

Tisha.

I do say. Scandalous!

Libby.

But not surprising. The late Mrs. Mayhew could have taken the booby prize at a cattle show.

Sarah.

Libby!

Tisha.

Libby Strong, what a team you and Fred Allen would make! (Slight pause.) Still, Betty Mayhew's grave hardly has grass on it.

Sarah.

How's your arthritis, dear?

Tisha.

In again, out again, gone again Finnegan . . . you know.

Sarah.

That's too bad, dear.

Tisha.

Well, my young doctor told me to expect it if I was determined to live so long.

Sarah.

He needs a lesson in bedside manners.

Tisha.

Oh, he's so cute, dear, I can forgive him almost anythin'.

The World of Sholom Aleichem

Arnold Perl

❦

The following scene is from A Tale of Chelm, *one of three short plays in* The World of Sholom Aleichem, *which opened in New York in 1953. This collection was adapted by Arnold Perl from the popular short stories of the beloved Yiddish satirist. The play is set in the small village of Chelm, known in Eastern European Jewish folkore as a village of fools. When it opens, Melamed, or "Scholar," is talking to his wife, Rifkele. Rabbi David has just exited. Mendele, a book peddler and the narrator, talks directly to the audience before, during, or after any dialogue. There are many small roles in this scene and if necessary or desired, one actor could read more than one part.*

*MELAMED, RIFKELE, MENDELE, FRIEND, DODI,
GOATSELLER, RABBI DAVID*

Mendele.
Such is the wisest man in Chelm. (Referring to
Rabbi David.) Now our Melamed.

Melamed.
(Sitting.) Rifkele, my darling.

Rifkele.
(Working at nearby table.) Did you say something?

Melamed.
Rifkele, I have been thinking. If I were the Czar,
Rifkele, I would be richer than the Czar.

Rifkele.
How, my fine Melamed?

Melamed.
I would do a little teaching on the side. (She nods
her head in appreciation.

           (Blackout.)

Mendele.
This is only one side of his character. For another
side, I must tell you, once the Melamed left Chelm
and forgot his slippers. So he wrote a letter to his
wife.

Melamed.
(Stage L.) Dearest Rifkele: Be sure to send me your
slippers. I have put down ''your slippers'' because
if I wrote ''my slippers'' you would read ''my slippers'' and would send me your slippers. Therefore,
I say plainly ''your slippers'' so you will know and
send me my slippers.

           (Blackout.)

Mendele.
Now Rifkele herself is someone, a person with very
definite opinions and ideas, a person of superior
mentality—even for Chelm. Once she was sitting,

figuring . . . (Rifkele is figuring on her fingers as a friend enters.)

Rifkele.

Now let's see—Four, three, (Aloud.) seven. Two, five—(Aloud.) seven. Two times seven is eleven.

Friend.

Excuse me, Rifkele, two times seven is fourteen.

Rifkele.

No, you're wrong, two times seven is eleven.

Friend.

I'm wrong?

Rifkele.

Of course. When I married the Melamed I was a widow with four children. He, at the time, was a widower and he also had four children. Since we're married, we have, together, three children. So he has seven children and I have seven children and altogether we have eleven. (The friend is duly impressed and he leaves. Blackout. Light on Rifkele and, in course of Mendele's remarks, on Melamed who enters scene carrying something in a large bag.)

Mendele.

By now we are almost ready for the story of the goat. I said almost. There is one last thing you must understand—the relationship between the Melamed and his wife. Listen carefully because this is not a simple matter.

Rifkele.

(Sewing—as Melamed approaches with bag.) Ah, you're back from the market, my Melamed.

Melamed.

Of course I'm back. I went—I'm back.

Rifkele.

So where's the chicken I sent you to buy?

Melamed.

Well—I went to the woman who sells chickens. She said her chickens were so fat that—"Oho," I said,

''Fat is better than chickens,'' so I went to the man who sells fat. He said his fat was so wonderful, it was like oil. ''Oil,'' I said. ''Aha! Oil is better than fat.'' When I got to the store, they said their oil was so pure, it was as pure as water. ''Uhuh,'' I said, ''water is better than oil.'' So instead of the chicken—(He takes out the pitcher from the bag.) I got a pitcher of water. (Blackout. Music. The introduction is over.)

Mendele.

Now we are ready for the story, unless—first—you insist on a few words about the goat. But the goat was only a goat. What can you say about a goat?— and besides this goat was not even in Chelm, but in the next village—famous for its goats. And that's the whole point of the story. So . . . one morning . . . (Lights on Rifkele and Melamed.)

Rifkele.

(Standing.) How would you like to have blintzes for supper?

Melamed.

(Preoccupied—sitting.) Blintzes? (In focus now.) Blintzes! Tonight!!

Rifkele.

Why not? Why should we scrape and scrimp from morning to night and deprive ourselves all our lives? Here is the money we've saved—go to the next village, buy us a goat, and we'll have blintzes tonight.

Melamed.

(Rises.) I'll go this minute.

Rifkele.

Not so fast. You remember with the chicken?

Melamed.

Of course I remember.

Rifkele.

So this time a goat.

Melamed.

Naturally a goat.

Rifkele.

And please. A female goat.

Melamed.

Does milk come from a billy goat?

Rifkele.

Does a pitcher of water lay eggs? (The Melamed kisses Rifkele and starts out on his trip. Light goes out on Rifkele as the Melamed makes a huge circle on stage.)

Mendele.

On the way he had to pass the inn which was run by his friend Dodi. Now Dodi served a nice glass of wine, inexpensive, he was pleasant to talk to— but he was, alas, given also to practical jokes. (By now the Melamed is seated with Dodi having a small glass of wine.)

Melamed.

. . . . So in a little while I'll have the goat.

Dodi.

Fine. Hold still.

Melamed.

What is it?

Dodi.

Hold still. (Dodi slaps him in the face.)

Melamed.

(Reacts.) What was it?

Dodi.

(Laughing.) I was wrong. It was nothing. I thought it was a fly. (Rubbing his face, the Melamed leaves, and for a brief moment lights are on both. Then the light on Dodi goes out and the Melamed continues his journey, arriving at the Goatseller's where he begins to examine the animal.)

Melamed.

It's a very shabby-looking animal. It's a wonder it's standing on its legs at all. And its eyes—awful.

Goatseller.

(Wipes hands.) This morning a man was in—he offered in exchange for our goat a cow. I turned him down.

Melamed.

She should only live till I get her home. (Turns away.) Sixty zlotys.

Goatseller.

As a matter of fact, she's not for sale. One hundred.

Melamed.

Well, in that case, good-bye. (He takes a step away from the Goatseller.) Sixty-five.

Goatseller.

I couldn't stand here talking with you anyhow. My children are sick. (She takes a step away from him.) Ninety.

Melamed.

I think I hear one of them crying. You better go. (Another step.) Seventy.

Goatseller.

All right, we'll call the whole thing off. (Another step.) Eighty.

Melamed.

I'm going. My wife'll wonder what happened to me. (Two steps.) Seventy-five.

Goatseller.

Sholom Aleichem. Seventy-seven.

Melamed.

Aleichem Sholom. Seventy-six. (By now the two are on opposite sides of the stage.)

Goatseller.

I see you're a man who appreciates value. Sold. (They come together, shake hands.)

Melamed.

All right, only one thing—there's no doubt—it's a she goat?

Goatseller.

You said a goat for milking. Would I sell you a billy goat?

Melamed.

Of course not.

Goatseller.

She'll give—at the very least—a pail of milk a day. (Scene ends, she hands him the rope, which is the goat, and he starts off for home, as the lights go out on the Goatseller. As he arrives at Dodi's, he wets his lips. Melamed ties the goat to a rail or chair just outside Dodi's area. Enters.)

Melamed.

So to make a long story short, when she said the goat gave at least a pail of milk a day I offered her forty zlotys and she sold it to me.

Dodi.

Fine, fine, very fine.

Melamed.

So tomorrow night, you'll come. We'll have blintzes together. Did you ever stop to think what you could make from goat's milk? (During this speech Dodi beckons and an Assistant comes over. Dodi speaks in a stage whisper while the Melamed continues to rave on.) . . . For example, an omelet. An omelet is an omelet, but with goat's milk—aha! Or else— You'll come?

Dodi.

(Stage whisper.) If we switched a male goat for his female, it might be very funny. Of course I'll come. Invite me. (The switch consists of substituting one piece of cord for another. This the Assistant does while the Melamed is talking.)

Melamed.

You're invited. Tomorrow night. (He leaves, makes a tour away from Dodi pulling the 'male' goat. Lights go out on Dodi and Assistant. And now the Melamed arrives back at home. Rifkele waits.)

Rifkele.

(Takes one look at the goat.) A Melamed you have to be! So tell me, my Melamed, you milk the goat.

Melamed.

What's the matter? A pail of milk a day, at least, she said—

Rifkele.

Maybe a pail a day—but not milk. It's a billy goat.

Melamed.

A genuine female, she said—

Rifkele.

Enough. Take it back already, and bring back what I sent you for—a lady-goat that gives milk. (Our Melamed shrugs, takes the goat and starts off again. Rifkele shakes her head as the light in her area goes out. The Melamed walks, scratching his head. After a while he wets his lips, and just then Dodi appears, his assistant just beside him. Again the Melamed ties the goat outside, enters Dodi's area. The following action is unspoken. It is done in pantomime.)

Melamed.

(Downcast.) Hello, Dodi.

Dodi.

What's the matter?

Melamed.

I'll tell you but—you wouldn't tell another living soul? (Dodi nods his head, he won't tell.) This woman sold me the goat—it was a billy goat.

Dodi.

(End of pantomime. Dodi winks at his assistant, who changes the goats back. The Melamed leaves, takes the rope, into the area of the Goatseller.)

Melamed.

Here—Give me back my money.

Goatseller.

Just a minute—what's the difficulty?

Melamed.

Please, do I look like a child? It strikes you that I was born only yesterday?

Goatseller.

Please, Melamed, I'm a busy woman.

Melamed.

So, if you're busy give me the money and take back your billy goat.

Goatseller.

What? (She inspects the goat.) Where are your eyes?

Melamed.

Never mind, I trusted you. I paid you the price you asked and you do this to me.

Goatseller.

I won't say another word. Watch. (She places a pail under the goat and "milks" her.)

Melamed.

It's impossible. Milk from a billy goat.

Goatseller.

This is milk. This is the goat that gave the milk. You're a Melamed. It's a lady-goat.

Melamed.

Only an hour ago it was a male goat.

Goatseller.

What have you been drinking?

Melamed.

Who drinks?

Goatseller.

All right, so take your goat and good-bye.

Melamed.

Listen. I'm convinced. I really am. It's a lady-goat. Only do me a favor. You have a Rabbi here?

Goatseller.

Such a question. You have a Rabbi in Chelm?

Melamed.

Are we godless people?

Goatseller.

Are we?

Melamed.

There's no need to get excited, I asked a simple question. You have a Rabbi?

Goatseller.

So?

Melamed.

So please ask him to do me a favor . . . to give me a certificate that says this is a female goat that gives milk.

Goatseller.

It's crazy. Of course it's a female. I just milked her. You saw me milk her. Here's the milk.

Melamed.

I know it, you know it, but for Rifkele, my wife—(Blackout—out of which the Melamed emerges, the certificate of authenticity in his hand. Pleased, he starts back for home, with goat and document. He trips off and the light comes on over Dodi who is smiling broadly. Dodi winks at audience and laughs aloud.)

Mendele.

Nu—do I have to tell you what happened? (The Melamed, without stopping, resumes his tripping walk. Then the light goes on over Rifkele. Rifkele looks at the goat, then the Melamed, then at the goat again.)

Rifkele.

I'm speechless. Absolutely speechless. For the first time in my life I can't say a word!

Melamed.

What did I do, Rifkele?

Rifkele.

Nothing, not a thing. Only do me a favor, the next time I send you for something, don't go.

Melamed.

You said a lady-goat that gives milk. Here's the goat, I saw the woman—

Rifkele.

Please, not another word. It's a billy goat.

Melamed.

Impossible.

Rifkele.

Listen to him.

Melamed.

Not only it's impossible, but I have here—wait— (He finds it.) here—a certificate that this is a lady-goat that gives at least a pail of milk a day. Signed by three expert witnesses, including the Rabbi.

Rifkele.

A paper signed by witnesses!

Melamed.

Would their Rabbi tell a lie? Would the goatherd lie too—would all three sign a paper bearing false witness—would they?

Rifkele.

Please somebody come and take him away!

Melamed.

Why excite yourself? The thing is beyond us. You say the goat is a billy goat; the certificate says it's a lady goat. We'll take the problem to Rabbi David, who is, after all, the wisest man in all Chelm—he'll settle it. Come.

(Blackout. Then immediately they are seen with the Rabbi David.) So you see, Rabbi David, the document proves the goat is a female.

Rabbi David.

(Examining the goat.) Well, the animal is—without question—there are certain unmistakable signs—a he-goat . . .

Rifkele.

Of course, I told you.

Rabbi David.

But still the document is not to be denied—don't forget three witnesses, including a Rabbi. So this is my decision—

Both.

Yes—

Rabbi David.

The law is on the side of the Melamed. The animal is a she-goat and beyond all question this is proved by the document. But it is equally clear and it must be so ordained, for can see no other explanation— that whenever a she-goat is brought into Chelm— by some process beyond my understanding—she becomes a—he-goat.

Both.

(In full appreciation.) Ohhhhh! (Blackout.)

Mendele.

And that settled it. And the townsfolk, who had, of course, heard all about the goat, marveled that a new Solomon was in Chelm. So the Melamed, his wife, Rabbi David and the goat—and all the other Chelmites—settled down to a normal life. And they would be at it still, to this day, except that all the Chelmites are no longer in Chelm. You see, they were scattered during a very heavy rain that nearly washed away their city, and they went to every part of the earth. Maybe you met at least one in your lifetime? Who knows, maybe there's one sitting next to you right now.

FADEOUT

The Young Man from Atlanta

Horton Foote

This moving play was first produced in New York in 1995. It takes place in Houston, Texas, in the spring of 1950. Will Kidder, sixty-four, is a successful southern businessman who has worked for the same firm since he was in his early twenties. He is a hearty, burly man with great vitality. His sixty-year-old wife, Lily Dale, is a warm, genuine woman, though with a limited awareness of and concern for the larger world around her. She has led a comfortable, protected life with her husband, but her world has taken a dramatic turn since their son Bill's death by drowning. This scene takes place in the den of Lily Dale and Bill's new home. Lily is talking to Will and her stepfather, Pete Davenport, seventy-two, who is visiting. Lily Dale is not aware that Will has been politely fired earlier in the day.

WILL, LILY DALE, PETE

Lily Dale.
  It was a lovely supper, wasn't it? I tell you, I believe Clara is the best cook we've ever had. During the

530

war, you know, Mrs. Roosevelt got all the maids in
Houston to join the Disappointment Club.

Pete.

Did she? I never heard about that.

Lily Dale.

You didn't? It was just awful. A maid would say
they were going to work for you. You would arrange the hours and the salary and she would be so
nice and polite; then the day she was supposed to
start work, she wouldn't show up, and that meant
she was a member of the Disappointment Club,
whose purpose was to disappoint white people.

Will.

And you think Mrs. Roosevelt was behind that?

Lily Dale.

I know she was. Everybody in Houston knows she
was. She just hated the South, you know. She took
out all her personal unhappiness on the South.

Will.

Shoot. Somebody sold you a bill of goods, Lily
Dale. I never cared much for either of the Roose-
velts, as you know, but I don't think Mrs. Roosevelt
organized the maids in Houston into anything.

Lily Dale.

Well, she did.

Will.

All right. She did.

Lily Dale.

Daddy?

Will.

What?

Lily Dale.

Why are you so cross?

Will.

I don't mean to be cross. I'm tired, I guess. I'm
sorry.

Lily Dale.
That's all right, Daddy. I guess you have a right to
be tired, as hard as you work. He's been so good to
me all my life, Pete. Anything I ever wanted, Will
got for me.
Pete.
I know that.
Lily Dale.
When is my new car going to be here, Daddy?
Will.
That may have to wait a while now, Lily Dale. The
house and the furnishing just cost more than I fig-
ured. I want to get them all paid for before I take
on any more debts.
Lily Dale.
The house is so beautiful, Will.

(A pause.)
I wish Bill could have seen it.

(A pause.)
I miss Bill so much, Daddy.
Will.
I know.
Lily Dale.
Not that we saw much of him these last years, but
it was just knowing you could call him on the phone
when you wanted to. Or that he'd be with us at
Christmas. The minute he'd come home for Christmas he'd ask me what new pieces I had composed,
remember? And then he'd say, play it for me. I'd
say, you haven't called your daddy at the office, and
he'd say, time enough for that. I want to hear your
new pieces right this very minute.

(A pause.)
I don't compose anymore, Pete.
Pete.
I know.

Lily Dale.

I haven't gone near the piano since Bill died. That all seems too frivolous to me now. Vanity. Vanity. Things of this world. Vanity. Vanity.

(Will gets up.)

Will.

I'm tired. I'm going to bed. Glad to have you here with us, Pete.

Pete.

Thank you. Nice to be here.

(Will starts out of the room, then pauses.)

Will.

Lily Dale, that roommate Bill had back in Atlanta is here in Houston.

Lily Dale.

Oh?

Will.

He called the office today. Has he called here?

Lily Dale.

No.

Will.

If he does, let him know we want nothing to do with him.

Lily Dale.

You told me that before, Daddy. I still don't understand what happened to turn you so against him. You seemed to like him so much at first. You seem—

Will.

I have my reasons, Lily Dale.

Lily Dale.

I'm sure you do.

Will.

Good night.

Lily Dale.

Good night.

Pete.

Good night. (Will goes.)

Lily Dale.

I don't know why he's turned against him. Do you?

Pete.

No.

Lily Dale.

What did you think of him, Pete?

Pete.

I didn't say more than two words to him, Lily Dale, the whole time he was here.

Lily Dale.

I don't care what Daddy says. I think he is a very sweet boy. I can't tell you what it meant to me when he told me how religious Bill had become. Why, he said every morning you could hear him pray all over the boardinghouse. He said they were the most beautiful prayers he had ever heard. He said everybody in the boardinghouse just stopped whatever they were doing to listen to him pray. (A pause.) Allie Temple committed suicide, I heard today. She took poison.

Pete.

She was from Harrison, wasn't she?

Lily Dale.

Yes, but she hadn't lived there for years. Her husband, Lawrence, killed himself. I guess it was twenty years ago. He hung himself. Alice was an atheist, you know. I went over to see her a month or so ago and I said, Alice, my son Bill told me the last time he was at home, there are no atheists in foxholes. Is that so, she said, very sarcastically. You aren't really an atheist, are you, Alice? I am, she said, confirmed. My heavens, I told her, I couldn't ever in this world be an atheist. God has been too good to me. He certainly has been good to you, she said, again most sarcastically. Only why did this good God let your son commit suicide? What on earth are you talking about, I said. His death was an accident. If it was an accident, she said, what was he doing in a lake over his head, when he couldn't swim? It was a hot day, I said, that's why he went for a swim. And how many swims had he ever gone to before? Ask your God to explain that. And she upset me so, Pete, that I couldn't stop trembling and my heart started racing so, I thought I would have a heart attack. And I just had to call that sweet roommate of his in Atlanta, even though Daddy had told me never to, and I told him exactly what Alice had told me. He said there was not a word of truth in it, and he had talked to him from Florida the night before on the telephone and the whole time they talked about God. So, I felt very relieved after that, and I thanked God, got on my knees and thanked God for sending this sweet friend of Bill's to tell me once again of Bill's faith in God. I could never be an atheist. Could you, Pete?

Pete.

No.

Lily Dale.

My cousin Willa Thornton is, you know. Least she says she is. She says all the terrible things that have happened to her family make her an atheist. Pete, you do believe in God, don't you?

Pete.

Yes, I do.

Lily Dale.

I'm glad of that. I wish you'd start going to church with me, Pete.

Pete.

Maybe I will one Sunday.

Lily Dale.

Will won't go with me to church. He says he believes in God, but he can't stand church. Don't ever tell Will I called that friend of Bill's. I've never done anything in my life I felt Will disapproved of, but this one time I had to disobey him. (A pause.) Pete, if I tell you something, promise you won't breathe it to another soul?

Pete.

I promise.

Lily Dale.

Every time I feel blue over missing Bill, I call his friend and I ask him to tell me again about Bill and his prayers and he does so so sweetly. And I've been helping him, too, Pete.

Pete.

How have you been helping him?

Lily Dale.

Loaning him money. Well, not loaning it to him exactly. Although he says that's how he feels about it. You know, He's been so blue and depressed since Bill died that he couldn't keep his mind on his job and he got fired and so I sent him five thousand dollars until he could get himself together, and then—

Pete.

Is that all you sent him, Lily Dale?

Lily Dale.

No, not all.

Pete.

How much have you given him, Lily Dale?

Lily Dale.

I don't know exactly. I've got it written down somewhere. His mother got sick and needed an operation and I sent him ten thousand for her and his sister's husband deserted her and she has three small children and so I sent—

Pete.

Lily Dale.

Lily Dale.

It's my money, Pete. I prayed about it and God said that's what Bill would want me to do, and Randy, that's the name of Bill's friend, said he was sure it was, because he said Bill was going to make him the beneficiary of his life insurance, and that's another reason he knew he didn't commit suicide, because he hadn't had time to change his life insurance making him the beneficiary.

Pete.

Lily Dale.

Lily Dale.

It's my money, Pete. Will gave me the money every Christmas and he always said, spend it like you want to, and I never spent any of it because there was nothing I needed or wanted and I kept it all untouched, just in case one day Bill might need something to buy a house when he got married. . . . (A pause.) Do you know what's troubling Daddy, Pete? He seemed so quiet at supper. So depressed. It's not like Daddy to be depressed.

Pete.

No.

Lily Dale.

Do you know what's troubling him?

Pete.

Yes, I do.

Lily Dale.

What is it, Pete?

Pete.

I don't think I can tell you.

Lily Dale.

Why can't you tell me, Pete?

Pete.

Because I think Will would be mad at me if I did.

Lily Dale.

Did he ask you not to tell me?

Pete.

Yes.

Lily Dale.

Do you think he'll ever tell me?

Pete.

I think he will. Yes, I do.

Lily Dale.

When?

Pete.

At the right time.

Lily Dale.

You scare me, Pete—is it something bad?

Pete.

I can't say any more, Lily Dale.

Lily Dale.

I won't sleep tonight now for worry. I've got lots to worry me, Pete.

Pete.

I'm sorry.

Lily Dale.

I haven't slept hardly a night through since Bill died.

Pete.

I'm sure.

Lily Dale.

Will just sleeps the whole night through. I know he misses Bill, but it doesn't seem to affect his sleep. (A pause.) I have another worry now, Pete. I knew Bill's friend was in Houston. He's been out here twice today. He needs a job so badly. I'm praying

that Will has a change of heart and finds a job for
him at his company. If he knows how Will feels
about him he doesn't let on. He told me he had been
calling him. He needs a job and he needs a father,
he's hoping Will will be a father to him. He said
Bill was like a father to him, gave him advice in all
things. He never knew his own father. He died when
he was two. I know what that's like, Pete, having
lost my own father when I was eight. But I was
lucky because Mama married you and you became
a wonderful father to me, but, unfortunately, his
mother married a man that was a drunkard and he
beat him and his sister. I've asked him to visit me
here in the afternoons while Will is at work, whenever he gets blue, but you mustn't ever tell Will this,
Pete, until God changes his heart, and he will
change his heart, that I know, because Will is a good
man, a kind man. Don't you think he will change
about this, Pete?

Pete.

Maybe so. I hope so, if that's what you want.

Lily Dale.

It's certainly what I want. (Will comes in. He is in
his robe and pajamas.) Couldn't you sleep?

Will.

No.

Lily Dale.

I thought you were sleepy.

Will.

I thought so, too. But I'm not.

Lily Dale.

Anything worrying you, Will?

Will.

To tell the truth there is. I was going to wait a day
or two before telling you this, but I guess I'd better
get it over with.

Pete.

You want me to leave, Will?

Will.

No, you stay. You know about it anyway. I've been fired, Lily Dale.

Lily Dale.

What?

Will.

Fired.

Lily Dale.

From the company?

Will.

Yes.

Lily Dale.

Why on earth—

Will.

They are replacing me with a younger man. Tom Jackson.

Lily Dale.

Tom Jackson. Why, you hired him, trained him.

Will.

I know. I know. He feels terrible about it.

Lily Dale.

Will, if he feels so terrible about it, why—

Will.

There's nothing he can do about it. If he didn't take the job they'd just give it to someone else. They want younger men.

Lily Dale.

Who does?

Will.

Ted Cleveland Jr.

Lily.

Oh, I think it's scandalous. What will you do, Will?

Will.

I'm going to start my own company if I can get one of the banks to finance me. They told me I could stay on at the company for three months, but I said I wanted to leave right away. I'll spend tomorrow talking to some of my banker friends about a loan. (A pause.) I hate to ask you this, Lily Dale, but I may need some cash. How much do you have left of those Christmas checks I've given you?

Lily Dale.

Let's see—

Will.

I'll just need to borrow it back for a month or so.

Lily Dale.

Well—and then you have Bill's money that you gave him that you were going to give to me after he died—

Will.

That money was all spent.

Lily Dale.

Spent?

Will.

Yes.

Lily Dale.

How? Bill never spent money on anything that I knew of. He spent no money on clothes; you gave him his car. He didn't even have an apartment—he lived in a boardinghouse.

Will.

That's perfectly true.

Lily Dale.

Then how did he spend it, Will?

Will.

I don't know how he spent it. There was nothing in his room.

Lily Dale.

I don't understand it.

Will.

Neither do I. But that's how it is. His life insurance barely paid the funeral expenses. Would you mind going down in the morning and getting your money? I gave you five thousand for fifteen Christmases, so you should have at least seventy-five thousand unless you've spent some of it. (A pause.) Have you spent any of it?

Lily Dale.

Not that I remember.

Will.

Thank God. I'm going to need every nickel I can get until I get this all straightened out, and don't look so upset, honey. I will get it straightened out. We'll be back on our feet before you can turn around good. You know your husband. I always land on my feet. (A pause.) Well, I feel better now that's off my chest. I think I can sleep now. Are you coming to bed, honey?

Lily Dale.

I'll be along later. (Will goes. There is a pause. Lily Dale goes to the door to listen to see if he has really gone to his room. When she thinks he has, she turns to Pete.) Pete, what am I going to do? Over half that money is gone.

Pete.

My God, Lily Dale.

Index

THE PHENOMENAL
NATIONAL BESTSELLERS
FROM TRACY KIDDER

A · M · O · N · G
SCHOOLCHILDREN

71089-7/$12.50 US/$16.50 Can

an entire year Tracy Kidder lived among twenty school-
children and their indomitable, compassionate teacher—
sharing their joys, their catastrophes, and their small but
essential triumphs.

The SOUL OF A NEW MACHINE

71115-X/$12.50 US/$16.50 Can

Tracy Kidder's "true life-adventure is the story of Data
General Corporation's race to design and build the Eagle,
a brand new 32-bit supermini computer, in the course of
just a year and a half…compelling entertainment."

Washington Post Book World

HOUSE

71114-1/$12.50 US/$16.50 Can

With all the excitement and drama of a great novel, Kidder
now takes us to the heart of the American dream—into the
intimate lives of a family building their first house.